ISBN: 978129021697

Published by:
HardPress Publishing
8345 NW 66TH ST #2561
MIAMI FL 33166-2626

Email: info@hardpress.net
Web: http://www.hardpress.net

ΜΕΤ·ΑΓΩΝΑ ΣΤΕΦΑΝΟΣ

LIBRARY

OF

ST. FRANCIS DE SALES.

IV.—LETTERS TO PERSONS IN RELIGION.

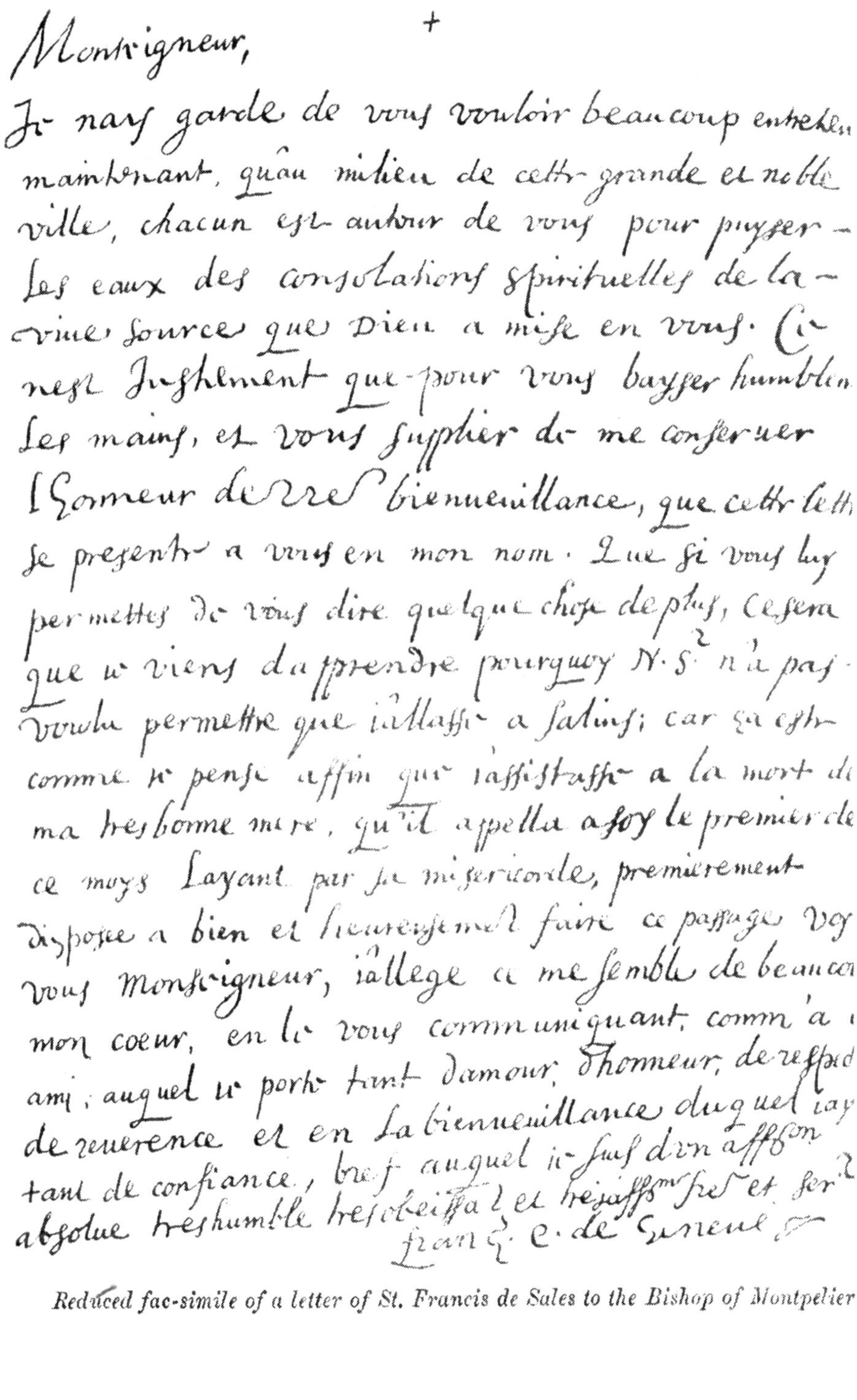

Monseigneur, +

Je n'ay garde de vous vouloir beaucoup entretenir maintenant, qu'au milieu de cette grande et noble ville, chacun est autour de vous pour puyser les eaux des consolations spirituelles de la vive source que Dieu a mise en vous. Ce n'est justement que pour vous bayser humblement les mains, et vous supplier de me conserver l'honneur de vostre bienveuillance, que cette lettre se presente a vous en mon nom. Que si vous luy permettes de vous dire quelque chose de plus, ce sera que je viens d'apprendre pourquoy N. S. n'a pas voulu permettre que j'allasse a Salins; car ça esté comme je pense affin que j'assistasse a la mort de ma tresbonne mere, qu'il appella a soy le premier de ce moys l'ayant par sa misericorde, premierement disposee a bien et heureusement faire ce passage. Voy vous Monseigneur, j'allege ce me semble de beaucoup mon coeur, en le vous communiquant, comme a un ami, auquel je porte tant d'amour, d'honneur, de respect et de reverence et en la bienveuillance duquel j'ay tant de confiance, bref auquel je suis d'un affection absolue treshumble tresobeissant et tresaffectionné frere et serviteur

Franç. E. de Geneve

Reduced fac-simile of a letter of St. Francis de Sales to the Bishop of Montpelier

LIBRARY OF ST. FRANCIS DE SALES.

WORKS OF THIS DOCTOR OF THE CHURCH TRANSLATED INTO ENGLISH.

BY THE

VERY REV. CANON MACKEY, O.S.B.

UNDER THE DIRECTION AND PATRONAGE OF
HIS LORDSHIP THE

RIGHT REV. JOHN CUTHBERT HEDLEY, O.S.B.
Bishop of Newport and Menevia.

IV.—LETTERS TO PERSONS IN RELIGION.

WITH INTRODUCTION BY BISHOP HEDLEY,

AND FACSIMILE OF THE SAINT'S HANDWRITING.

Fourth Edition

"Ah! how happy are these well-beloved hearts of my daughters, in having given up some years of the false liberty of the world, in order to enjoy eternally that desirable slavery in which no liberty is taken away save that which hinders us from being truly free."—p. 151.

LONDON: BURNS & OATES, LIMITED.
NEW YORK, CINCINNATI, CHICAGO: BENZIGER BROTHERS.
1909.

ST. FRANCIS OF SALES AND THE RELIGIOUS LIFE.

IT is a great pleasure to introduce to Catholic readers, and to others, this, the fourth, volume of the Rev. Henry Benedict Mackey's translation of the complete works of St. Francis of Sales. It comprises a very complete selection of the holy Doctor's Letters to "religious" persons. These letters are characterised not only by that depth, sweetness, and attractiveness which we find in all his utterances, but also by matured and powerful instructions, worthy of so great a spiritual director, on the subject of the religious life of persons consecrated to God.

Although St. Francis was not himself a religious, and was indeed occupied during his whole life rather with the care of souls, with anxious missionary work and with the reformation of people of the world, than with monks or nuns, yet it is well known that the religious state shared in his solicitude, his lights and his prayers. It is only necessary to mention the Order of the Visitation for religious women, which he founded, and which still happily flourishes, and to recall to mind the history of the vocation and direction of St. Jane Frances de Chantal.

But in truth the influence of St. Francis of Sales on the religious life is far more deep and widespread than most people imagine. The beginning of the seventeenth century, when he lived (he died in 1622), was a time when religious life for women was beginning to take new shapes and directions. The moment had come, in God's providence, when women were to be uncloistered, yet true religious, and were to be formed into societies which should spread far beyond this or that particular diocese. It was not given to St. Francis to establish, or even perhaps to foresee, the new condition of things. For the history of his own foundation is very curious and instructive. His first idea was to found a society of pious women under the diocesan Bishop; a mere Congregation, not a religious order, with simple and not solemn vows, without any formal or canonical enclosure, wearing the dress of secular women, and devoting their lives to the "visitation" of the sick and the poor. The scene at Annecy, when he finally declared to St. Jane Frances what she was called to, places before us in the most striking manner what was passing in his thoughts. She had fallen on her knees before him, and he said, in order to try her, "You are to be a Poor Clare." "Father," she replied, "I am ready." "No," he continued, "you are not strong enough—you must be a Sœur hospitalière." "Father, whatever you please." "Not that either," said the Saint, "you must be a Carmelite." "Father, I am ready to obey." "No," he said, "what God wants from you is something different; he destines you to establish an order which shall be ruled over by the charity and sweetness of Jesus Christ, into which shall be admitted the weak and the infirm, and whose work shall be to tend the sick and to visit the poor." When the holy Bishop uttered these words,

St. Jane Frances tells us that she felt herself interiorly moved to acquiescence, and filled with light and gentle satisfaction, such as she had not experienced when he made the preceding proposals; so that she knew that this was truly God's will. It was God's will; but it was to be fulfilled in a way which, as it would seem, neither of them was given to comprehend even at that moment of divine impulse and illumination. It was all to come true; but the reality was to be far more wonderful than their saintly humility then suspected. St. Francis of Sales was finally overruled by Monseigneur de Marquemont, Archbishop of Lyons, and consented that the Visitation should be a regular religious Order. By a special bull of Pope Paul V., he erected it as such in the year of our Lord 1618.

There were, perhaps, four things as to which St. Francis thought that a change would be good for religious women. Two of them I have already alluded to. The modification of enclosure he gave up, in as far as regards his own foundation. The authority or influence of a Mother-General seems at first sight a point to which he attached no importance; for he insists, over and over again, that every house of religious women ought to be under the immediate jurisdiction of the diocesan Bishop. Nevertheless, it is clear to any one who studies his Letters and his method of directing foundations, that he held it to be of the utmost moment that the different houses of the Institute should be one in spirit and in practice. We have a letter—translated at p. 232 of this volume—in which he expresses himself most decidedly on the subject of a rumour that the Archbishop of Lyons is going to introduce new laws into the Visitation in that city. In another letter, we have directions to St. Jane Frances as to her "visitation" of the Houses of France (p. 234). Not that the Superioress of the Mother House, or even the Bishop of that House, had any absolute authority over foundations in another diocese; but that it was essential that there should be such communication between the Houses that a kind of moral authority should be acknowledged as belonging to the chief seat of the traditions of the Order. The Visitation is the most conspicuous example in the Church of a religious Order of women holding together in spirit and flourishing in numbers through two centuries by the power and virtue of the instructions of its saintly founders and the intercommunication of the Houses with one another and with the Mother House at Annecy. The government of women by women, admitted from the beginning of the Church in each particular convent, was not recognised on a larger scale till some time afterwards; but the principle has worked in the Visitation since the time of St. Jane Frances. It is she who has been the perpetual Mother-General.

The third point in which the holy Bishop of Geneva made an innovation was the obligation of the Divine Office. This he endeavoured, and with success, to change, in the Visitation, into the Little Office. For his reasons, the reader may find some of them in Letter XXXIV. of the present translation (p. 161). He did not conceal his opinion that in more than one convent the recitation of the Divine Office was got through in a way that might "well make the Huguenots laugh."

The fourth point relates to what he calls the very spirit of the Visitation. When he yielded to the representations of the Archbishop of Lyons, and allowed his little Congregation to pass into the state of an Order, he reserved two things—which, indeed, as far as our present purpose is concerned, may be put down as one. He tells Mother Favre—the generous Savoyard who was among the first three admitted to the vows—that he had yielded without reserve to the Archbishop, except as regards the "principal end" of the Congregation, viz. "that widows should be admitted into the monasteries, these to live in their secular dress till they were free from encumbrance and able to take the habit, and that secular women might come in and live there for a time for devotional purposes." Thus did he carry out, in spite of all, that inspiration of charitable "visitation" which he received in the beginning. His daughters were not to "visit" outside, but to receive within their own walls those who needed their help. It was the same loving thoughtfulness for others which made him prescribe that consideration of health and strength should not be allowed to exclude from the habit such candidates as were otherwise suitable. "Je suis grand partisan des infirmes," he writes to a Sister of the Visitation:—

"And am always afraid lest the inconveniences which they cause should excite a spirit of prudence in the houses, and a tendency to desire to dismiss them without getting leave from the spirit of charity, under which our Congregation has been founded, and for which there has been expressly made the distinction of sisters which is seen therein. I favour then the cause of your sick person, and provided that she is humble and acknowledges herself indebted to charity, you must receive her, poor daughter. It will be a continual holy exercise for the charity of the sisters" (p. 189).

To St. Francis, indeed, the monastery was a refuge,

an infirmary, in which poor sick and suffering souls were to be treated and cured, and infirm bodies cherished and ministered to. He says, in the thirteenth *Entretien*, that the Spirit of the Visitation is the humble love of God and "extreme sweetness" towards our neighbour.

It is interesting, and by no means fanciful, to trace the influence of these four points of St. Francis of Sales on the development of Institutes for religious women during the two centuries and a half which have elapsed since his time. These institutions may perhaps be roughly classified under three different heads. First there are the associations, which are not strictly "religious congregations," because they only take private, and generally temporary vows, such as the Sisters of Charity of St. Vincent de Paul. Next there are the Institutes, which have more or less followed the rule and spirit of St. Ignatius, such as the English Virgins, with those widespread Irish branches which have sprung from them; also the Sacré Cœur, the Sisters of Mercy, &c. In the third place come the Orders, chiefly French, on the model of the Congregation of Charity and Refuge founded by Père Eudes. A moment's consideration will show that the three great legislators for religious in these latter centuries have been St. Vincent de Paul, St. Ignatius, and St. Francis of Sales. Perhaps the word "legislator" is not the right one; these great Saints have, two of them at least, legislated for women; but their influence has mostly come from their firm grasp of certain principles which Divine Providence inspired them to see clearly. The need for a society in which women might live in strict obedience, and yet wholly devoted to charity, was made known to St. Vincent de Paul almost at the same time as to St. Francis. Does not the congregation of the Sisters of Charity seem almost to correspond to the ideal which the latter Saint showed to St. Jane? But God's thoughts are richer and more fertile than all that even his Saints can take in, and St. Vincent carried out that inspiration in one way, St. Francis in another. The work of St. Ignatius has been not less wonderful, though more indirect. It is worthy of remark, that at the very moment when St. Francis was taking steps to have the Visitation approved at Rome, Mary Ward was in Rome also, and pleading her cause before the tribunals. The "innovations" proposed by that great foundress have nearly all been accepted now; but at the time they were thought to be very doubtful indeed; and what is worse, the behaviour of some at least of her associates was not calculated to inspire the authorities with confidence. Mary Ward wanted to do away with canonical enclosure, to let her nuns go about the country almost like missionaries, to undertake the teaching of catechism, and to have all the convents of her institute placed under one Mother-General. Her vision has been realised, in the Presentation, the Loretto Sisters, the Irish Sisters of Mercy, and those innumerable offshoots or modifications of these Orders which are even yet multiplying. St. Ignatius, in spite of the Pontifical privilege that his Order should never have to govern nuns, is the patriarch of these active Orders, and has given them their statutes, their discipline, and their freedom for every charitable work. The devoted Congregations which I have called French, with their offshoots, have inherited the spirit of St. Francis of Sales. For example, the Constitutions of Père

Eudes's institute are almost word for word those of the Visitation, although it is true that he has added one or two which St. Francis himself might have signed. The holy Doctor wished his daughters to "visit" the poor and sick. God has brought the poor and the sick to the very doors of their cells, under the very roof of their chapels. That loving sweetness and devoted sacrifice which were his characteristics are multiplied day by day, all the world over, wherever communities of white-robed nuns gather around them the miseries of nature, of misfortune, or of sin, and practise upon their alleviation the lessons which St. Francis of Sales dictated to the first daughters of the Visitation.

The book now offered to the reader contains these lessons, not in the form of a cold abridgment, but in the warm and living words of the Saint himself. Most of the Letters are naturally addressed to Sisters of the Visitation—many to St. Jane Frances herself. But there are a few also to members of other religious orders. Those in which he speaks so prudently and tenderly of "reformation" are addressed mostly to the Abbess of Puits d'Orbe, a house which was Benedictine in name, but from which secular troubles had banished the Benedictine spirit for a century past. The "general instructions" at the end of this volume contain those treasured instructions which the Saint had either written for particular sisters in a more formal shape than a letter, or which the sisters themselves had reduced to writing in the shape of memoranda for the spiritual life. Among them is the "Livret," or book of answers given by St. Francis to various questions on the spirit and practice of the Visitation.

The Letters translated by Father Mackey in this

volume are of every kind—from trivial to weighty, from playful to severe, from the first instructions of beginners to the deepest counsels of mystical theology. The series of Letters to St. Jane Frances with which the Third Book opens are like a commentary on the sublimest parts of the *Amour de Dieu.* The letter in which he replies to some sister who had naively asked him how *he* would behave if he lived in her community, is such as one would expect from a finished master to a simple and well-meaning soul. We have letters to superiors, letters to "officers" of a house, letters to novices; letters to the tempted, to the suffering, to the faint-hearted, to the over-busy. The volume is a series of illustrations of his well-known views—of detachment from earth, of abandonment to God, of patience with ourselves, of "extreme sweetness" for others. Like every great spiritual doctor, he does not trouble himself whether his teachings are "new things" or "old." There is little that can be called absolutely new in spiritual learning, unless it is also false; but St. Francis leaves in the heart the impression of one who has been raised up to teach the importance of interior acts over exterior, of simple and direct "views" of God as against complicated spirituality, and of the ever-presence of Christ in every human creature around us. Of all this the book is full. Let me give one specimen—a passage in a letter probably written to Mother de Chastel, at Grenoble, in 1620; it is on the subject of trust in God and tranquillity:—

"You go considering your steps too much for fear of falling. You make too much reflection on the movements of your self-love, which are doubtless frequent, but which will never be dangerous so long as, tranquilly, not letting yourself be annoyed by their importunity nor alarmed by their multitude you, say No. Walk simply ; do not desire repose of spirit too earnestly, and you will have the more of it. Why do you put yourself in trouble? God is good, he sees very well what you are ; your inclinations cannot hurt you, bad as they may be, since they are only left to you to exercise your superior will in making a more profitable union with that of God. Keep your eyes uplifted, my dear daughter, by a perfect confidence in the goodness of God. Do not be anxiously solicitous for him, for he told Martha that he did not wish it, or at least that he was better pleased that there should be no solicitude even in doing good. Do not examine your soul so much about its advancement. Do not want to be so perfect, but in simple earnest spend your life in your exercises, and in the actions which come to be done in their time. *Be not solicitous for to-morrow.* As to your path, God, who has guided you up to the present, will guide you to the end. Remain in entire peace, in the holy and loving confidence which you ought to have in the sweetness of heavenly Providence" (p. 199).

This volume will therefore serve as an admirable manual of spiritual reading for religious, especially for those whose institute is modelled on the Visitation, or carries out the great principle of mercy and compassion which lies at the root of all that St. Francis wished religious women to do.

Perhaps it may be necessary to make one observation here. If one wished to have a true idea of the perfection of a holy person, one would hardly get it from that person's letters to her confessor, or from the director's instructions to herself. We must not then judge of the advanced state of the first Mothers of the Visitation from what we read in these letters of their saintly founder and father. We know from other sources how holy and perfect many of them were. Their imperfections, such as they were, or as they seemed to be, have become our instruction, in drawing from one of the greatest of spiritual directors a series of golden teachings, which will lift up and purify to the end of time souls much more in need of help than were those to whom they were first imparted.

But to many of us the great merit and satisfaction of this book of holy Letters will be that it keeps before us St. Francis himself. Nothing displays a human soul like a genuine letter. We have here St. Francis in every paragraph. We have even innumerable hints and suggestions of his outward life and occupations. We see him snatching a minute as the messenger waits to write "four lines" to his beloved daughters. We see him interrupted in his writing the *Love of God*, and just at the moment when he was filled with a "kind of realisation of the feelings of the blessed when they first see God in Paradise" (p. 166). We can follow him to his father's house, at Sales, where on a winter's day, Ash Wednesday of the year 1615, he is all alone in the gallery and the chapel, and where he sees the snow lying a foot deep in the court-yard, and John clearing a space to feed those pigeons which have furnished him with so many an illustration. One letter is written at Grenoble, where he is preaching the Lent in the cathedral known to so many of us, and it relates how all the previous night he had been lying awake revolving "a thousand good thoughts of sermons." He promises a lady his portrait—"I cannot refuse you anything, my dear daughter! . . . Why have I not striven to preserve the image of our heavenly Father in my soul!" (p. 290). Sometimes he reveals his interior. "I must tell you," he says to St. Jane Frances, in the year 1621, "that this morning, having a little solitude (at Annecy), I have made an incomparable act of resignation, but one which I cannot write. . . . Oh how blessed are the souls which live by the will of God alone!" (p. 240). "I would never excite myself," he writes to one of his daughters; "that, thank God, I do already; for I never let myself become excited" (p. 395). And the following passage is very interesting to those who have been struck, as we all have been, by the tone of effusive tenderness which is sometimes perceptible in his communication with his spiritual children:—

"There are no souls in the world, as I think, who love more cordially, tenderly, and (to speak in all sincerity) more lovingly than I; and I even somewhat abound in affectionateness, and words thereof, particularly at the beginning. You know that it is according to the truth and the variety of that true love which I have for souls; for it has pleased God to make my heart so. But still I like souls that are independent, vigorous and not feminine; for such great tenderness disturbs the heart, disquiets it, distracts it from loving prayer to God, hinders entire resignation and the perfect death of self-love. That which is not God is, for us, nothing. How can it be that I feel thus, I who am the most affectionate person in the world, as you know? Yet in truth I do feel it; but it is a marvel how I reconcile it all together; for it is my idea that I love nothing at all but God, and all souls for God. Ah! Lord God, do yet this grace to my whole soul that it may be in you only!" (pp. 203–4).

The saints derive from their association with Christ the power which belongs in its fulness to him, of transforming the heart of those who gaze upon them into their own likeness and the likeness of their Master. No saint seems to have this gift more marvellously than St. Francis of Sales. Therefore, every chance of looking upon him is most precious and acceptable to all who aspire to devotion.

I think the reader will approve of the translation, which has been made with very great care. The

Saint's words and expressions are often archaic and sometimes obscure, and his language has not unfrequently a trait of directness and simplicity which our modern usages hardly tolerate. But Father Mackey seems to have fairly hit the mean between slavish literalness and too great freedom. The division into six books will be found useful. All the letters to the Visitation are kept together, viz., in Books II. and III., and arranged according to date. Book I. contains letters previous to the founding of the Visitation; Book IV. letters to persons outside the Visitation; Book V. "general instructions" for the Visitation, and Book VI. letters on various festivals. The index and analysis will make it easy to find passages and subjects. Father Mackey has added one or two excellent paragraphs of introduction and explanation. He has in many cases put for the first time the real names of the persons to whom the letters are addressed. He has also corrected many dates, and added others. The date will generally enable the reader to find the original letter in the French editions; the few undated letters will mostly be found in the French collections after the dated ones. The headings of the letters are by the translator himself, those found in the French editions being very often wrong or misleading. The book, therefore, is much more than a mere translation. Father Mackey, in executing his task, has made use of all that minute knowledge of the life and writings of St. Francis of Sales which many years of patient study have put him in possession of, and which we may expect to bear still more abundant fruit in the future if his life be spared.

JOHN CUTHBERT, O.S.B.,
Bishop of Newport and Menevia,

TABLE OF CONTENTS.

Book II.

EARLIER LETTERS TO SISTERS OF THE VISITATION.

Book III.

LATER LETTERS TO SISTERS OF THE VISITATION.

Book IV.

FURTHER LETTERS TO RELIGIOUS OUTSIDE THE VISITATION.

Book V.

GENERAL INSTRUCTIONS TO SISTERS OF THE VISITATION.

Book VI.

LETTERS FOR VARIOUS FESTIVALS.

CLASSIFIED INDEX.

[*The Roman numerals refer to the Book, the Arabic to the Letter.*]

BOOK I.

Letters Previous to the Founding of the Visitation.

LETTER I.

To the Filles-Dieu at Paris.

[These were Benedictine nuns of the order of Fontevrault. They succeeded (1485) certain sisters, who, having been established there by St. Louis to serve a hospital or *hôtel-Dieu,* were hence called "Filles-Dieu," a title which the new inmates of the house inherited. They were also called "Ladies of the Mother of Mercy." The Saint had made their acquaintance when at Paris, and wrote to them immediately after his return to Savoy, during his retreat before consecration.]

Exhortation and instruction on reforming their practice of poverty.

From Sales, 22d November 1602.

My very Reverend Ladies and dear Sisters—I have conceived so great a confidence in your charity that I seem no longer to require a preface or introduction when I speak to you, whether absent, as I am now obliged to do, or present, in case God should ever so dispose as to give me the blessing of seeing you again. In everything I love simplicity and candour; I believe that you love them too; and I beseech you to continue to do so, because this is very becoming to your profession. I consider that the white tunics you wear are a sign thereof. I will say simply to you, then, what has led me to write to you all together.

I beg you to be assured that I am greatly urged by the extreme affection which I have for the good of your house; for even here, where I can render you but slight service, it ceases not to suggest to me a multitude of desires which are useless to you and to me. Still, I dare not reject these inclinations, because they are good and sincere, and above all because I firmly believe that it is God who has given them to me. If they tend to make me suffer some disquiet, it is not from their own nature, but through the weakness of my spirit, still subject to the movement of the winds and tide. Now there is a wind which agitates my spirit in the affection which it bears you, and I cannot restrain myself from telling you of it; for it is the only subject which has made me steal leisure to write to you from amidst the pressing business which surrounds me in this beginning of my office.

I quitted Paris with the satisfaction of having in some sort manifested to you the esteem in which I held the virtue of your house, the thought of which gave me much consolation and interior profit, animating me to the desire of my own perfection. The sacred Word says * that Jonas found the shade of the ivy exceeding grateful, but that a hot and burning wind withered it up in an instant. A wind had almost the same effect on the consolation which I had in you; but be assured, I beseech you, that it was the south wind of charity.

* Jonas iv. Precisely speaking, it was "the worm" which destroyed the ivy or gourd, as the Saint himself says further on. [Tr.]

It was a report which I was forced to believe when I considered all the circumstances. God knows how grieved I was, both for what was said to me and because it only became known to me at a time when I had not leisure to treat of it with you; for, unless my affection deceives me, I think that you would have given me a favourable hearing, and would not have been displeased with any remonstrance I might have made, since you would never have discovered in my soul or in any of its movements aught save full and pure affection for your spiritual progress and the good of your monastery.

But, as it was my duty not to stop for this, being called here for a greater good, I have decided to write to you on this subject, although I debated some time with myself whether this would be good or no. On the one hand, it almost seemed to me that it would be useless, seeing that my letter would give occasion to replies from you, and would require others from me; that it would perhaps arrive unseasonably; that it would not exactly represent either my aim or my affection; that you are where you will have counsels by word of mouth from a multitude of persons who deserve to be in greater esteem with you than I am, and that if you do not believe Moses and the Prophets who speak to you, you will hardly believe this poor sinner who can but write to you; and, further, seeing that, as I hear, certain other preachers, better and more experienced in the conduct of souls than I am, have spoken to you on this subject without effect.

But, on the other hand, all these reasons had to give way to my affection, and to the duty which my extreme desire of your good imposes on me. God oftentimes employs the weakest instruments for the greatest purposes. How do I know but that he may will to convey his inspiration into your heart through the words which he will give me to write to you? I have prayed; I might say much more and only say the truth; but this shall suffice,—I have wetted my lips with the blood of Jesus Christ in the Mass to be able to send you suitable and fruitful words. These, then, I will here place on this paper: may God graciously introduce and adapt them to your spirits to advance his glory therein.

My dear sisters, I am told that there exist in your house private pensions and allowances which cause differences in the treatment of the sick; that those in health have particular indulgences in food and dress without necessity; and that your conversations and recreations are not entirely edifying. I have heard all this, and much more which follows from it. And I upon it have many things to say; but have patience, I beg you; do me the honour of reading attentively and calmly what I am going to represent to you about it; favour in this my zeal to serve you.

My good ladies, you should correct your house of all these defects, which are without doubt contrary to the perfection of the religious life. The paschal lamb had to be without stain; you are lambs of the Pasch, that is, of the passage, for you have passed from the Egypt of the world into the desert of Religion, on your way to the Land of Promise. Without doubt you must be free from all appearance of stain or blemish. But are these not very dark and manifest stains, these faults and grave irregularities which I have noted above, particularly in such a house? They must be corrected, then. You must, it seems to me, correct them because they are, apparently, little, and therefore must be opposed while they are so; for if you wait till they grow, you will not easily be able to mend them. It is easy to divert rivers at their source, when they are as yet weak; but farther on they get beyond our power. *Catch us*, say the Canticles,* *the little foxes which destroy the vines.* They are little; do not wait till they become great; for if you wait it will not only not be easy to catch them, but by the time you would catch them they will already have spoilt everything. The children of Israel say in one of the Psalms:† *O daughter of Babylon miserable. . . . Blessed he that shall take and dash thy little ones against the rock!* The disorder, the irregularity, of religious bodies is truly a daughter of Babylon and of confusion. Ah! how blessed are those souls who suffer no more than the commencement of these things, or rather, who dash and shiver them on the rock of reformation! The asp of relaxation and irregularity is not yet within the enclosure of your monastery, but take good heed to yourselves, these faults are its eggs; if you warm them in your bosoms, they will break out some day unto your loss and perdition when you are least expecting it.

But if these defects are small, as some may fancy, are you not much less excusable for not correcting them? How sad, said St. Chrysostom to-day, in his homily on the Gospel of this feast of St. Cecilia which we are celebrating,—how sad to see these virgins, who have put down and triumphed over the most powerful enemy of all, which is the ardour of the flesh, let

* ii. 15. † cxxxvi.

themselves be overcome by that puny enemy, Mammon, god of riches! And certainly proprietorships, that is, enjoyment of private means, in religion, come under the head of Mammon of iniquity. That is why, said he, these poor virgins are all called foolish,—because after having conquered the stronger they yield to the feebler.

Your house excels in many other points of perfection, and in them is beyond comparison with all others; will it not be a sad reproach to let its glory be tarnished by these miserable imperfections? You are called, by an ancient glory and prerogative of your house, *Filles de Dieu*, Daughters of God; would you lose this honour by failing to reform these little defects?—will you for a mess of lentils lose the birthright which your name would seem to have given you with the consent of entire France?

It is, surely, a mark of very great imperfection in the lion and the elephant, that after having conquered tigers, oxen, rhinoceroses, they quail, grow terrified, and tremble, the one before a little fowl, the other before a rat, the mere sight of which makes them lose courage. That is a great flaw in their nobleness, and similarly it is a great tare (which signifies deduction) off the goodness of your house, that in it there are particular pensions, and the like weak points, while it is seen to deserve praise in so many other things. Be faithful, then, in the reformation of these little imperfections, in order that your Spouse may place you over many perfections, and bring you one day to his glory.

Now, however, I beg you to let me tell you my opinion concerning these defects. It is true they are small if put in comparison with greater ones; for they are only beginnings, and a beginning, whether in evil or in good, is always small. But if you consider them in comparison with the true and entire religious perfection to which you ought to aspire, they are undoubtedly very great and very dangerous. Is that, I ask you, a small evil which affects and injures a noble part of your body, namely, the vow of poverty? One can be a good religious without reciting in choir, without wearing this or that particular habit, without abstinence from such or such things; but without poverty and community of goods no one can be so.

The worm which gnawed the gourd-tree of Jonas seemed to be little; but its venom was so strong that the tree died from it. The defects of your house seem very slight; but their effect is so evil that it spoils your vow of poverty.

Ismael was a little child, but as soon as he began to vex and trouble Isaac, the wise Sara made him depart, with Agar his mother, from out of the house of Abraham, that is, of the great heavenly Father. Here have been a Sara and an Agar; the superior, and in a certain way superhuman, part, and the other lower and human; the spirit and the interior, the body and exterior. The spirit brought forth the good Isaac—the vow which you have offered on the mountain of Religion; as Isaac, on the mountain of Vision, voluntarily offered himself in sacrifice. The flesh and corporal part only brings forth Ismael, that is, the care and the desire of exterior and temporal things. So long as this Ismael, this care and desire, attacks not your Isaac, that is, your vow and profession, although he remain with you and in your house, I am satisfied, and, which is the chief thing, God is not offended;

but when he troubles your vow, your poverty, your profession, I beg you, nay, I conjure you—send him off, drive him away. Be he little as you will, as merely a child as you please, let him be no bigger than an ant, still he is evil, he is mischievous, he will ruin you, he will subvert your house.

Moreover, I consider this evil very great in your house because it is *maintained* there, because it is in repose and dwells there as an ordinary resident. It is the chief evil I see in the case that these proprietorships are already citizens. *Dying flies*, says the Wise Man,* *spoil the sweetness of* balm and *ointment.* If all they did were to pass over the ointment and suck it as they passed, they would not spoil it; but staying in it dead and as it were buried, they corrupt it. I will grant that the shortcomings and defects of your house are only flies; but the evil is that they stay upon your ointment, they stay and are buried therein with your approval. However small the evil may be, it easily increases when it is cherished and maintained. No enemy, say soldiers, is little when he is despised.

Such are the reasons which God has given me for beseeching you to resolve to reform your house in these little or great faults which I am told are in it; and I cannot assuage my desires on this point.

Then I have turned to consider what impediments might be making the holy work difficult, and to tell you my opinion about them. I suspect that you therefore consider there is no proprietorship contrary to your vow, because perchance all is done under the permission and license of the superior. This word, permission, or license, has already a bad sound by the

* Eccles. x. 1.

side of spirit of perfection. It would be better to live under laws and ordinances than to introduce exemptions, licenses, and permissions. Here you have already a subject for reformation.

Moses had given a permission and license concerning the integrity of marriage. Our Lord, reforming this holy sacrament and restoring it to its purity, declared that Moses had only given the permission under force and compulsion—*for the hardness of your hearts.** Often enough superiors bend what they cannot break, and allow what they cannot hinder: and the permission has afterwards this artfulness and malice, that having lasted some time it extends itself, and, unlike other things that get old, it gets stronger, and seems little by little to lose its ugliness and its deformity. *Permissions enter into monasteries only by favour; but having got foothold they stay on by force, and never leave but by severity.*

Besides, I say that there is nothing so like as two drops of water—yet the one may be from roses, the other from hemlock; one cures, and the other kills. There are permissions which may be to a certain extent good; but the present one is not; for at last it is a proprietorship, though veiled and hidden; it is the idol which Rachel had hidden under her garments. Persons say: the superior allows this, and it is by her good pleasure—this is Rachel speaking; but this pension belongs to one certain sister and not to another—there is the idol of proprietorship. If it be not proprietorship for one to have more necessity without the means of supplying it, and the other less necessity with more means, how comes it that while you are all sisters your

* Matt. xix. 8.

pensions are not sisters? One suffers, and the other suffers not; *one is hungry*, I will almost say, with St. Paul,* *and another* abounds. There is no community of Our Lord's there. Call it what you like, but it is a pure proprietorship; for where there is no proprietorship there is no *mine* and *thine*—the two words which have produced the misery of the world. *The religious who has a penny is not worth a penny*, said the Ancients.

The love and tender affection you bear to your house may also be a great hindrance to the reformation of it; because this passion cannot permit you to think ill of it, nor to listen in a good spirit to reprehensions which may be given you about it. But take care, I pray you; for self-love is cunning; it pushes and insinuates itself into everything, while making us believe it is not there at all. The true love of our houses makes us jealous of their real perfections, and not of their reputation merely. The wife of good Tobias took offence at a caution of her husband's, because it seemed to imply a doubt as to the honour of his family. She was too touchy; if there was no fault in the matter she should have praised God; if there was, she should have amended it, We must *eat butter and honey*, like Our Saviour, make our spirits meek and humble, *choose the good and refuse the evil.*† Bees love their hives, which are, as it were, their convents; I said to you once that they were like nature's nuns in the animal creation; and they fail not to keep a jealous watch over all that is in their hives, and to clean them out at certain periods.

Nothing is so constant under heaven but it tends to

* 1 Cor. xi. 21.

† Isa. vii. 15.

dissolution; nothing is so clean but it contracts some dust. It is good not to mention without reason the defects one may see in a house, nor to show them to others; but to be unwilling to acknowledge them, or to confess them to those who may be of use in mending them, is an ill-regulated love. The spouse in the Canticles * confesses her imperfection: *I am black,* she says, *but beautiful, . . . do not consider me that I am brown, because the sun hath altered my colour.* I think you can say the same of your house; it is fair and virtuous indeed, but the course of time and the long years have altered its colours. Why will you not restore them by a holy reformation? When there is some little passing fault in a house, one may take no notice; but when it is permanent and customary, then it must be driven out, those being called in who can help to do so. It was an ill-regulated love in David to be unwilling to have Absalom put to death, in spite of his wickedness and rebellion. Whoever loves his house procures its soundness, purity, and reformation.

I think there is another obstacle to the reform of your house; viz., that you perchance consider it could not maintain itself without these pensions, because it is poor. On the contrary, I think that this monastery is poor because it has these pensions. There are in Italy two noble republics, Venice and Genoa. In Venice the private individuals are not so rich as at Genoa. The wealth of private persons hinders that of the public. If once you were really poor in particular, you would afterwards be rich in common.

God will have us trust in him, each according to his vocation. It is not required for a layman and

* i. 4, 5.

ordinary man to depend upon the Providence of God in the way that we must, who are churchmen; for to us it is forbidden to amass wealth by engaging in trade, whereas to persons in the world it is not forbidden: the secular clergy, again, are not bound to trust in this same Providence as much as religious are; for religious must trust in it so strongly as to have no care whatever, individually, about their means of subsistence: and amongst religious those of S. Francis excel in this point, viz., the confidence and resignation they have towards Divine Providence, having no means of support either in particular or in common, but perfectly fulfilling that of the Psalmist: * *Cast thy care upon the Lord, and he shall sustain thee.*

Each one ought to cast all his care on God, who indeed sustains the whole world; but each one does not cast it on God with the same degree of resignation: some cast it on him through the labour and occupation which God has given them, and through which God sustains them; others aim at it more simply, without any intermediate way of getting their living: *They sow not, neither do they reap, and your heavenly Father feeds them.*† Now your condition as religious obliges you to resign yourselves to God's Providence without the help or favour of any private pensions or proprietorships; which, therefore, you should give up.

David is in admiration of the way in which *God giveth the young ravens their food*:‡ and indeed it is a thing most admirable. But does he not feed the rest of the animal creation? Of course; yet not in that way, nor immediately; the others are helped by their fathers and mothers, and have some means of working.

* Ps. liv. 23. † Matt. vi. 26. ‡ Ps. cxlvi. 9.

But those our Lord feeds almost miraculously, and so does he ever feed those, his devout servants and creatures, who by the condition of their state and profession have devoted themselves to common life with individual poverty, using no intermediate means contrary to their condition.

The Cordeliers considered that they could not live in that strict poverty which their primitive rule required; the Capuchins have clearly shown them that they could. So long as St. Peter trusted in him who called him he was safe; when he began to doubt and to lose confidence he sank in the waters: let us do what we ought, each in his condition and profession, and God will not fail us. Whilst the children of Israel were in Egypt he fed them by the food which the Egyptians furnished; when they were in the desert, where there was no food, he gave them the manna, a food common to all and particular to none, and which, if I am not mistaken, represents a certain common life. You have come out of the world of Egypt, you are in the desert of religion; seek worldly means no longer; firmly hope in God; he will sustain you, undoubtedly, even if he have to rain down manna for you.

Then I doubt whether there may not be another hindrance to your reformation. Perhaps those who have proposed it to you have handled the sore somewhat roughly; but would you therefore reject your cure? Surgeons are sometimes obliged to enlarge the wound in order to lessen the mischief, when under a small sore the flesh is much bruised and crushed: perhaps that was why they sent the lancet somewhat deeply into the living flesh. I praise their method, although it is not mine, particularly with noble and well-trained souls, as yours are. I think it is better simply to show them the mischief, and to put the knife into their hands to make the incision themselves. Do not, however, on that account cease to reform yourselves. I am wont to say that we should receive the bread of correction with great respect, even though he who brings it may be disagreeable and unacceptable. Just as Elias ate the bread brought by ravens, so must he be welcome to us who procures our good, though he may be in every other respect disagreeable and unwelcome. Job scraped off the corruption of his sores with a potsherd; this was a hard humiliation, but it was a useful one. Good advice ought to be well received whether steeped in gall or preserved in honey.

Let not all these hindrances be powerful enough, I beseech you, to keep you back from undertaking this your most necessary reformation. I pray God to send his Angels *to bear you up in their hands, lest perhaps you dash your feet against the stones* * of stumbling. It remains for me to tell you my opinion concerning the order you should follow.

Ask God, by common and express prayers, to let you see the defects of your house, and the means of remedying them and of receiving grace. Since he is the God of peace, pacify your spirits, put them in repose; do not let the spirit of contention, which may have possessed your souls with regard to those who have up to this time tried to correct you, form any obstacle to the celestial light; cling no longer to your own cause, or to that of your house; do just as you would if you wanted to institute a new Congregation. According to your order and your rule, treat one

* Ps. xc. 11.

another in this matter with a spirit of gentleness and of charity. Then will your Beloved, with his Angels, regard you as we do the bees when they are sweetly busy with the making of their honey, and I doubt not that this holy Lord will speak to your heart, saying to you what he said to his servant Abraham, *Walk before me and be perfect.** Go farther into the desert of perfection: you have already made the first day's journey by chastity, and the second by obedience, and a part of the third by some sort of poverty and common life; but why do you stop in so excellent a path, and for so slight a cause as private pensions? Go farther; finish the journey; have all in common; renounce private proprietorship, so that, according to the sacred Word, you may make a holy immolation and entire sacrifice in spirit and in goods.

After you have treated of your affair with your Spouse and with one another, call to your assistance and direction some of the more spiritual persons who are round about you; they will not fail you. I would name some of them; but you will name them better than I, and I dare say the very ones whom I should wish to name: they are persons extremely good for this purpose, gentle and gracious souls, indulgent when it comes to the point, though their rebukes may seem a little harsh and bitter. To these should you entrust this your affair, that they may decide what may seem most suitable; for your sex is subject, since the creation, to the condition of obedience, and never succeeds before God save by submitting itself to direction and instruction. Look at all the estimable Ladies of the Mother of Mercy up till this present, and you will

* Gen. xvii. 1.

find that I say the truth. In everything, however, I am presupposing that the authority of Madame de Fontevrault holds its place.

I am perhaps speaking and writing too much on a subject which you very likely have already had too much dinned into your ears; but God, in whose presence I write to you, knows that I have much more affection than I use words in this matter. I am unworthy to be heard, but I think your charity to be so great that you will not despise my advice, and I believe that the good Jesus has not given me so much love and confidence towards you without giving you a reciprocal affection, in order to take in good part what I propose to you for the service of your house, which I esteem and honour equally with any other, and think one of the best I have seen. This it is which has made me desire that it should be better, and perfect. It grieves me to see such grand qualities as those of your house subject to such paltry imperfections, and, as the Scripture says,* to see your *strength delivered into captivity*, and your *beauty into the hands of the enemy.* It is sad to see a precious liquor lose its worth through the presence of a little dirt, and an exquisite wine by the admixture of water: *thy wine*, says the prophet, *is mingled with water.*†

I will speak to you as did your holy Patron St. John, who was ordered to write to the Bishops of the East: ‡ *I know your works*, which are almost all good—you are almost such, good religious—*but I have a few things against you:* something is wanting to you. I praise you on the whole, said St. Paul to his Corinthians, but *in this I praise you not.*§ I pray and

* Ps. lxxvii. 61. † Isa. i. 22. ‡ Apoc. ii. § 1 Cor. xi. 22.

beseech you by the charity which is between us, take from your house what is in excess, and add to it what is wanting. Give me, I humbly beg of you, this consolation, to read my letter in repose and tranquillity of mind, and to weigh it not in the ordinary balance, but in the scales of the sanctuary and of charity; and I beseech God to give you the resolution necessary for your good, for the greater sanctification of his holy name amongst you, in order that you may be in name and in fact his true daughters. I promise myself the help of your prayers for my whole life, and more particularly for this entrance which I am making into the laborious and dangerous office of bishop, in order that *while preaching to others I may not myself become a castaway.**

May God be our peace and consolation.

I am, and will be throughout my whole life, Reverend Ladies and most dear sisters in Jesus Christ, yours, &c.

LETTER II.

To a Novice-Sister.

The signs by which we may know whether what we feel comes from God or from the evil one: the way of tending to perfection.

Annecy, 16*th January* 1603.

My very dear and beloved Sister and Daughter in Jesus Christ—May God be your repose and your consolation.

I have received your two letters by the President

* *Ib.* ix. 27.

Favre, a little later than you expected and I desired, but soon enough to give me consolation, in that I see therein some evidence that your mind is more at ease. May God be eternally blest for it!

In answer, I will first say that I do not want you to use any phrase of ceremony or of excuse with me, since by the will of God I bear you all the affection you could desire, and I cannot help it. I love your soul with a strong love, because I think God so wills, and tenderly, because I see it still weak and young. Use all confidence, then, and liberty in writing to me, and ask what you may think proper for your good. Let this be said once for all.

I see in your letter a contradiction which you have put in without noticing it; for you tell me that you are delivered from your disquiet, and yet I see you thoroughly disquieted by seeking to acquire perfection all in a moment. Have patience; I will tell you by-and-by what to do.

You ask me if you are to receive and yield to feelings [of devotion]. You say that without them your spirit languishes, and that still you cannot receive them without suspicion; and it seems to you that you ought to reject them. Another time that you write to me on such a subject as this, give me an example of the matter which you ask my advice about; that is to say, of some one of those feelings which has given you the most reason for doubting whether it should be received; for I shall much better understand your meaning. In the meantime here is some advice on your question.

Feeling and sweetness may come from the friend or from the enemy, that is, from the evil spirit or from the good one. Now, we can tell whence they come by certain signs, all of which I cannot well name to you; but here are some of them which will suffice.

When we do not stay in them, but simply use them by way of recreation, to enable us afterwards to fulfil our duties, and the work with which God has charged us, more courageously, it is a good sign; for God gives them sometimes for this purpose. He bends down to our weakness; he sees that our spiritual taste is out of order; he gives us a little sauce, not that we may eat the sauce only, but that he may tempt us to eat the solid meat. It is, therefore, a good sign when we do not stop at feelings; for the evil one, when it is he who gives the feelings, desires that we should stay in them, and that eating only the sauce our spiritual appetite should be weakened, and, little by little, ruined.

Secondly, good feelings do not inspire thoughts of pride, but, on the contrary, they strengthen us to reject those which the evil one may take occasion from them to whisper to us, so that the superior part ever remains entirely humble and lowly. It understands that Caleb and Josue would never have brought back the grapes from the Promised Land, to entice the Israelites to conquer it, unless they had considered their spirits to be weak and in need of stimulating; and so, instead of thinking itself to be something on account of these feelings, it argues and acknowledges its weakness, and humbles itself lovingly before its Beloved, who pours out his balm and his perfume that the young maidens and weak souls like itself may perceive, love, and run after it. But when they are evil feelings that possess us, instead of making us think of our weakness, they make us think we are getting them as a reward and prize.

Good feelings, when they depart, do not leave us weakened, but strengthened, not afflicted, but cheered; evil ones, on the contrary, when they arrive, give us some joy, and departing, leave us full of distress. Good feelings, when they go away, recommend that during their absence we should cherish, serve, and follow virtue, for the increase of which they had been given to us; evil ones make us believe that with them virtue goes away, and that we are unable to observe it as we should.

In short, good feelings do not want us to love them, but to love him who gives them (not that they are unworthy to be loved, but that is not what they *seek*); whereas evil ones would have themselves loved above all things. Hence the good ones do not make us eagerly seek them or cherish them; but bad feelings encourage us ever to seek virtue with eagerness and disquiet.

By these four or five marks you will be able to tell whence your feelings come from; and if they come from God you must not reject them, but, acknowledging that you are as yet but a poor little infant, take the milk of your Father's breasts, who, from the pity which he feels for you, fulfils also to you the office of mother. *Thy breasts*, says the spouse to her Beloved,* *are better than wine, smelling sweet of the best ointments.* They are compared to wine, because they rejoice, invigorate, and put in good order the spirit, which without these little consolations would sometimes be unable to digest the travails which it must receive.

* Cant. i. 1, 2.

Receive them, then, in God's name, with this sole condition, that you be ready not to receive them; and do not love them, but reject them, when you know by the decision of your superiors that they are not good and not for the glory of God; and be ready to live without them, when God shall consider you worthy and able. Receive them, then, I say, my dear sister, thinking yourself weak as to your spirit, since the doctor gives you wine, in spite of the fevers of imperfections which are in you. If St. Paul recommends wine to his disciple for his corporal weakness, I may well advise you to take spiritual wine for your spiritual weakness.

Such is my answer, clear enough, I think; to which I add that you must never make a difficulty as to receiving what God sends you on the right or on the left, with the preparation and resignation that I have said: and if you were the most perfect being in the world, you ought not to refuse what God gives you, provided that you are ready to refuse it if such were his pleasure. At the same time you must believe that when God sends you these feelings it is for your imperfection, and it is this you must fight against, not the feelings which tend against it.

As for me, I have only one scruple—that you tell me these feelings are from the creature. I believe you meant to say that they come to you through the creature and yet from God; for in the rest of your letter you give me reasons to think thus. But even if they were from the creature they would not therefore have to be rejected, since they lead to God, or at least they are led to God; you have only to take care not to let yourself be taken by surprise, according to the general rules for using creatures.

I will now tell you what I promised. I seem to see you agitated and restlessly anxious in your seeking after perfection; for this it is which has made you afraid of these little consolations and these feelings of devotion. But I tell you in truth, as is written in the Book of Kings,* God is not in the strong wind, nor in the earthquake, nor in those fires, but in the soft and tranquil breathing of a wind that can scarce be felt.

Let yourself be governed by God; think not so much for yourself. If you desire me to command you, since your mistress wishes it, I will do so willingly, and will first order that, having a general and universal resolution to serve God in the best fashion you can, you do not busy yourself with examining and minutely analysing what is the best fashion. This is a drawback incident to the nature of your spirit, which seeks to tyrannise over your will, and to guide it by lower and narrow rules.

You know that God wills in general that we should serve him by loving him above all things and our neighbour as ourselves. In particular he wills that you should keep a rule; that is enough. You must do it in good faith, without narrowness and subtlety; the whole after the way of this lower world, in which perfection resides not; in human way, and according to time, waiting for a day on which to do it after divine and angelic manner, and according to eternity.

Eagerness, agitation, does not help on an undertaking at all. Here the desire is good, but let it be without agitation. It is this eagerness which I expressly forbid you as the mother-imperfection of all imperfections.

* 3 Kings xix.

And therefore do not examine so anxiously whether you are in perfection or not. For this I give you two reasons: the one, that our inquiry will be useless, because if we were the most perfect people in the world we ought never to know or recognise it, but ever esteem ourselves imperfect; our examination should never aim at learning whether we are imperfect or not, for we must never have a doubt about it. Whence it follows that we must not be astonished to see ourselves imperfect, since we must never see ourselves otherwise in this life; nor must we vex ourselves about it, for there is no help for it; but we must humble ourselves for it, for by this we shall repair our defects; and we must quietly correct ourselves, because this is the discipline for which our imperfections are left us; and though we are not excusable if we do not strive to correct them, yet we are excusable if we do not entirely succeed—the case of imperfections being different from that of sins.

The other reason is, that this examination, when it is made with anxiety and perplexity, is but a waste of time; and those who make it resemble soldiers who in training for battle should have so many encounters and bouts among themselves that when it came to right down earnest they would find themselves tired and spent; or they are like musicians who should get hoarse with practising to sing a motet; for the spirit wearies itself over such a searching and continual examination; and when it comes to the moment of execution it can no more. Such is my first commandment.

The second, following the first: *If thine eye be simple thy whole body will be lightsome,* says our

Saviour.* Have a simple judgment; make not so many reflections and returns on self, but walk simply and with confidence. For you, there are but God and yourself in this world; all the rest ought to touch you not, save in so far as God commands, and in the way he commands. I beg you, do not look about you so much; keep your gaze fixed on God and on yourself; you will never see God without goodness, nor yourself without misery; you will see his goodness favourable to your misery, and your misery the object of his goodness and mercy. So do not look at anything except this,—I mean with fixed, settled, and deliberate gaze; only glance at all the rest.

Wherefore, study but little what others do, or what will happen to them; but regard them with a simple, kind, gentle, and affectionate eye. Do not require more perfection from them than from yourself, and do not be surprised at the diversity of imperfections; for imperfection is not more imperfection for being extravagant and odd. Do as the bees do; suck honey from all flowers and herbs.

My third commandment is, that you do as little children do; whilst they feel their mothers holding them by the sleeve they go boldly and run about, and do not alarm themselves when the weakness of their legs makes them slip a little to one side; in the same way, as long as you perceive that God holds you by the goodwill to serve him which he has given you, walk boldly, and do not alarm yourself about those little baulks and stumbles you make, and do not distress yourself about them, provided that at certain intervals you throw yourself into his arms, and kiss

* Matt. vi. 22.

him with the kiss of charity. Walk joyously and open-heartedly as far as you can; and if you do not walk joyously, at least walk courageously and faithfully.

Do not give up the company of the sisters, although it may not be according to your taste; rather give up your taste when it may not be according to the general way of the sisters. Love the holy virtue of forbearance and self-adapting; for thus, says St. Paul,* *you will fulfil the law of Christ.*

Lastly, God has given you a temporal father, from whom you may receive much spiritual consolation. Love your spirit better than your body; follow out his advice as that of God; for God will give you many blessings by his instrumentality. He has sent me his translation of Blosius's *Institution;* I have had it read at table, and have enjoyed it exceedingly: read it, I beg you, and dwell upon it, for it deserves it.

For the rest, when there occur to you doubts in this life which you have undertaken to lead, I admonish you not to let yourself wait for me; for I am too far off you to help you, and this would make you delay too much. There is no want of spiritual fathers to help you; employ them with confidence. I do not say this from any wish not to have your letters, for they give me consolation, and I wish to have them, yea, with all the details of the movements of your spirit, and the length of this letter will testify sufficiently that I do not grow weary of writing to you; but I say it in order that you may not lose time, and that whilst awaiting help from such a distance you may not be overcome and injured by the enemy.

* Gal. vi. 2.

As to my sacrifices, doubt not that you have part in them continually. Every day I offer you on the altar with the Son of God; I trust that God will deign to be pleased thereat.

Assure our Sister Anne Seguier, my very dear daughter in Jesus Christ, of the same, and madame your mistress, whose salutations I have presented to good M. Nouvelet, who was much gratified. If you knew the great multitudinousness of my affairs, and the embarrassment which this charge causes me, you would take pity on me, and would sometimes pray to God for me; and He would be greatly pleased. I beg of you and of Sister Anne Seguier that you often say to God, like the Psalmist, *I am thine, save me;** and, like Magdalen, when at his feet, *Rabboni*—Ah! my Master!—and then let him act as he pleases. He will make of you, in you, without you, and yet by you and for you, the sanctification of his name, to which be honour and glory.—Your affectionate servant in Jesus Christ, &c.

LETTER III.

TO M. ANTOINE REVEL, NAMED TO THE SEE OF DOL.

On the virtues necessary for the episcopal office, and the way to acquire them.

ANNECY, *end of* 1603.

SIR,—I have received two of your letters, but I have not yet answered them because when they arrived I was not here, but in Piedmont, whither I was obliged

* Ps. cxviii. 94.

to go on account of the temporal revenues of this see. Now, sir, I send you the document from Rome which you desire. I have opened it to see whether it contains all you want, and I see all is there, and something more which does not concern you, and does not affect the document as to what is required for you. So there is my promise fulfilled in that particular. If any difficulty remain, please use the same confidence with me about it. I assure you, sir, that I shall never weary of doing services for your pleasure and for your soul, which I hope God will employ for the service of many others.

The other part of my promise is harder for me to put into effect, on account of the incessant occupations which overwhelm me; for I think I am in an office more burdensome than any other of its kind. But still I give you here an outline of what I have to put before you.

You are entering upon the ecclesiastical state, and at the same time you mount to the very summit of that state. I will say to you what was said to a shepherd who was chosen to be king over Israel: *Thou shalt be changed into another man.** You must be other, in your interior and in your exterior; and to make this great and solemn change you must revolutionise your spirit and alter it throughout. Would to God that our charges, more tempestuous than the sea, had also that property which the sea has of making those who embark upon it cast up and vomit forth all their evil humours! But it is not so here; for very often we embark and spread our sails to the wind in very sickly state, and the farther we sail and voyage

* 1 Kings x. 6.

over the high seas, the more evil humours we beget. Well, praised be God, who has given you the desire not to do thus! I hope that he will also give you the power not to do it, that his work may be perfect in you.

To help you in this alteration you must use the living and the dead. The living, because you must find one or two thoroughly spiritual men of whose conversation you may be able to avail yourself. It is an extreme benefit to have those to whom we can give our spiritual confidence. I pass over M. du Val, who is good at all things and universally fitted for such offices. I tell you another—M. Galemant, *curé* of Aumale. If by chance he were at Paris, I know that he would help you much. I mention to you a third, a man to whom God has given much, and whom it is impossible to approach without great profit—M. de Berulle. He is entirely such as I would wish to be myself. I have hardly seen a soul which pleases me as his does; in fact, I have not seen one nor come across one; but there is this drawback, that he is extremely occupied. You may make use with as much confidence of him as of any one, but with some regard for his engagements. I have a great friend whom M. Raubon knows, M. de Soulfour; he is very capable in these matters. I should like you to know him, as I consider you would get much benefit from him.

As to the dead, you must have a little library of spiritual books of two kinds—the one for you as an ecclesiastic, the other for you as bishop. Of the first sort you should have some before entering on your charge, and should read them and reduce them to practice; for we must begin with the private (*monas-*

tique) life before coming to the active and public life. I beg you to have the entire works of Granada, and to make them your second breviary. Cardinal [St. Charles] Borromeo had no other theology to preach with, and yet he preached excellently. But that is not its chief utility: the chief is, that it will train your soul to the love of true devotion, and to all the spiritual exercises which are necessary for you. My advice is, that you begin to read him in his large *Guide to Sinners,* then that you proceed to the *Memorial*, and then read him all; but to read him with fruit you must not simply hasten to get him down; you must weigh him and see his value, and, chapter after chapter, you must ruminate him, and apply him to your soul with many considerations and prayers to God. You must read him with reverence and devotion, as a book containing the most useful inspirations which the soul can receive from on high; and in this way must you restore all the powers of your soul, purging them by the detestation of all their bad inclinations, and applying them to their true end by firm and high resolutions.

After Granada, I strongly recommend to you the works of Stella, particularly on the vanity of the world, and all the works of Francis Arias, a Jesuit. The *Confessions* of St. Augustine will be extremely useful to you, and if you follow my advice you will take them in French, in the translation of M. Hennequin, bishop of Rennes. Bellintani, a Capuchin, is also very good for expressing with clearness many excellent considerations on all the mysteries of our faith, and it is the same with the works of Costerus, a Jesuit. And at the last moment I remember to recommend to you the

Spiritual Letters of John of Avila, in which I am certain you will find many useful considerations for yourself and others; and at the same time I recommend to you the Epistles of St. Jerome, in his excellent Latin.

As bishop, to help you in the management of affairs, have Cardinal Toletus's book of *Cases of Conscience*, and study it well; it is short, easy, and safe; you will find it enough for the beginning. Read the *Morals* of St. Gregory, and his *Pastoral Care;* St. Bernard in his letters, and in his books *On Consideration.* Or if you choose to have an abridgment of both, get the book entitled *Stimulus Pastorum*, by the Archbishop of Braga, in Latin, printed by Kerner. The *Decreta* of the Church of Milan is necessary for you; but I do not know whether it is printed at Paris. Also I want you to have the life of the Blessed Cardinal Borromeo, written by Charles *a Basilica Petri*, in Latin, for therein will you see the model of a true pastor; but, above all, have always in hand the Council of Trent and its Catechism.

I do not think that will be too little for you during the first year, for which alone I speak; afterwards you will be better instructed, and this from the very fact of having made progress in the first year, if you confine yourself within the simple limits I propose. But please excuse me for treating so confidently with you; for I cannot act in any other way on account of my high opinion of your goodness and friendliness.

I will yet add these two words: the one is, that it is of immense importance for you to receive consecration with a great reverence and devotion, and with a thorough appreciation of the greatness of your ministry. If you were able to get the discourse of Stanislaus

Scolonius upon it, entitled, at least according to my copy, *De sacrâ episcoporum consecratione et inauguratione*, it would help you much; for in truth it is an excellent piece. You know that the commencement in all things is very important; and one can truly say, *the first in each kind is the measure of the rest.*

The other point is, that I earnestly wish you much confidence and a particular devotion with regard to the holy Angel, guardian and protector of your diocese; for it is a great consolation to have recourse to him in all the difficulties of one's charge. All the Fathers and theologians agree that bishops, besides their own particular Angel, have the assistance of another, who is deputed for their office and charge. You must have much confidence in the one and the other, and by frequently invoking them contract a certain familiarity with them, and specially, for affairs, with the one of the diocese, as also with the holy patron of your cathedral. For the rest, sir, you will gratify me if you love me intimately, and give me the consolation of writing to me familiarly; and be assured that you have in me a servant and brother in vocation as faithful as any one.

I forgot to say to you that you should by all means take the resolution of preaching to your people. The most holy Council of Trent, after all the Ancients, has decreed that a bishop's first and chiefest office is to preach, and let no consideration divert you from this. Do not do it in order to become a great preacher, but simply because it is your duty and God's will. The paternal sermon of a bishop is worth more than all the art of the elaborate discourses of other kinds of preachers. There is needed very little for good preaching, in a bishop; for his sermons should be on necessary and useful, not on curious or recondite, things; his words simple, not studied; his manner paternal and natural without art or effort; and short as he may be, or little as he may say, it is always a great thing.

Take all I have said as the beginning, for the beginning will afterwards teach you the rest. I see that you write your letters so well and fluently, that, in my opinion, you will, with but a little determination, make good sermons; still, sir, I say that you must have no little resolution, but much, and of a good and invincible kind. I beseech you to recommend me to God; I will return you an equivalent, and will all my life be, sir, your, &c.

LETTER IV.

To Madame Rose Bourgeois, Abbess of Puits d'Orbe.

[This was a Benedictine Abbey in Burgundy, ten miles from Châtillon-sur-Seine. The Abbess, on whose name, Rose, the Saint frequently plays, was daughter to M. Bourgeois de Crépy, president of the parliament of Burgundy. One of her sisters was married to M. Brulard, another was prioress in the same Abbey. Madame de Chantal also called them sister, and they her. St. Francis, who made the acquaintance of them all when he preached the Lent of 1604 at Dijon, adopted the same style, and calls them all, indifferently, sisters.

Many of these letters are wrongly dated and arranged by the French editors. The dates are here restored, as far as possible, by the internal evidence of the letters themselves, resting on the following ascertained facts. The first could not have been earlier than May 1604, the date of the Saint's return to Annecy. An interview at Saint-Claude which is mentioned took place on 24th August 1604. Jeanne de Sales went to Burgundy with Madame de Chantal in May 1605. The Saint was commissioned to reform the Abbey in August 1608.]

On the devotion proper to a religious, and the means to obtain it : also on the method to be observed by a religious superior in reforming her community.

May 1604.*

YOU have two sets of duties, Madame my dear daughter; for you are a religious and you are an abbess; you must serve God in each capacity, and to this end must be directed all your aims and exercises and affections.

Remember that there is nothing so blessed as a devout religious, nothing so miserable as a religious without devotion.

Devotion is simply the promptitude, fervour, affection, and agility which we have in the service of God: and there is a difference between a good man and a devout man; for he is a good man who keeps the commandments of God, although it be without great promptitude or fervour; but he is devout who not only observes them, but does so willingly, promptly, and with a good heart.

The true religious ought to be devout, and to aim at acquiring a great promptitude and fervour. To do this, it is necessary, first, to have the conscience uncharged with any sin; for sin is a heavy burden, which makes its bearer unable to walk uphill. On which account it is necessary to confess often, and never to let sin sleep in our bosom.

Secondly, we must take away all that can tie the feet of our soul, which are the affections. These must be unfastened and withdrawn from every object which is, I do not say bad, but not entirely good; for a horse that is shackled or tethered cannot run.

* The French says, "Before 3rd May 1604." [Tr.]

Further, we must beg this promptitude from our Lord, and for this purpose exercise ourselves in prayer and meditation, letting no day pass without making it during the space of a short hour. And as regards prayer, I remind you (1) that you must never omit the ordinary Office which is prescribed by the Church; you must rather omit every other prayer: (2) after the Office you must prefer meditation to all other prayers, for it will be more profitable to you and more pleasing to God: (3) make it a practice to use ejaculatory prayers, which are sighs of love breathed out before God to ask his help and protection. It will greatly help you in this to keep before your imagination that point of your meditation which you have most relished, in order to ruminate over it throughout the day, as one uses lozenges for physical benefit. You will find the same help from a cross, or from a pious image suspended from your neck, or your Rosary, if you often touch and kiss it in honour of the person represented, or from saying, when the clock strikes, a little word with your heart or your lips, such as, *Vive Jesus!* or, *Now is the hour to arise from sleep*, or, *My hour approaches*, and the like. (4) Pass no day, as far as possible, without reading a little in some spiritual book, and the same before meditation, to put yourself into a spiritual frame of mind.

Make it a custom to put yourself in the presence of God in the evening before you go to sleep, thanking him for having preserved you, and making the examen of conscience, as spiritual books direct. Do the same in the morning, preparing yourself to serve God all the day long, offering yourself to his love, and offering to him your own.

I wish that your meditation should be made in the morning, and that on the day before you should read the point that you intend to meditate on in Granada, Bellintani, or a similar author.

In order to acquire a holy promptitude in the practice of virtue, let no day pass without some particular act of it with this intention; for practice serves marvellously to facilitate our performance of all sorts of operations.

Never fail, at this commencement, to communicate every first Sunday of the month, besides the chief feasts; go to confession the night before, and excite in yourself a holy reverence and spiritual joy, as being about to have the happiness of receiving your sweet Saviour; and then make a new resolution of serving him fervently, confirming this, when you have received him, not by vow, but by a good and firm resolution.

On the day of your Communion, keep yourself as devout as ever you can, sighing after him who will then be yours and in you; and with the interior eye perpetually regard him lying in your heart, or seated in it as on his throne; and make your senses and your powers come one after another to hear his commandments and to promise him fidelity. This should be done after Communion by a short half-hour's meditation.

Take care not to let yourself be moody and out of humour with those about you, lest, attributing this to devotion, they despise devotion; on the contrary, give them the greatest pleasure and satisfaction you can, in order that they may thus be brought to honour and esteem devotion, and to desire it.

Have in you the spirit of sweetness, joy, and humility, which most befit devotion; as also tranquillity, not disturbing yourself either for this or for that, but going your way of devotion with an entire confidence in the mercy of God, who will lead you by the hand into the heavenly country, and by this means keep yourself from vexations and from contentions.

As regards your quality of abbess, that is, of mother of a monastery, it obliges you to procure the good of all your religious in the perfection of their souls, and consequently to reform their manners and the whole house.

1. The method of doing it, at this beginning, ought to be sweet, attractive, and cheerful. You must not commence with the reprehension of things which have been tolerated up to now, but you yourself, without saying a word to them, must show the exact contrary in your life and conversation, employing yourself before them in holy exercises, such as saying prayers sometimes in the church, or possibly making your meditation there, saying the Rosary, having some spiritual work read to you while working with your needle; exhibiting to them meanwhile a more sweet and unaffected love than ever, with special marks of friendship for those who are giving themselves to devotion, yet not failing also to show every sign of affection to the others, in order to attract and lead them into the same path.

2. Be chary as to worldly conversations, and do not allow them in your own room further than you can possibly help, so that little by little you may get the sisters' dormitory entirely cleared of them;—that is most requisite, and your example is a great means towards it.

3. At table, have some good spiritual book read; such as Granada *On the Vanity of the World*, Gerson, Bellintani, and others of the kind; and make this a custom for every day.

4. At Office your own devout behaviour must set the law of modesty and reverence to all the religious. This you will easily do if you put yourself in the presence of God each time you begin the Office. I think that to introduce the Breviary of the Council of Trent will be a useful and profitable thing.

5. Do not adopt too austere an air at the outset, but be amiable with every one save very worldly persons; with these you must be short-spoken and reserved.

6. It will be good to employ one of your religious to help you in the management of temporal affairs, in order that you may have so much the more opportunity of giving yourself to the spiritual and to duties of charity.

7. Lastly, do not be in a hurry at this commencement, but do all that you will do so cheerfully and with such sweetness that all your daughters may come gradually to desire to embrace devotion; and when you see they have entered upon this you must treat more thoroughly of the re-establishment of the perfection of your Rule, which will be the greatest service you can do Our Saviour. But all must proceed not so much from your authority as from your example and gentle leading.

8. God calls you to all these holy works; hear him and obey. Consider that you can never take too much pains nor practise too much patience in the pursuit of so great a good. How happy will you be

if at the end of your days you can say with Our Lord: * *I have finished* and perfected *the work thou gavest me to do!* Desire it, effect it; think of this, pray for this; and God, who has given you the will to desire it, will give you strength to execute it.

LETTER V.

TO THE SAME.

Same Subject.

ANNECY, *between May and end of August* 1604.†

MADAME—I have sent to President Brulart's wife, your sister, a writing which I wish to be communicated to you; not that the one I have given you is no longer of use for you and for the present time, but that you may ever have more and more illumination in your soul, to the advancement of which I feel myself so much bound that there is nothing in the world I desire more, not only on account of the great confidence God has given you in my regard, but also on account of that which he gives me, that you will greatly serve for his glory: have no doubt of this, madame, and have good courage. I am extremely consoled by the pleasure you take in reading the life of St. Teresa, for you will see the great courage which she had in reforming her Order; and this will doubtless aid you to reform your monastery, which will be much easier for you than she found it, since you are perpetual superior. But keep to the method I recommended to you, of commencing by example; and

* John xvii. 4. † The French says, "3rd May 1604."

though it may seem to help you but little at first, yet have patience, and you will see what God will do. I recommend to you above all the spirit of sweetness, which is what ravishes hearts and gains souls. Hold tightly and resolutely, in this beginning, to the good performance of all your exercises, and prepare yourself for temptations and contradictions. The evil spirit will excite innumerable such, to hinder the good which he sees is about to come from your resolution; but God will be your protector, as I beseech him to be with all my heart, and will beseech him all the days of my life. I beg you to recommend me to his mercy, and to believe that I am, as greatly as you can desire and as I can be,—Madame, yours, &c.

My companion told me on the journey that you wished to come to Saint-Claude, and that I shall then have the advantage of seeing you. I beg you in that case to let me know beforehand, that I may be able to be in a place and in a state of leisure suitable for your consolation.

LETTER VI.

To the Same (The Abbess of Puits d'Orbe).

Advice on her own conduct, on the introduction of certain community exercises, and the general reformation of the Abbey.

Autumn of 1604.*

Madame—I have kept your messenger, Philibert, a long time, but it is because I have never had a single day to myself, although I have been in the country;

* The French says, "9th October 1604."

for the charge which I hold carries its martyrdom with it everywhere, and I cannot say that any single hour of my time is my own, except my hours of Office; so much the more earnestly do I desire to be recommended to your prayers.

I send to you, my dear daughter (such is the name that you desire and that my heart dictates), a paper on what seems to me the easiest and most profitable method of making mental prayer. I have inserted for you some exercises and ejaculatory prayers. This will amply suffice to teach the form which you must follow for spending the day. I want you to communicate it to Madame the wife of the President, your sister, and to Madame de Chantal; for I think it will be useful to them.

As to the matter of your meditations, I should like it to be, as a rule, on the life and death of Our Lord; for these are the most simple and most useful.

The books which I recommend you are Bruno, a Jesuit; Capiglia, a Carthusian; Bellintani, a Capuchin; but above all Granada in the *True Way*—to begin with. Bruno and Capiglia may serve you for feasts and Sundays, the other two for the common days of the year. But although you may look at these authors, who are excellent, do not depart from the form which I have sent you.

Always enter upon prayer by putting yourself in the presence of God, invoking him, and proposing to yourself the mystery; and after the considerations always make acts of the affections, not of all, but of some, and the resolutions; after that the thanksgivings, the offering, the prayer; lastly, read carefully the little memorial which I send you, and put it in practice.

As to meditation on death, judgment, and hell, it will be very useful to you, and you will find materials for it in Granada at great length. Only, my daughter, I beg you to let all these meditations on the four last things end always with hope and confidence in God, and not with fear and terror; for when they end with fear they are dangerous, particularly those on death and hell.

Therefore, after having considered the greatness of the torments and their eternity, and after having excited yourself to the fear of them, and made a resolution of serving God better, you must represent to yourself the Saviour on the cross, and running to him with outstretched arms, you must go and take hold of his feet, with interior exclamations full of hope: O, harbour of refuge, ah! your blood shall be my safety; I am yours, Lord, and you will save me: and leave off in this affection, thanking Our Lord for his blood, offering it to his Father for your deliverance, and beseeching him to apply it to you. But never at any time fail to finish by hope, otherwise you would draw no profit from such meditations; and ever keep to this rule of finishing your prayer with confidence; for it is the virtue which is most required for gaining God's help, and the one which honours him the most. So you may make these meditations on the four last things once every three months, during four days.

Touching the order of prayer for the day, I think I have given you sufficient instruction in this little paper which I send you. I will, however, tell it you here a little more particularly.

Knowing that you are a very early riser, I say that in the morning after you rise you ought to make your meditation and the morning exercise which I have called preparation, with the proviso that the whole shall not last longer than three-quarters of an hour at most, as I do not want the meditation and exercise to take an hour. After this you can proceed with the day's business until Office, if there is any time.

At the Mass, I advise you to say your chaplet rather than any other vocal prayer; and while saying it you can break off when you have to observe the points I have marked—the Gospel, the Credo, the Elevation,—and then take it up where you left off, and have no fear but that it will be the better said for these interruptions; and if you cannot finish it at the Mass, it will do at some other time of the day, but you need only go on from where you stopped.

At dinner, I should approve of your arranging to have the *Benedicite* said, and the ecclesiastical grace which is at the end of the Breviary. This you can introduce at the same time that you introduce the Tridentine Breviary, or before, if you think well; and little by little get each sister to take her turn in saying it, for the Church has not given the order except for us to observe it. When at Annecy I always observe it.

A little before supper it would be very useful for you to take a quarter of an hour's recollection to ruminate the morning's meditation, unless at that time they are saying Compline in the monastery.

In the evening, before going to rest, I recommend that if the church be not too far removed from your rooms, and if not inconvenient, you should all go there together, and that when you get there, and are on your knees and in the presence of God, the one whose week it is should make the examination of conscience thus: *Paternoster*, and the rest said secretly; *Ave Maria* and *Credo*, and at the end *Carnis, resurrectionem, vitam æternam, Amen.* Then all together the *Confiteor*, up to *meâ culpâ*, and stop for about half a quarter of an hour to make the examen; then finish the *meâ culpâ* and the rest, *Misereatur* and *Indulgentiam.* After that the Litany of the Blessed Virgin, and the prayer of Our Lady, or that which follows: *Visita quæsumus Domine, habitationem istam*, &c. The others answer: *Dormiam et requiescam.* V. *Benedicamus Domino.* R. *Deo Gratias.* V. *Requiescant in pace.* And from that time let each one retire to her cell, after all have saluted one another together.

For the rest, dear madame, it is above all necessary that yourself first should keep a fixed order, not only for the Offices, but also as to rising and retiring; otherwise you cannot continue in health: and it is so arranged in all communities. Night vigils are dangerous for head and stomach. I should advise that dinner should not be later than ten, nor supper than six, nor bed-time than nine to ten, and getting up from four to five, unless some constitutions require more time for sleep, or cannot take so much. But for not sleeping so much the cause must be well approved; because for young women it seems that six hours are almost required, and if they do not take it they are without energy the whole of the day.

Do not make mental prayer after dinner, at least not for four hours after, and never after supper. On fast-days collation may be taken at seven; and as to fasting, for yourself it will suffice to begin with Friday, and to be satisfied with this for some time, particularly because you must be with the rest, and must lead them on little by little.

When you are ill make only ejaculatory prayer. Take care of yourself, obeying the doctor scrupulously, and be sure that this is a mortification agreeable to God; and when your sisters are ill be very affectionate in visiting them, assisting them, getting them served and comforted. Similarly, if some of them are sickly, show to them a tender compassion, easily dispensing them from their duty, from Office, according as you judge fitting; for this will gain their hearts wonderfully.

As to Communion and confession, I approve that it should be every week, and that on the evening of the Saturday you should add to the *Visita* the prayer of the Blessed Sacrament.

I sent you a little formula for confession, which I have prepared expressly for you. I do not put everything into it, but only what I have thought suitable for your instruction. You can communicate it to Mesdames Brulart and de Chantal, and to the religious whom you may see disposed to profit by it. I have not here the books which treat of it, and perhaps they say it better than I do; but it matters not, if you find it elsewhere so much the better.

As to the reformation of your house, my dear daughter, you must have a great and durable courage, and you will succeed without doubt, if God gives you his grace and some years of life. You are the one who will be employed on this sacred business, and without great trouble. I am glad that you are but few sisters; multitude breeds confusion. But how are you to begin? My idea is this.

The exact reformation of a monastery of women

consists in obedience well kept, poverty, and chastity. You must be closely on your guard to give no alarm, either loud or low, of your intention of making a reform; for that would cause all the hasty and busy-minded people to take up arms and set themselves against you. Do you know what must be done? It is necessary that the sisters should reform themselves under your guidance, and bind themselves to obedience and poverty. But how? Walk very little at a time; gain those young plants which are there; inspire into them the spirit of obedience; and to do this use three or four artifices.

The first is to give them commands often, but in things very little, pleasant, and light, and this before others; and then gracefully to praise them about it, and to call them to obedience with expressions of love,—my dear sister, or child, and the like; and just before doing this to say: If I ask you to do this or that, will you not do it well for the love of God?

The second is to put before them some books which will help them, and amongst others there are three admirable ones which I counsel you to have, and to read the most suitable points from, sometimes to them by themselves. These are Platus, *On the Advantages of the Religious State*, which is printed in French at Paris; *The Gerson of Religious*, composed by Père Pinel, printed at Lyons and at Paris; *The Desiring [soul], or Treasure of Devotion*, printed at Paris and Lyons. Also, to speak often of obedience, not as if wanting it from them, but as wanting to render it to some one. For example: Ah! how much happier are those abbesses who have superiors to command them! They are not afraid of erring; all their actions are much more agreeable to God ; and the like little baits.

The third is to command, so sweetly and amiably, as to make obedience an object of love, and after they have obeyed you to add: May God reward you for this obedience—and so to make yourself very humble.

The fourth is to make profession yourself of wishing to do nothing save by the advice and counsel of your spiritual father, to whom, however, you must attribute no right at all of commanding, just as you must not give to what you do under his direction any title of obedience, for fear of exciting contradictions, and of making unkind people raise jealousy in the minds of those who are superiors of your monastery. That would spoil all; and I have had my experience in such accidents through having seen them happen in France, in monasteries wherein there was no little difficulty in appeasing these tempests.

I say the same of poverty. It is necessary to lead them to it step by step in such way, that, inspired after this sweet fashion, after some time all their pensions may be placed together in one purse, from which they will draw all that is necessary, equally and as required, according to each one's need, as is done in many monasteries of France which I know. But above all you must not in any way give the alarm about all this, but lead them to it by gentle and sweet inspirations, towards which, also, the above-named books will assist.

As to chastity, you must begin thus. Declare that you yourself are never so content as when you are alone with them ; that it seems to you the greatest of pleasures to be thus in your private sisterly society amongst yourselves; that you like every one to be in his or her place, people of the world by themselves, and you with the sisters; or that worldly people only come to a religious house to get something to carry away and spread about here and there, and such-like little words to influence their minds—which, however, must be so said as to seem to be only your own personal ideas. You will see that, little by little, they will be very glad to give up going out into the world, and letting the world come in to them; and at last some day (it may well be after a year, or even two) you will get this passed into a constitution and rule; for, after all, enclosure is the guardian of chastity.

I am pleased to know that almost all of you are young, for this age is suited to receive impressions. At the monastery of Montmartre, near Paris, the young, with their abbess still younger, have effected a reformation.

When you encounter difficulties and contradictions, do not try to break them, but prudently let them pass, and bend them with sweetness and time: if all do not show themselves disposed, have patience, and advance as far as you can with the rest. Do not show any desire to conquer; excuse in the one her infirmity, in the other her age; and say as little as you possibly can that there is a want of obedience.

But tell me—do you think it little that you have done already for the Office, the veil, and the like? Good heavens! Our Saviour was three and a half years forming the college of his twelve apostles, and there was, after all, a traitor and much imperfection when he died. We must possess our heart in longanimity; great designs are not effected save by virtue of patience and duration of time. Things which grow in one day decay in another. Courage, then, my good daughter! God will be with you.

My daughter, I approve the charity you are willing to show to this poor misguided creature, provided that she return with a spirit of gratefulness and penitence; and if she come in this way she will find it sweet as sugar and honey to be placed in the lowest rank, and to have no part in the honours of the house, until the virtues she may display to balance her past faults may raise her back into new honours—except her order, which it is reasonable for her to lose absolutely. In particular, I am thoroughly of opinion that you should lift up her heart by gentleness, and that you invite all the other sisters to do likewise; for the Apostle says * quite plainly that *those who are spiritual* must lift up those who have been *overtaken in any fault in the spirit of mildness*, when they come in dispositions of penitence. Thus are we to mingle justice with kindness, after the manner of our good God, in order that charity may be practised and discipline observed.

I should approve that the exercise of the examen of conscience should not be made till a good half-hour or three-quarters after supper, and that during this three-quarters of an hour there should be recreation in innocent conversation, or even in singing spiritual songs, at any rate in this beginning.

Your children ought to receive Communion at eleven, at latest, supposing that they have the discretion which is ordinarily had at that age. And the first time they go to Communion it is well that you should yourself take pains to instruct them as to the reverence they

* Gal. vi. 1.

ought to have, and to make them mark the day and year in their prayer-book, to thank God for it each following year.

And now, it seems to me, I have answered all you asked me, madame my dear sister. I have only to say that I am, without ceremony, entirely yours and your abbey's, throughout which I hope one day to see holy devotion flourishing; in what I can, I will contribute both, what God will give me of his Spirit, and my feeble prayers. I never fail to make good room for you all in the *Memento* of holy Mass; and be sure that if you desire to be near me, I also greatly desire to be near you. But we are near enough, since God unites us in the desire to serve him. Let us live in God, and we shall be together. I beseech him with all my heart to strengthen you more and more in his love, with all the ladies your religious, whom I salute and beg not to forget me in their prayers, but to bestow on me some of the breathings of devotion which they direct towards heaven, where their hope is. Amen.

Meditation for the Beginning of each Month.

Place yourself in the presence of God; beseech him to inspire you. Imagine that you are a poor servant of Our Lord, and that he has placed you in this world as in his house.

1. Ask him with humility why he has placed you there; and consider that it is not for any need he may have of you, but in order to exercise his goodness and liberality upon you, for it is to give you his Paradise; and in order that you may have it, he has

given you an understanding to know him, a memory to be mindful of him, a will and a heart to love him and your neighbour, an imagination to represent to yourself him and his benefits, all your senses to serve him, your ears to hear his praises, your tongue to praise him, your eyes to contemplate his wonders, and so of the rest.

2. Consider that, being created for this end, all actions contrary to it ought to be utterly avoided, and those which do not conduce to it ought to be held in no esteem.

3. Consider what an evil thing it is to see in the world that men for the most part think not of this, but suppose they are in the world to build houses, lay out gardens, possess vineyards, amass gold, and the like transitory things.

4. Represent to yourself your misery, which was so great at such time as you were of this number. Alas! must you say, what was I thinking of when I was not thinking of thee, O Lord? Of what was I mindful when I was forgetting thee? What did I love when I loved not thee? Was I not unhappy in serving vanity instead of truth? Alas! the world, which was only made to serve me, ruled me, and was mistress over my affections! I renounce you, vain thoughts, useless memories, faithless friendships, lost and miserable services.

Make your resolutions, and a firm purpose of henceforward applying yourself faithfully to what God wants from you, saying to him: Thou shalt henceforth be my only light in my understanding; thou shalt be the object of my memory, which shall occupy itself solely in representing to itself the greatness of thy goodness, so sweetly exercised in my regard; thou shalt be the sole delight of my heart, and the only well-beloved of my soul.

Particular Application.

Ah! Lord, I have such and such thoughts; I will refrain from them in future: I have too keen a memory of injuries and slights; I will give it up from this time: I have my heart still attached to such or such a thing which is useless or hurtful to thy service, and to the perfection of love which I owe thee; I will entirely withdraw and disengage it, by the help of thy grace, that I may be able to give it all to thy love.

Fervently beseech God to give you this grace, and practise what you can in something which concerns this point.

Often repeat the saying of S. Bernard; and in imitation of him, stirring up your heart, say often: Rose, what hast thou come into this world to do? What art thou doing? Do that which thy Master hath charged thee to do, that for which he has put thee into this world and preserves thee in it. No one shall be crowned with roses who has not first been crowned with thorns by Our Lord.

One who desires your perfection in God, in whose tender mercies he is yours, &c.

LETTER VII.

TO THE SAME.

Further instructions on the same subjects. Announces the death of (Ven.) Ancina, and the intention of the Saint's mother to send her youngest daughter to be educated at Puits d'Orbe.

13*th October* 1604.

MADAME, MY VERY DEAR SISTER AND DAUGHTER IN OUR LORD—I want to mention some points to you privately, and I wish you to keep them to yourself.

I beg you by the words of our Lord to believe, without any doubt whatever, that I am entirely and irrevocably at the service of your soul, and that I will apply myself therein to the whole extent of my powers, with all the fidelity that you could ever wish. God wills it, as I know full well; more I could not say. On this good foundation I will employ my spirit and my prayers in thinking out all that will be useful and necessary for making a thorough reformation of all your monastery; only have a great courage, full of hope. This is all we need at present; for you will undoubtedly be attacked; but with a spirit of gentle bravery we shall achieve this good design, God helping. And for the present you must firmly establish the interior of your hearts, your own above all, for this is the true and solid method; and after some time we will establish the exterior to the edification of many souls. Be sure that I will think of this in good earnest. As to your desire to make your vows again in my hands, and to give me a writing to this effect, since you think this will give you so much repose, I am willing, provided that you add to the writing this condition, in that part where you speak of me—"saving the authority of lawful superiors"—and you must not let anything of this be known.

I am writing to your and my honoured father a letter calculated, in my opinion, to gain over his spirit to our design, which I am not making out to him so great as it is, because it would turn him against it to propose it all at once, whereas little by little he will undoubtedly approve it. I use some liberty about you in that letter, but you well know that all this is for nothing but the glory of God and your advantage, which alone I regard herein. I know that you hold me too much yours to interpret anything coming from me otherwise than as well and kindly meant.

We must have patience over his wanting his opinions to be followed, for he does all in excess of loving-kindness; and I hope that in the way that I am writing we shall greatly gain him over. I am writing a word to madame your sister, whom I cannot help loving extremely, being what she is. Your honoured father seems to desire it, by the letter which he has written to me.

I am much afraid that the writing of the Meditation is so badly done that you will not be able to read it. You must please take the trouble to get it copied out clearly, so as to be able to use it with more fruit. I was so much indisposed when I had it written that I could not use my hand to write it, and contented myself with dictating it.

There is no human likelihood that I shall ever have the consolation of seeing Puits d'Orbe; but the great desire with which I am moved towards your spiritual service makes me hope that Our Lord will conduct me thither by his Providence when the time requires, if my poor co-operation is required for your good design.

Persevere in having reading at table, and likewise sometimes in your room in company with your sisters. You must, little by little, dispose the matter of the entire reformation; and the chiefest preparation is to render hearts gentle, tractable, and desirous of perfection.

Take advantage of the help of the good Father de Villars, who writes to me, in answer to the note which I gave you at Saint-Claude, that he will take particular pains to help you. You will do well to keep to the devout practices which I have given you, and not to vary them without letting me know. God will be pleased with your humility towards me, and will make them fruitful to you.

My Lord the Bishop of Saluces [Ancina] has lately died. He was one of the greatest servants of God there has been in this age, and one of my most intimate friends: he was made bishop the same day as myself. I ask you for a Rosary for him; for I know that if I had died before him he would have done me the like charity wherever he had credit. If I had had time to myself I would have written to you in better order; but all that I am writing is only in morsels, according to the leisure I can get. Believe that I greatly need your prayers.

The books which you might have for the present are: Platus *On the Excellence of the Religious State; The Gerson of Religious*, by Luce Pinel; Paul Morigie

On the Institution and Commencement of Religious Orders; the works of Granada, newly printed at Paris; Bellintani *On Mental Prayer;* the *Meditations* of Capiglia, a Carthusian; those of St. Bonaventure; *The Desiring Soul;* the works of Francis Arias, and particularly *The Imitation of Our Lady;* the works of the Mother [St.] Teresa; the *Spiritual Catechism* of Cacciaguerra, and his other works. This, or a part of it, will suffice you, with those which I know you have already. May God, our dear sister, be your guide, protector, and preserver, your aim and your confidence. Amen.—Yours, &c.

Madame, I was almost forgetting to tell you that my mother and I have formed the plan of sending to you, after this next winter, my young sister, whom you saw at Saint-Claude, with the intention that, if God favour her with the inspiration of being a religious, she may be so in due time, with your favour and help; and too happy will she be to arrive in this house at the same time that devotion will be kindled there. Or, if she be not worthy of this place, nor I of this satisfaction, at least she will have this happiness, wherever she may go, of having been in so good a place. And it will all be, with God's help, without any inconvenience to any one save what may arise from her own disposition. See, madame my dear sister, whether or no we want to bind ourselves strongly to your service. I say it without ceremony.

LETTER VIII.

TO THE SAME (THE ABBEY OF PUITS D'ORBE).

How to sanctify corporal suffering: Instructions on peace and humility.

1605, *about April.**

MY VERY DEAR SISTER—The great word which makes me so absolutely yours is this: God it is who wills it, and I have no doubt thereof. There is no better title than this in all the world. You will already have known all the news about my cure, which is so complete that I have preached the Lent right through. Indeed my illness was nothing much, as I think; but the doctors, who thought I had been poisoned, caused so much fear to those who love me that it seemed to them I was going to slip out of their hands. As soon as ever I was up I wrote to you, and I feel sure you had the letter. Again since then I have written to you, but amid the press of a world of affairs which prevented me from giving you much time, as I should much have wished to do; subject never failing me, on account of the extreme satisfaction which I find in it.

Not only your messenger, but also our good and dear father, has informed me how many evils you suffer, and the compassion which they cause him for you. May Our Lord be blessed for it! Here is the safest and most royal way of heaven for you; and, from what I understand, you have to stay in it some time, since, according to what our good father writes to me, you are still in the hands of the doctors and surgeons. I

* The French says, "After 18th April 1604." [Tr.]

have certainly an extreme compassion for your sufferings, and recommend them often to Our Lord, that he may make them useful to you, and that when you come out of them it may be able to be said of you as of the holy man Job: *In all these things Job sinned not,** but hoped in God.

Courage, my good sister, my good daughter! Look at your Beloved, your King, how he is crowned with thorns, and all torn to pieces on the cross, so that *they* could *number all* his *bones.*†

Consider how the crown of the bride ought not to be better than that of the Bridegroom; and if they so tore away his flesh that all his bones might be counted, it is reasonable indeed that one of yours may be seen. *As the* rose *among thorns so is my love among the daughters.*‡ It is the natural place of that flower, and it is also the most suitable to your Bridegroom. Accept this cross a thousand times a day, and kiss it willingly for love of him who sends it to you. There is no doubt that he sends it to you from love, and as a rich present. Often represent to yourself your Saviour crucified just before you, and think which of the two suffers the more, and you will find your trouble much less. Oh! how happy will you be eternally if you suffer for God this trifling evil which he sends you!

You will not err in fancying that I am near you in these tribulations. I am so in heart and affection, and often *I declare before* your Beloved your sufferings and *trouble,*§ and feel in this a great consolation. But, my dear daughter, have confidence, be strong: *If you believe, you shall see the glory of God.*|| What do

* Job i. 22. † Ps. xxi. 18.
‡ Cant. ii. 2. § Ps. cxli. 3. || John xi. 40.

you think the bed of tribulation is? It is simply the school of humility: thereon we learn our miseries and weaknesses, and how vain, delicate, and infirm we are. And truly, my dear daughter, on that bed have you discovered the imperfections of your soul. And why, I pray you, rather there than elsewhere, save because elsewhere they stay within the soul, and there they come outside? The agitation of the sea so upsets the humours, that those who enter upon it thinking they have none, after sailing a little find by the convulsions and retchings which this irregular tossing excites that they are full of them. It is one of the great benefits of affliction to see the depths of our nothingness, and to make the scum of our bad inclinations float to the top. But still, are we for this to be troubled, my dear daughter? Certainly not; it is then that we must yet more cleanse and purify our spirit, and make more earnest acknowledgment of them than ever.

This important trouble, and the other troubles with which you have been beset, do not alarm me, so long as there is nothing worse. Do you, then, not disquiet yourself, my well-beloved daughter. Are we to let ourselves be swept away by current and by whirlwind? Let the enemy rage at the gate, let him knock, let him push, let him cry, let him howl, let him do his worst; we know for certain that he cannot enter save by the door of our consent. Let us keep this shut up, often looking to see that it is quite close; and about all the rest let us not trouble ourselves, for there is nothing to fear.

You ask me to send you something touching peace of soul and humility; I would do so willingly, my dearest daughter, but I do not know whether I shall be able to do it in the little space of leisure which I have for writing to you ; but here are four or five words about it, my well-beloved daughter. It is by divine inspiration that you ask me about peace of soul and humility both together; for it is indeed the truth that the one cannot be without the other.

Nothing troubles us except self-love, and the esteem in which we hold ourselves. If we have not feelings of tenderness in our heart, relish and sensible feeling in prayer, interior sweetnesses in meditation, we fall into sadness; if we find some difficulties in doing well, if some obstacle crosses our good designs, at once we anxiously hasten to overcome it all, and with disquieted minds to free ourselves from it. Why is all this? There is no doubt it is because we love our own consolation, our own pleasure, our own comfort. We want our prayer to be steeped in orange-flower water, and we would be virtuous in eating sugar; and we do not regard our sweet Jesus, who, prostrate on the earth, sweats blood and water in agony over the deadly conflict which he feels within him, between the affections of the inferior part of his soul and the resolutions of the superior.

Self-love, then, is one of the sources of our troubles; the other is the esteem in which we hold ourselves. What is the meaning of our being disappointed, troubled, and impatient when we fall into some imperfection or sin? Without doubt it is because we were thinking ourselves to be good for something, resolute, steady; and therefore, when we see that in reality it is all a mistake, and that we have fallen flat down, we find ourselves deceived, and consequently are troubled, vexed, and disquieted. If we only knew what we were, instead of being astonished at finding ourselves on the ground, we should marvel how we can remain standing up. And there is this other source of our disquiet; we want consolations only, and we are taken aback when we lay our finger on our misery, our nothingness, and our weakness.

Let us do three things, my dear daughter, and we shall have peace. Let us have a thoroughly pure intention of willing, in all things, the honour of God and his glory; let us do the little we can for that end, according to the advice of our spiritual father; and let us leave to God the care of all the rest. He who has God for the object of his intentions, and who does what he can—why does he torment himself? Why does he trouble himself? What has he to fear? No, no; God is not so terrible to those whom he loves; he is content with little, for he well knows we have not much.

And know, my dear daughter, that our Lord is called *Prince of Peace* in the Scriptures,* and that, therefore, wherever he is absolute master he holds all in peace. Though it is true that before placing peace anywhere he causes war there, separating the heart and the soul from its most cherished, familiar, and ordinary affections, such as an inordinate love of self, confidence in self, complacency in self, and the like affections. Now when Our Lord separates us from affections so fondly and passionately cherished, he seems to be flaying the heart alive, and the acutest pains are felt; we can scarcely help resisting with the whole soul, because this separation is most sensibly felt. But yet

* Isa. ix. 6.

all this resistance of the spirit is not without peace, even if we are at last overwhelmed with this distress, so long as we fail not on this account to hold our will resigned to that of Our Lord, and keep it there nailed to his divine good pleasure, and in no wise let go our obligations or the fulfilment of them, but execute them courageously. Of this Our Lord gave us an example in the Garden; for, all overcome with interior and exterior anguish, his whole heart was calmly resigned to his Father and the divine will, saying: *Yet not my will but thine be done*;—and, for all his agony, he did not omit going three times to see and admonish his disciples. It is to be "Prince of Peace" indeed, to be in peace amid wars, and to live in sweetness amid bitternesses.

From this I want you to draw these conclusions. The first, that very often we think we have lost peace because we are in bitterness, and yet we have not lost it all; as we know if on account of bitterness we cease not to renounce ourselves, and to keep our will dependent on the good pleasure of God, and fail not to fulfil the duties of the charge in which we are.

The second, that of necessity we must suffer interior pain, when God tears away the last skin from the old man to renew him in *the new man who is created according to God*.* Wherefore we must not be disquieted about this, nor think that we are in disfavour with God.

The third, that no thoughts which cause us disquiet and agitation of spirit are from God, who is Prince of Peace, but are temptations of the enemy, and there-

* Ephes. iv. 24.

fore we are to reject them, and take no notice of them.

We must in all things and everywhere live peacefully. If trouble, exterior or interior, come upon us, we must receive it peacefully. If joy come, we must receive it peacefully and without throbbings of heart. Have we to avoid evil ?—we must do so peacefully, without disquieting ourselves; for otherwise we may fall as we run away, and give time to our enemy to kill us. Is there some good to be done ?—we must do it peacefully; otherwise we should commit many faults in our hurry. Even our repentance itself must be made peacefully: *Behold in peace is my bitterness most bitter,** said the penitent.

Read, my good daughter, chapters 15, 16, and 17 of the *Spiritual Combat*, and add them to what I have said, and for the present this will suffice. If I had my papers here I would send you a treatise on this subject which I made at Paris for a spiritual daughter, a religious of a good monastery, who needed it both for herself and for others. If I find it I will send it you on the first opportunity.

As to humility, I can say little more than that your dear sister De N. must show you what I have written to her about it. Read carefully what Mother [St.] Teresa says of it in the *Way of Perfection*. Humility causes us to avoid troubling ourselves about our own imperfections by remembering those of others: for why should we be more perfect than others ?—and in the same way to avoid troubling ourselves over those of others when we remember our own: for why should we think it extraordinary for others to have imper-

† Isa. xxxviii. 17.

fections since we have plenty? Humility makes our hearts gentle towards the perfect and the imperfect; towards those from reverence, towards these from compassion. Humility makes us receive painful things sweetly, knowing that we deserve them, and good things with lowliness, knowing that we do not deserve them. As to the exterior, I should recommend you to make every day some act of humility, either in words or in deed—I speak of words that come from the heart; in word, as by humbling yourself to an inferior; in deed, as by doing some lower work or service, either for the house or for some particular person.

Do not distress yourself about staying in bed without meditation; for to endure the scourges of Our Lord is not a less good than meditating. No, undoubtedly; for it is better to be on the cross with Our Lord than to look at him only. But I know well that there, on your bed, you cast your heart a thousand times a day into the hands of God, and it is enough. Obey the doctors exactly; and when they forbid you some exercise, whether fasting, or mental or vocal prayer, or even Office, or any prayer beyond ejaculatory, I beseech you as earnestly as I can, both by the respect and by the love you are good enough to bear me, to be very obedient; for God has so ordained it. When you are cured and have got back your strength, resume your journey quietly, and you will see that we shall advance far, with God's help; for we shall go where the world cannot reach, beyond its limits and confines.

My dear daughter, you write me that you are in every respect the last, but you are mistaken; the fruits I expect from you are greater than from any of the others. Believe, I beg you, that I have nothing more at heart than your advancement before God, and if my blood would further this you would soon see in what rank I hold you. I leave on one side the extreme confidence you have in me, which obliges me to an extreme zeal for your welfare. You say you would like to send me your heart. Be sure that I should see it with satisfaction, for I love it tenderly, and it seems to me that it must be good because it is vowed to Our Lord. But you know the spot where our hearts meet; there they can see one another in spite of the distance of places.

Speak to this good father whom I mentioned about your interior: he will have enough in common with me, and I with him, not to distract your soul by a diversity of paths, which indeed would be very hurtful to it. In a word, receive him as another myself. But at the same time I ask you so to manage that, that other good father who wanted to help you, may not recognise that you do not wish his direction, because in the future he will be of service in the work that you and I desire, by obtaining something from the Holy Father.

But let not this last word excite you, for above all things it is necessary to go quietly and step by step; the edifice will be all the firmer for it. And you must give no alarm whatever about anything which takes place, so that the blessings of heaven may come upon earth like the dew upon the grass, which one sees on the ground without seeing it fall; and thus imperceptibly must you conduct your whole design up to the very height of its perfection. And courage, my dear and well-beloved daughter; God will give us this grace. As to that other good father, I approve of your listening to him and hearing him, and also of your making use of his advice by putting it in practice, but not when it is contrary to the design we have formed of following in everything and everywhere the spirit of sweetness and of mildness, and of thinking more about the interior of souls than the exterior. But in everything you ought to communicate with me, as I am your poor father.

No, my dear daughter, I have never thought it fitting for religious to have anything of their own if it could be helped; though I may have said that, in so far as superiors permit, individuals may use this liberty, so long as they are ready to leave all and put it in common should superiors order it. It is expedient, then, to take away private possession, and to make necessaries and conveniences common and equal among the sisters, and so to let the corn of Egypt fail before the manna which falls in your desert.

My mother, who offers you her own service and that of all who belong to her, continues in her desire of the honour of seeing my sister with you. It is one of our ardent desires: God grant that it may be with as willing consent on your part!

There was, indeed, no necessity for making excuses to me about the open letter; for my very heart would like to be open before your eyes, if its imperfections and weaknesses would not give you too much distress. Be ever quite safe, I beseech you, as far as I am concerned; and be certain that I desire nothing so greatly as to see you with a soul quite full of charity, which is totally frank and holily free. And why do I say this? Because I seem to see that you have some fear of offending me. I am by no means tender or sensitive in that direction, and particularly in cases where my friendship is rooted on the Mount of Calvary, by the cross of our Lord.

I am writing to that daughter of yours whom you ask me to write to, in a way as suitable to her trouble as I can. Oh how divinely does our St. Bernard say, that the exercise of the charge of souls has not to do with strong souls !—for those go by their own feet; but it is concerned with feeble and fainting souls, who have to be borne and supported on the shoulders of charity which is all-strong. This poor little one is of the latter sort, languishing under the depression and difficulties of various weaknesses, which seem to overwhelm her virtue. We must help her as much as we can, and leave the rest to God. I should never finish writing to you if I followed my inclination; it is full of affection. But enough; Mass calls me, in which I am going to present Our Lord to his Father for you, my dear daughter, and for all your house, in order to obtain from his divine goodness his Holy Spirit, to direct all your actions and affections to his glory and for your own salvation. I beseech him to preserve you from vain sadness and disquietude, and to repose in your heart that your heart may repose in him. Amen.

LETTER IX.

TO THE SAME.

Advice on meditation, on sleep, on having Mass in bedrooms: further advice on the way to sanctify corporal sufferings.

April or May 1605.*

MY VERY DEAR SISTER—May Our Lord grant you his Holy Spirit, to do and to suffer all things according to his will! Your messenger urges me so strongly to despatch him that I do not know whether I shall be able to answer you fully. At any rate I will say something to you, according as God shall give me the grace. I was glad that N. arrived so opportunely with my letters. All your repugnances do not alarm me; they will cease one day, God helping: and if it is true that you have given little satisfaction to this good father, I feel certain that he will not be vexed about it; for I esteem him capable of understanding the different accidents of a soul which is beginning to walk in the ways of God. As for me, my dear sister and daughter, you could not be troublesome to me: and if Our Lord had given me as much liberty and convenience for assisting you as I have desire and affection, you would never find me tired of serving you unto the glory of God; for I am completely yours, and you cannot be too fully convinced of this.

Touching meditation, I pray you not to distress yourself, if sometimes, and even very often, you do not find consolation in it; go quietly on, with humility

*The French says, "Before 9th October 1604." [Tr.]

and patience, not on this account doing violence to your spirit. Use your books when you find your soul weary, that is to say, read a little and then meditate, then read again a little and meditate, till the end of your half-hour. Mother [St.] Teresa thus acted in the beginning, and said that she found it a very good plan for herself. And since we are speaking in confidence, I will add that I have also tried it myself and found it good for me. Take it as a rule that the grace of meditation cannot be gained by any effort of the mind; but there must be a gentle and earnest perseverance full of humility. Continue all your other exercises in the manner I have marked them out for you.

With regard to going to bed, I will not change my opinion, if you please; but still, if you do not like bed, and cannot stay in it as long as the rest do, I will permit you to rise an hour earlier; for, my dear sister, it is incredible how dangerous long night vigils are, and how much they weaken the brain. It is not felt during youth; but it comes to be felt so much the more afterwards, and many persons have rendered themselves useless in this way.

I come to the question of the lancing of that poor limb. This will not be without extreme pain, but, my God! what an occasion does his goodness here give you of exercise in his commandments! Courage, my dear sister; we belong to Jesus Christ: see how he sends us his livery; take care that the iron which will open your leg be one of the nails which pierced Our Saviour's feet. What an honour! He has chosen this sort of favours for himself, and has loved them so greatly that he has carried them into Paradise, and behold he shares them with you; and you say that you leave me to think how you can serve God during the time that you will be in bed. And I am glad to think of it, my good daughter. Do you know what I think? In your opinion, my dear sister, when was it that Our Saviour chiefly served his Father? Without doubt it was when lying on the tree of the cross, with his hands and feet pierced. And how did he serve him? In suffering and in offering; his sufferings were an odour of sweetness to his Father. And here, then, behold the service which you are to do to God while on your bed of pain; you will suffer, and will offer your sufferings to his Majesty. He will certainly be with you in this tribulation, and will console you.

Here is your cross come to you; embrace it and love it for the love of him who sends it to you. David in his affliction said to Our Lord: * *I have been silent and have not opened my mouth, because it is thou*, O my God, *who hast done me* this evil that I suffer. As if he said: If any other but thou, O my God, had sent me this affliction, I should not love it, I should reject it; but since it is thou, I say no word more, I receive it, I honour it.

Have no doubt but that I will earnestly pray to Our Lord for you, that he may give you a share of his patience, since he pleases to give you a share of his sufferings. I ought to do this, I will do it, and I will be near you in spirit during all your illness; no, I will not abandon you.

And here is a precious balm to soften your pains. Take every day a drop or two of the blood which distils from the wounds of the feet of Our Lord, making

* Ps. xxxviii. 10.

it flow by your meditation; and in imagination reverently dip your finger in this liquid and spread it over your sore place, with the invocation of the holy name of Jesus, *which is oil poured out*, said the spouse in the Canticles,* and you will find that your pain will lessen.

During this time, my dear daughter, give up saying your Office for as many days as the doctors advise, although you may seem not to have need to do so. I ordain it thus for you, in God's name.

If these letters reach you before the painful moment, get them to look everywhere for the treatise of Cacciaguerra *On Tribulation*, and read it to prepare yourself, or have it read quietly to you by one of your more pious daughters while you are in bed. Never have I been so much touched by any book as I was by that during a very painful malady which I had in Italy.

The obedience which you will pay to the doctor will be extremely agreeable to God, and will be placed to your advantage at the day of judgment.

I cannot send you the writing on Communion just now, because your man presses me too much. I will send it you soon, for I shall have an opportunity; but meantime you will find in Granada all that you require, and in the *Spiritual Exercises*.

How pleased I was to see that you have overcome all difficulties in doing all that I wrote to you touching your vows and confession! My dear sister, you must always act so, and God will be glorified in you. You shall have letters from me very often and by every opportunity.

* i. 2.

Whilst I think of you suffering in bed, I shall have for you—and, indeed, I speak in good earnest—I shall have for you a particular reverence, and shall greatly honour you as a creature visited by God, clad in his livery, and as his special spouse. When Our Lord was on the cross he was declared King, even by his enemies, and souls which are on the cross are declared queens.

You do not know what the angels envy us in? Truly in this only, that we can suffer for Our Lord, while they have never suffered anything for him. St. Paul, who had been in heaven, and amid the beatitudes of Paradise, gloried in nothing save his infirmities, *and in the cross of our Lord.** When the lancing is over, say to your enemies the words of the same Apostle: † *From henceforth let no man be troublesome to me; for I bear the marks* and signs *of the Lord Jesus in my body.* O leg, which, being well used, will carry you higher in heaven than if it were the soundest in the world! Paradise is a mountain whose summit one reaches better with broken and wounded legs than with whole and healthy ones.

It is not good to have Masses said in bedrooms. Adore from your bed Our Lord on the Altar, and be satisfied. Daniel, being unable to go to the Temple, turned towards it to adore God: ‡ do you the same. But I certainly consider that you should communicate in bed on all Sundays and chief feasts, so far as the doctors permit. Our Lord will willingly visit you on the bed of affliction.

I have received the note which was attached to your letter. Be very sure that it was quite pleasing

* Gal. vi. 14. † *Ibid.* 17. ‡ Dan. vi. 10.

to me. I accept it with all my heart, and promise you that I will take the care of you that you desire, as far as God will give me the strength and ability. I beseech his divine Majesty to load you with his graces and benedictions, and all your house. May God be eternally blessed and glorified about you, in you, and by you! Amen. I am, my very dear daughter, your most affectionate servant in our Lord, &c.

I beg you to please to get a good work which I want to see done recommended to God, and, above all, to recommend it yourself during your sufferings; for at such time your prayers, though short and only in the heart, will be extremely well received. Ask from God at this time the virtues which are most necessary to you.

LETTER X.

To the Same (the Abbess of Puits d'Orbe).

Encouragement and consolation in bodily sufferings, and in the difficulties she finds in reforming her Abbey.

16th November 1605.

My Sister and very dear Daughter—Oppressed and overwhelmed with affairs in this Visitation of my diocese which I am making, I yet fail not to beseech our good God or to offer the Holy Sacrifice every day to the end that you may not be overwhelmed by the sufferings which your leg causes you, nor by the difficulties which our holy enterprises meet with, and must meet with, in these beginnings.

Our good respected father often writes me news of you: and nothing more desirable can reach me when it is good news, as it always is according to God—on whom I know your interior gaze is entirely fixed, into whose good pleasure all your designs and all your desires come to merge. Courage, my dear daughter; God will without doubt be propitious to you provided that you are faithful to him. What a happiness that his divine Majesty deigns to make use of you in his service, not only acting but suffering!

Take care to preserve the peace and tranquillity of your heart: let the waves growl and roar all round about your back, and fear not; for God is there, and by consequence, safety. I know, my dear sister, that little troubles are more distressing, on account of their multitude and their importunity, than great ones, and troubles at home than those abroad; but, at the same time, I know that victory over them is oftentimes more agreeable to God than over many others which in the eyes of the world seem to be of greater merit.

Adieu, my dear sister: they are seizing my letters to carry them off, and I have only time to sign myself, Your brother and servant, very affectionate and still more faithful, &c.

LETTER XI.

To the Same.

On religious enclosure and on charity towards her sister the Prioress.

About 1606.*

I was pleased to have news of you (after so much time without receiving any), my very dear daughter, from yourself: for what can anybody else tell me for certain of you or of your affairs? And so, my dear daughter, all human remedies have been found ineffectual for the cure of this poor limb, which gives you a pain which must wisely be converted into a perpetual penance. In truth, I have always had the impression that all these applications would succeed very ill, and that this was a blow which heavenly Providence has given you in order to furnish you a subject of patience and mortification. What treasures can you amass by this means! Henceforth you must do so, and live as a true *Rose* amongst thorns.

But I am told that you were at Puits d'Orbe, with some of your daughters, and that the rest had stayed at Chastillon; that is true, for I should have guessed it. But this was for a short time, you tell me, and for a good and legitimate cause; I believe it; but believe me also, my dear daughter, that as women who have left the world ought to wish never to see it again, so the world which has left them never wants to see them again, and every little it sees of them it gets vexed and grumbles. It is the truth also that one ever loses something by going out whenever it can

* The French says, "6th November 1604." [Tr.]

(even with some temporal loss) be avoided. Wherefore, if you listen to my advice, you will go out as little as possible, even to hear sermons, since you have every right to have sometimes a preacher in your chapel, who will say things entirely appropriate to your congregation. It certainly behoves to pay attention to common report, and to do things in order to avoid the talk of the children of the world. *Wherefore*, said that great exemplar of religion and devotion, St. Paul,* *if meat scandalize my brother, I will never eat flesh, lest I should scandalize my brother.* Content in this your honoured relatives, and I think that then you can with confidence ask their assistance to provide you good accommodation; for it seems to me I hear some of them saying, Why make a comfortable dwelling for persons who go out and about in the world? And their dislike for this going abroad leads them to make out the worst of its quantity and its quality. It is the ancient custom of the world to judge it lawful to talk of ecclesiastics as much as ever they like; and it thinks that, provided it has something to say about them, there will no longer be anything to say about its own associates.

Well, now, is there no way of finding the side by which to take and to preserve the heart of Madame the Prioress, our sister?—for although, according to the world, it is for inferiors to seek the goodwill of superiors, yet according to God and the Apostles it is for superiors to go after inferiors, and to gain them. For so acted Our Redeemer, so did the Apostles, so do and will ever do all prelates who are zealous in the love of their Master. I own that I do not at all

* 1 Cor. viii. 13.

wonder that your relatives are scandalised to see what coolness of friendship there is between two sisters by nature, two spiritual sisters, two sisters in religion. It is necessary to remedy this, my dearest daughter, and not to let this temptation subsist. It may be that the wrong is on her side; but at any rate there is this on yours, that you do not win her back to your love by the continual and irresistible manifestation of that which you owe her according to God and the world.

You see what liberty I take in telling you my sentiments, my dear daughter, whom I wish to be totally victorious with the victory which the Apostle announces: * *Be not overcome by evil, but overcome evil by good.* If I spoke otherwise to you, I should betray you; and I neither can nor will love you save altogether paternally, my dear daughter, whom I beg Our Lord to deign to load with his graces and consolations. I salute very humbly all your dear company.—Yours, &c.

LETTER XII.

TO THE SAME (THE ABBESS OF PUITS D'ORBE).

The Saint's extreme solicitude for her, and for the success of her efforts to reform her Abbey.

About 1607.†

MY VERY DEAR DAUGHTER—I am impatiently expecting better news of your health than I have received

* Rom. xii. 21.

† The French says, "December 1608." [Tr.]

up to the present; it will be when Our Lord pleases, of whom I earnestly ask it, believing that it will be employed to his glory and to the advance and perfection of the work begun in your monastery.

I am always in trouble to know whether you have not yet found some person proper for the guidance of this flock of souls, who otherwise doubtless cannot be without much disturbance and disquiet, which are the plants which grow readily in ill-cultivated monasteries, and principally in those of women. But before all, I should greatly like to understand what progress you hope for the enclosure, whether it will be possible to keep the door shut to men, at least in that moderate way which I wrote to you about, which was only too easy, I think, and such as your respected father could not find objectionable. Certainly you must work very quietly, my dear daughter, but very earnestly; for on this depends the good order of all the rest.

Courage, my dear daughter; I know how many troubles, how many contradictions there are in such affairs, but it is because they are great and full of fruit. Take care of your health, that it may serve you to serve God. Be painstaking, but keep from eager solicitude. Present to God your little co-operation, and be certain that he will accept it and will bless it with his holy hand. Adieu, my dear daughter; I beseech his holy goodness to help you always, and I am extremely, and with all my heart, all yours, and more than yours.

LETTER XIII.

To the Same.

[This letter seems to have been formed, by M. Maupas, from various letters.]

The evil of pride amongst religious: method to be used by superiors in introducing reforms: care in admitting subjects.

About 25*th August* 1608.

Would you like to know what I think on the matter, madame? Humility, simplicity of heart and affection, and submission of mind, are the solid foundations of the religious life. I would rather cloisters were filled with all vices than with the sin of pride and vanity; because in other offences one can repent and get pardon, but the proud soul has in itself the principle of all vices, and never does penance, considering itself to be in a good state, and despising all the advice which is given to it. Nothing can be done with a soul that is vain and full of self-conceit; it is no good either to self or others.

To make government good it is further needed that superiors should resemble shepherds feeding their flocks, and should not neglect the smallest chance of giving edifying example to their neighbour, because, as there is no little stream which does not run to the sea, so there is no deed which does not lead the soul to that great ocean of the wonders of God's goodness.

Madame, your leading of your daughters in this holy work should be sweet, gracious, compassionate, simple, and persuasive; and, believe me, the most perfect guiding is that which most closely follows God's ordering of us, which is full of tranquillity, quietude, and repose, and which, even in its greatest activity, has no emotion, and makes itself all to all things.

Moreover, the diligence of superiors ought to be great in applying a remedy to the very lightest murmurings of the community. For as great storms are formed from invisible vapours, so in religion great troubles come from very light causes.

Again, nothing is so destructive to Orders as the want of care which is used in examining the spirit of those who throw themselves into the cloister. People say, he is of a good house, he has a good head; but they forget that he will with great difficulty submit to religious discipline.

Before admitting them one should represent to them the true mortification and submission which religion demands, and not dwell so temptingly on the numerous spiritual consolations. For just as a stone though thrown upwards returns downwards by its own movement, so the more a soul whom God wants in his service is repelled, the more it will be urged to what God wants from it. Besides, those who choose this path as it were disappointed because they have high aspirations with low fortune, ordinarily bring more disorder than good order into the cloister.

LETTER XIV.

To the Same.

Directions on enclosure, extraordinary confessors, administration of revenues: how to behave to a disobedient subject: advice as to her own perfection.

1608 *or* 1609.*

Yes, my daughter, I say it in writing as well as by word of mouth, be joyful as far as possible in well-doing, for it is a double grace of good works to be well done and to be cheerfully done. And when I say in well-doing, I do not mean to say that if some defect happen you are to give yourself to sadness on that account; for God's sake, no! for this would be to add fault to fault; but I mean that you must persevere in wishing to do what is good, and must always return to good as soon as you realise that you have left it, and in general that you must live joyfully by virtue of this fidelity.

I have to tell you that, besides the former writing which I send you, you must keep the cloister and the dormitory closed to men; thus will the enclosure be established gradually.

The Council of Trent commands all superiors and superioresses of monasteries that at least three times a year they should make all who are under their charge go to confession to extraordinary confessors, as is strongly required for a thousand good reasons. Wherefore you must observe it, getting some good monk or very devout priest, to whom all must on

* The French says, "1st May 1606." [Tr.]

that occasion confess. I have told you the reason why all must confess, but this will be a grievance to no one; for those who like need only confess the faults of a day or two, going to confession previously, and those who like can act otherwise.

It must be your place, my dear daughter, to administer the pensions, but depute one of the sisters to the office of keeping account of what may be used.

It will be good, in your little chapters, to recommend the mutual and tender love of one another, and to testify that you have it towards them, but particularly towards her of whom you write to me, whom you must by charity recall to a good understanding and sweet confidence with the rest. I write her a little word.

You will no doubt find the first instructions I gave you, five years ago, on the way by which you must gently bring all these souls to your good design. You will see there many things which for the sake of brevity I will not say now.

As to her who is absent, you must write to her or her brother, that for the greater glory of God, the salvation of your souls, the edification of your neighbour, and the honour of your monastery, you have resolved, with all your religious sisters, to live more retiredly within your house than you have done hitherto; that, this thing being so reasonable and becoming, you have no doubt she will agree to it; that you request and summon her to do this by the obedience which she has vowed to you, outside of which she cannot effect her salvation; promising her that she will find nothing in yourself or in others except a sweet and very loving mutual intercourse, which alone, besides her duty, would invite her to a holy retreat, and the like. If upon this she return not, you must cite her twice more with intervals of three weeks. But if after all she return not, you will say to her that she determines then not to be received again and to be shut out from her place. I think, however, that her friends will make her return, and when she does, you will treat her sweetly and with great patience.

If I forget anything I will say it to our sister, who will infallibly go to see you, and she loves you very strongly. As for your private self, do not fail to make mental prayer every day, at the same time as it is being made in choir, if you cannot attend there; and this for half an hour. Do not torment yourself when you cannot have feelings as strong as you would desire, for it is the goodwill which God wants. Read spiritual books for a quarter of an hour each day before going to Vespers, or before saying them when you cannot go to them.

You will go to bed every day at ten, and rise at six. When you are obliged to be in bed, get some one to read from time to time as suits you. Often kiss the cross which you wear; renew the good purposes which you have made of being all God's, immediately before going to rest, or while you are going, or in your oratory, or elsewhere; and make one fuller renewal by half a dozen aspirations and humiliations before God.

I give you for your special patron of this year the glorious St. Joseph, and for your patroness St. Scholastica, sister of St. Benedict, in whose life you will find many actions, as in that of St. Benedict, worthy of being imitated.

See now, my very dear and good daughter, undertake

to gain for yourself a great courage in the service of Our Lord; for assuredly his goodness has chosen you to make use of you, provided that you will it, for the true re-establishment of his own glory and that of souls. In your house you could not hold a safer path than that of holy obedience; wherefore I greatly rejoice that you are attached to it, for the reason you tell me. Remember well, then, what I have recommended to you on the part of Our Lord, to whom I commend you, beseeching him, by his death and passion, to crown you with his holy love, and to make you more and more entirely his own.

As for me, my dear sister, my well-beloved daughter, I have a very entire will to love, honour, and serve you; and nothing will ever take away from me this affection, since it is in this same Saviour and for him that I have taken it up, being ever your humble brother and servant, &c.

LETTER XV.

To a Young Lady.

Counsels relating to a vow of chastity.

ANNECY, 18*th May* 1608.

MADEMOISELLE—I consider that the desire which you have of vowing your chastity to God has not been conceived in your heart without your having first and for a long time considered its importance: for this reason I approve your making it, and making it on Whit Sunday itself. Now to make it well, use your leisure time during the three days beforehand to prepare your vow properly by prayer, which you can form on these considerations.

Consider how agreeable a virtue holy chastity is to God and the angels, he having willed that it shall be eternally observed in heaven, where an end is put to every sort of carnal pleasure and to marriage. Shall you not be very happy to begin in this world the life which you will continue eternally in the other? Bless God, then, who has given you this holy inspiration.

Consider how noble is this virtue, which makes our souls white as the lily, pure as the sun; which makes our bodies consecrated, and gives us the advantage of belonging wholly and entirely to his divine Majesty, heart, body, spirit, and feelings. Is it not a great delight to be able to say to Our Lord: *My heart and my flesh have rejoiced* * in your goodness, for the love of which I give up all love, and for the pleasure of which I renounce all other pleasures? What a happiness to have reserved no earthly delights for this body, in order to give our heart entirely to Our God!

Consider that the Blessed Virgin was the first to vow her virginity to God, and after her so many virgins, men and women. But with what ardour, with what love, with what affection, was this their virginity, this chastity, vowed! Ah! it cannot be described. Humble yourself greatly before this heavenly band of virgins, and by humble prayer beseech them to receive you amongst them, not indeed as professing to equal them in purity, but at least that you may be acknowledged as their unworthy servant, imitating them as nearly as you can. Beseech them to offer with you your vow to Jesus Christ, King of virgins, and by the merit of their

* Ps. lxxxiii. 3.

chastity to make yours acceptable. Above all, recommend your intention to Our Lady; and then to your good Angel, that it may please him thenceforward to preserve with a particular care your heart and your body pure from everything contrary to your vow.

Then on Whit Sunday, when the priest is elevating the sacred Host, offer with him to God the eternal Father the precious body of his dear child Jesus, and together with this your body, which you will vow to keep in chastity all the days of your life. The form of making the vow might be such as this: "O eternal God, Father, Son, and Holy Spirit, I, N., thy unworthy creature, here in thy presence and in that of all thy heavenly court, promise to thy divine Majesty, and vow, to keep and observe, all the time of mortal life which it shall please thee to give me, an entire chastity and continence, through the favour and grace of thy Holy Spirit. Vouchsafe to accept this my irrevocable vow as a holocaust of sweetness, and since it has pleased thee to inspire me to make it, give me the strength to perfect it, to thy honour, for ever and ever."

Some persons write this vow, or get it written and sign it, then hand it to some spiritual father, in order that he may be, as it were, the protector and sponsor of it; but this, though useful, is in no way necessary.

Then you will communicate, and you will be able to say to Our Lord that he is indeed your Spouse.

But speak of this to your confessor; for if he tell you not to do it you must believe him, since he, knowing the present state of your soul, will be able to judge better than I what is expedient.

But, my good daughter, when this vow is made, it is

necessary that you never permit any one to solicit your heart with any proposal of love or marriage, and you must have a great respect for your body, not now as your own body, but as a most sacred body, a most holy relic. And as one dares no longer to touch or profane a chalice after the Bishop has consecrated it, so when the Holy Spirit has consecrated your heart and your body by this vow, you must show it a great reverence.

For the rest, I will recommend all this to God, who knows that I love you very affectionately in him; and on the same day of Pentecost I will offer him your heart and what may proceed from it unto his glory. May Jesus be for ever your love, and his holy Mother your guide! Amen.

Your servant in Jesus Christ, &c.

LETTER XVI.

TO F. CLAUDE DE COEX, PRIOR OF THE BENEDICTINE MONASTERY OF TALLOIRES.

Instructions for the beginnings of a reform in his community.

ANNECY, 10*th July* 1609.

SIR—Since God has chosen a very small number of persons, and, moreover, from amongst the least of the house in age and standing, it is needful that all be undertaken with a very great humility and simplicity, and that this little number do not reprehend or censure the others in words or in exterior gestures, but simply edify them by good example and conversation.

The beginning being so small, great longanimity is needed in the execution, and a remembrance how that Our Lord after thirty-three years left only six-score disciples really collected together, amongst whom also there were many hard of teaching. The palm-tree, queen of trees, only produces its fruit a hundred years after it is planted. It is well, then, to be furnished with a generous and persevering heart in a work of such great importance. God has made reformations with less beginnings, and you must aim at nothing short of perfection.

And, to come to particulars, my advice is, that your holy band be careful to communicate devoutly at the very least once each week. Let them be taught to examine their consciences well and duly every night; let them be shown how to make mental prayer suitably, according to the disposition of the subject, and, above all, let them be instructed to obey their director very willingly, very closely, and very perseveringly.

As to the habit, I do not think that it will be well to change it till after the year has expired, although I should like it to be in all things as uniform as it can be, both in shape and in material, and that the tunic should be wide, after the fashion of the reformed Benedictines. I think that the shirt should be kept to, for cleanliness, provided always that the collar be not extravagantly lengthened, but cut low and in a uniform manner. Each one, also, will wear a belt and hood of the same fashion, the whole to be very neat.

As regards the beds, the more simple they are the better. Let each have his own, and let them be so arranged that in getting up or retiring to rest persons may not see one another, so that even the eyes also be clean and modest. I should greatly approve that those who have a beard should be well shaved on head and chin, according to the ancient custom of Benedictines, and that, as far as possible, they should no longer go out by themselves, but always with a companion.

It will be expedient that at the Divine Office the little flock enter, remain, and go out all together, with uniform behaviour and ceremony, inasmuch as the exterior comportment, whether at the Office, at table, or in public, is a powerful incentive to good.

In this beginning it is not necessary to add any abstinence to that of Fridays and Saturdays, unless it be that of Wednesdays, according to the old custom and mitigation observed in the monastery.

Such is my modest advice for this commencement; the end arrived at will be a very different thing, please God; for, as you know, the first thing in intention is the last in execution. But to work well in this business, there is needed an unconquerable courage and to await the fruit in patience. I know and see your Rule, which speaks wonders; but it is not expedient to pass from one extremity to the other without a mean.

Plant deep down in your heart, sir, this affection—to build up again the walls of Jerusalem: God will help you with his hand. Above all, take care to use milk and honey, because meat cannot yet be masticated by the weak teeth of your guests. Adieu! Have good hope of being one of those by whom salvation will be made in Israel.

LETTER XVII.

To Madame de Chantal.

Praise of a future lay-sister of the Visitation: spirit of that Order.

November 1609.

Your Anne Jacqueline pleases me more and more. The last time she went to confession she asked leave, in order to prepare herself to be a religious, to fast on bread and water in Advent, and to go barefoot all the winter. O my daughter! I must tell you what I answered her, for I consider it as good for the mistress as for the servant,—that I should like the daughters of our congregation to have the feet well shod, but the heart bare and naked of terrestrial affections; to have their heads properly covered, and their soul all uncovered by a perfect simplicity and an offstripping of their own will.

LETTER XVIII.

To a Person of Piety.

On humility, resignation, and simplicity: remedies against drowsiness at prayer.

5*th January* 1610.

You tell me three good things, my very dear daughter, in the letter which I have received from you,—that you do yourself great violence to keep down the swellings of your heart and to practise love of abjection;

that this is what you are striving after now; and that you have your desires more accommodated to the divine will than formerly. You must be sure always to act so, my dear daughter; for, as Our Lord says: *The kingdom of heaven suffereth violence, and the violent bear it away.** The more pains holy humility costs you, the more graces it will give you. Continue, then, courageously to bring down your heart by humility, and to exalt it by charity; for so you will ascend and descend like the angels on the holy ladder of Jacob. Study this lesson deeply, for it is the one lesson of our sovereign Master: *Learn of me, because I am meek and humble of heart.*† How happy will you be, my dear daughter, if you resign yourself fully to the will of Our Lord! Yes; for this holy willing is all good, and its disposing all good. Better can we not walk than under its providence and guidance. But do you know what pleases me? Your saying that you speak to me with open heart. For, my dear daughter, it is a good condition, if we want to advance according to the Spirit, to be open-hearted, and so to make the communication which must be between us faithful and simple. As also Our Lord, who is so greatly pleased to communicate his Spirit to his servants, is, moreover, greatly pleased to see that our spirits communicate themselves one to another, for mutual aid and solace. Walk then so, my dear daughter. And do not distress yourself about your fits of drowsiness, against which you must do two things. One is, often to change your position in prayer; as, to keep the hands sometimes crossed, sometimes clasped, sometimes folded; sometimes to stand, sometimes to go on your knees,

* Matt. xi. 12. † *Ibid.* 29.

now on one knee, now on the other, when the drowsiness attacks you. The other thing is, frequently to utter words out loud, interjected more or less amidst your prayer, according as you find yourself more or less beset by these inclinations to doze. May God be ever favourable to you, my dear daughter, in order that you may advance very far forward in his love, for the sake of which I will love you all my life; and recommending myself more and more to your prayers, I am, your humble servant, &c.

BOOK II.

Earlier Letters to Sisters of the Visitation.

[The Visitation Order was founded at Annecy on 6th June 1610. Mother de Chantal [St. Jane Frances] was the superioress and co-foundress. Her first companions and daughters were Mother Favre, Mother de Bréchard, and the out-sister Anne Jacqueline Coste. Mother de Chastel joined them after a few weeks, and within two years came, amongst others, Mothers Joly de la Roche, de Blonay, and Rosset. There exist letters addressed to all these. The sisters were in the first months called Oblates. Their work was to practise the interior life and to visit the sick poor. From the latter practice arose their name of Visitation sisters, given them first not by their founder, but by the poor. Their institute was confined to Annecy until the end of 1614, and during this first period we have but few letters of St. Francis to them, as they were under his own eye. On 25th January 1615, Mother de Chantal, Mother Favre, and three others started to make the foundation of Lyons. Towards the end of 1615 M. de Chantal returned to Annecy, leaving M. Favre superioress at Lyons. This first foundation from Annecy led to a notable change in the institute, as St. Francis, taking the advice of the Archbishop of Lyons, gave up external active work and adopted enclosure. The next foundation was Moulins, 25th August 1616, M. de Bréchard being appointed superioress. The fourth foundation was Grenoble, 8th April 1618; superioress, M. de Chastel. The fifth was Bourges, 15th November 1618; superioress, M. Rosset. The sixth was Paris, founded by Mother de Chantal herself, 1st May 1619. This important event opens a new period in the development of the Order, and furnishes a natural line of division between St. Francis's earlier and later letters to his spiritual daughters.]

LETTER I.

To Mother de Chantal.

On entire devotion of self to God: St. Francis's extreme affection for her.

5th June 1610.

To-morrow, then, you will have thoughts and cares, for I am beginning to have very particular ones about your future house, as regards temporal things; as to the spiritual, it seems to me that Our Lord will have care of them without our solicitude, and that he will pour out over them a thousand blessings.

My daughter, I must tell you that I never saw so clearly how much you are my daughter as I see it now; but I say that I see it in the heart of Our Lord; so do not fancy there is any failure of confidence in those few words which I wrote to you the other day—but we will talk of them another time.

O my daughter! what a desire have I that we be one day annihilated in ourselves to live wholly to God, and that our life be *hidden with Christ in God!* * Oh! when shall we live, now not we, and when shall Christ live wholly in us? † I am going to make a little prayer on this, and I will beseech the royal heart of Our Saviour for our heart.

I am ever more yours in Jesus Christ, and I marvel at this growth of affection. Yes, I say it in earnest, I did not know that I could do what I can do in this, and I find a source which ever supplies me more abundant waters. Ah! it is God, undoubtedly. We must certainly put ourselves on our highest mettle, to serve

* Col. iii. 3. † Gal. ii. 20.

God as nobly and valiantly as we can, for why do we think he has willed to make one sole heart out of two except that this heart might be extraordinarily bold, brave, spirited, constant and loving in its Creator and its Saviour?—by whom and in whom I am, yours, &c.

LETTER II.

To the Same.

The excellence of her vocation: the Saint praises God for it.

In proportion as the sovereign goodness of the divine Trinity renews the spirit of his adoration * in the Holy Church, it seems to me to renew that of the sacred vocation of my dearest, best, and most honoured mother, who going out from her country, without knowing whither she was going, but believing God, who had said to her: *Go out from thy country and thy father's house,*† came in to the mountain whose name was "God will see her;" ‡ and God did see her, multiplying her spiritual offspring like the stars of heaven.

May God be ever glorified, my very dear mother, with whom I rejoice, yea, in whose heart my heart rejoices as in itself. May it, this heart of my mother, be eternally fixed in heaven like a fair star, the centre of a constellation. Is it possible that we shall eternally sing the canticle of Glory to the Father, to the Son, and to the Holy Ghost? Yes; the soul of my mother shall sing it for ever and ever, Amen. And God shall be blessed thereby unto eternity of

* Adoption? [Tr.] † Gen. xii. 1. ‡ *Ibid.* xxii.

eternities, Amen. *Vive Jésus!* Glory be to the Father, and to the Son, and to the Holy Ghost, for the gathering together of all these hearts for his honour. But, alas! what confusion for mine, which has co-operated in so holy a work with so slight a fidelity! But still, this same most holy Trinity, who is so sovereign a goodness, will be gracious to us, and we will in future do his will. Amen.

LETTER III.

To the Same (Mother de Chantal).

That she should receive her son with signs of love.

It is I, I think, who will be the first to announce to you, my very dear daughter, the coming of the well-beloved Celse Benigne. He arrived yesterday evening very late, and we had a difficulty in restraining him from going to see you in bed, where you doubtless were. How sorry am I to be unable to be witness of the caresses which he will receive from a mother who is insensible to all that is of natural love! For I think they will be terribly mortified ones. Ah! no, my dear daughter, be not so cruel; manifest to him some pleasure at his coming, to this poor young Celse Benigne. It is not right all at once to show such strong signs of this death of our natural passion.

Well, then, I will go to see you, if I can, but I will not be in a hurry; for we ought not to be insensible in the presence of objects which so strongly call for love. Friendship rather goes downwards than upwards. I will content myself with not ceasing to cherish you for my daughter as much as you cherish him for your son, and, moreover, I defy you to do better than I.

LETTER IV.

To the Same.

On entire submission to God in spiritual trials.

25th January 1611.

St. Paul, that glorious and marvellous Saint, has awakened us early, my dearest daughter, crying out thus loudly in the ears of my heart and of yours: *Lord, what wilt thou have me to do?* *

My most dear mother and all-dear daughter, when will it be that, dead before God, we shall live again to this new life in which we shall no more will to do anything, but shall let God will all that we have to do, and shall let his will living act upon ours quite dead?

Well, my dear daughter, keep yourself close to God, consecrate to him your labours, await in patience the return of your fair sun. Ah! God has not shut us out from the enjoyment of his sweetness: he has only withdrawn it for a time, that we may live in him and for him, and not for this sweetness, that our afflicted sisters may find in us a compassionate assistance and a sweet and loving support, that from a heart denuded, dead, and immolated he may receive the agreeable odour of a holy holocaust.

O Lord Jesus! by your incomparable sadness, by

* Acts ix. 6.

the unequalled desolation which filled your divine heart on Mount Olivet and on the cross, and by the desolation of your dear Mother while deprived of your presence, be the joy, or at least the strength, of this daughter, while your cross and passion are most singularly united to her soul.

I send you this outburst of our heart, my dearest daughter, whom may the great St. Paul bless. I think you must be very good to the sister of Sister N.; for, after all, sweet charity is the virtue which spreads abroad the good odour of edification, and persons of lower position receive it with more profit.

LETTER V.

To the Same.

Change of name for the sisters: St. Frances of Rome their patroness and model.

9th March 1611.

Yes, my dear daughter, yes, we will yield and change the name of Oblate Sisters, since it displeases those gentlemen so much; but never will we change the eternal design and vow of being for ever the most humble servants of the Mother of God. Renew the promise of it in your Communion; I will do the same in the Sacrifice of the Mass. Ah! it is twelve years to-day since I had the grace of celebrating Mass in the monastery of this holy Roman widow, with a thousand desires of being devout to her all my life. As she is our holy patroness, she must be our model.

She loved her little Batiste as well as you love your Celse Benigne; but she left to God the entire disposal of him, to do with him as he willed, and he made of him a child of salvation: so do I hope for the most dear son of my most dear mother.

LETTER VI.

To Mother de Bréchard, acting as Superioress at Annecy.

That she should moderate her activity and her solicitude, trusting in God.

Autumn of 1611.

My very dear Daughter—You must take rest, and sufficient rest; must lovingly leave some work to others, and not seek to have all the crowns: our dear neighbours will be glad enough to have some. The ardour of holy love, which urges you to want to do everything, ought also to keep you back and make you leave others something to do for their consolation. God will be good to us, my daughter; I hope he is threatening you without intending to strike, and that the dear person of our mother will complete her journey back to her very dear lieutenant, her well-beloved daughter. I want you to labour in a spirit ardent yet gentle, fervent but moderate, expecting the good conclusion of sicknesses and of all affairs not from your labour, not from your care, but from the loving goodness of your Spouse. May he deign to bless you eternally, with all the flock of my dearest mother, absent, yet so present to us in heart, in the presence of him who is the supreme all of the heart of mother and of daughters: beseech him to be this also to the father, that all may be holily equal in our poor dear little Visitation. Amen.

LETTER VII.

TO MOTHER DE CHANTAL.

On Holy Communion and abandonment to God.

17th January 1612.

M. MICHEL is going to start a little sooner than usual, in order that you may take your tablet * at least an hour before dinner. But, my dear daughter, both these things which you will take are tablets of cordial virtue, particularly the first, composed of the most excellent powder that ever was in the world. Yes, my dear daughter; for Our Saviour has taken our true flesh, which is in substance powder, but in him is so excellent, so pure, so holy, that the heavens and the sun are but dust in comparison of this sacred powder. Now, the tablet of the Holy Communion is precisely that; and it has been made into a *tablet* that we may take it better, though in itself it is the most divine and very great *table* which the Cherubim and Seraphim adore, and at which they eat by real contemplation as we by real communion.

Oh! what happiness that our love, whilst waiting

* Referring, apparently, to some medicine which Mother de Chantal was taking. Afterwards the Saint speaks of the tablet of Holy Communion which she was to take next day, and plays on the words *table, tablette* (table, little table). [Tr.]

for that visible union which we shall have with Our Lord in heaven, is by this mystery so admirably united to him! My dearest daughter, keep your soul in peace, do not look where its little maladies come from, do not put yourself into any trouble about its cure, but divert your spirit, as far as possible, from returning upon itself.

The great St. Anthony, whose intercession has an extraordinary influence to-day, will make you, by God's goodness, rise to-morrow quite strong. It is a great joy to the heart to picture to oneself this great Saint among his hermits, drawing from his mind deep and sacred sayings, and pronouncing them with extreme reverence, as oracles from heaven: but, amongst other things, it seems to me that he says to our soul what he said among his disciples, taken from the Gospel: *Be not solicitous about your soul*, or, *for your soul.** No, my dear daughter, remain in peace; for God, to whom it belongs, will console it.

Meantime, my well-beloved daughter, I cease not, in the depths of my soul, to form holy hopes that after God has proved us by this occasional little abandonment, and has exercised us in interior mortification, he will revive us by his sacred consolations. He, this dear love of our heart, only abases us to lift us up: he holds back, and hides himself, and looks through the lattices to see how we are behaving. Ah! Lord and Saviour, I half see, meseems, the brightness of your gentle eye, which promises us the return of your rays, to make fair spring appear again on our earth. Ah! my daughter, we have got well through worse: why shall we not have the courage to surmount

* *Animæ.* Matt. vi. 25.

this difficulty also? Believe, my daughter, that I pray to Our Lord for you with all my heart, for my soul is knit to yours, and I cherish you as my soul, as is said of Jonathan and David.* May God be for ever gracious to this heart, all vowed, all dedicated, all consecrated to heavenly love!

Good-night, my most dearly sole daughter: keep Jesus crucified tightly within your arms, for the spouse held him there as *a bundle of myrrh*,† that is, of bitterness: only, my dear daughter, it is not he who is bitter to us, he merely permits us to be bitter to ourselves. *For behold*, says Ezechias, *my most bitter bitterness is in peace.*‡ May the God of sweetness deign to make your heart sweet, or at least make your bitterness to be in peace.

This good sister wants to open her heart to you somewhat fully, but says she does not know how to do it; you must help her, then, and you may tell her that I said so. Blessed be God. Amen.

LETTER VIII.

TO THE SAME.

On abandonment to God's pleasure, even as to the exercise of faith, hope, and charity.

28th March 1612.

WELL, my dearest daughter, it is fully time that I should, if I can, answer your long letter. Ah! yes, my dearest, most truly dearest daughter, but it must

* 1 Kings xviii. 1. † Cant. i. 12. ‡ Isa. xxxviii. 17.

really be in haste, for I have very little leisure; and unless the sermon which I am about to preach were already formed in my head, I should not write to you anything more than the note attached to this.

But let us come to the interior trial which you write to me about. It is in reality a certain insensibility, which deprives you of the enjoyment, not only of consolations and inspirations, but also of faith, hope, and charity. You have them all the time, and in a very good condition, but you do not enjoy them: in fact, you are like an *infant*, whose guardian takes away from him the administration of all his goods, in such sort, that while in reality all is his, yet he handles and seems to possess no more than what he requires for living, and, as St. Paul says, in this *he differeth nothing from a servant, though he be lord of all things.** For in the same way, my dear daughter, God does not want you to have the management of your faith, of your hope, or of your charity, nor to enjoy them, except just to live and to use them on occasions of pure necessity.

My dear daughter, how happy are we to be thus tied and kept close in by this heavenly guardian! And what we ought to do undoubtedly is what we do, namely, adore the loving Providence of God, and then throw ourselves into his arms and into his bosom. No, Lord, I no longer desire the enjoyment of my faith, of my hope, or of my charity, save to be able to say in truth, though without pleasure or feeling, that I would rather die than give up my faith, my hope, and my charity. Ah! Lord, if such is your good pleasure, that I should have no pleasure in the

* Gal. iv. 1.

practice of the virtues which your grace has bestowed upon me, I consent with my whole will, although against the inclinations of my will.

It is the supreme point of holy religion to be content with naked, dry, insensible acts, exercised by the superior will alone ; as it would be the superior degree of abstinence to content oneself in never eating save with disgust and reluctance, not simply without taste or relish. You have described your suffering to me very well, and you have nothing to do as remedy save what you are doing, protesting to Our Lord, even in spoken words, and even sometimes in song, that you will live on death itself, and will eat as if you were dead, without taste, without feeling and knowledge.

At last, this Saviour wishes that we should be so perfectly his, that nothing may remain to us save to abandon ourselves entirely to the mercy of his Providence without reserve. Well, let us then stay so, my dearest daughter, amid this darkness of the Passion. I say rightly amid this darkness, for I leave you to think—Our Lady and St. John being at the foot of the cross, amid the wonderful and dreadful darkness which occurred, no longer heard Our Lord, no longer saw him, and had no feeling save of bitterness and distress ; and although they had faith, it also was in darkness, because it behoved that they should share in the dereliction of Our Saviour. How happy are we to be slaves of this great God, who made himself a slave for us !

But it is the hour for the sermon ; adieu, my dear mother, my daughter in this Saviour. May his divine goodness live for ever ! I have an incomparable ardour for the advancement of our heart, for which I resign all my other satisfactions into the hands of the sovereign and paternal Providence.

Good-night again, my dear daughter. May Jesus, sweet Jesus, sole heart of our heart, bless us with his holy love. Amen.

LETTER IX.

To a Superioress of the Visitation.

Founders of a house must act according to the spirit of the Order: what the spirit of the Visitation is: blessed are poor communities.

22nd April 1612.*

My dear daughter, in a few words I say to you that those souls who are so fortunate as to desire to employ for God's glory the means which he has given them ought to accommodate themselves to the designs which they form, and to resolve to put them into effect accordingly. If they are inspired to found a convent of Carthusians, they must not want to have schools there, as with Jesuits; if they want to found a college of Jesuits, they must not desire to have entire solitude and silence observed therein.

If this good lady, whom you do not name, desires to found a monastery of sisters of the Visitation, she must not burden them with long vocal prayers, nor with many exterior exercises; for this is not to desire sisters of the Visitation. It should suffice, in my opinion, that the whole interior and exterior of the

* The French has this date. The letter, however, seems to belong to a much later time, say 1615 or 1616. [Tr.]

daughters of the Visitation is consecrated to God; that they are victims of sacrifice, and living holocausts; that all their actions and resignations are so many outward or inward prayers; that all their hours are dedicated to God, yes, even those of sleep or recreation, and are fruits of charity. All this being employed for her soul, and the glory which accrues to God from the retired lives of so many daughters being applied to the increase of the charity of that heart, there results an almost infinite sum of spiritual riches.

Such are my sentiments. To charge the monasteries of the Visitation with practices which lead off from the end for which God has established them, I consider not a good thing to do. To seek to gather olives from a fig-tree, or figs from an olive, is unreasonable. Let him who wants figs plant fig-trees, and him who wants olives plant olive-trees.

My dear daughter, you are entirely of my way of thinking: in receiving subjects I far prefer the meek and humble, although poor, to the rich who are less humble and less meek, although they be rich. But it is useless to say: *Blessed are the poor in spirit;** human prudence will not cease saying: Blessed are the monasteries, chapters, houses, which are rich. Even in this we must cultivate the poverty which we esteem, that we lovingly suffer it to be disesteemed.

You have received two new, yet old, daughters of your house: the return is always more agreeable to mothers than the departure of their children. I am with all my heart, my dear daughter, most entirely your very humble father and servant, &c.

* Matt. v. 3.

LETTER X.

Sacred challenge (cartel de défi) *to my dear daughters of the Visitation of Sainte-Marie, as a good New Year's present for this year,* 1614.* *Francis, Bishop of Geneva.*

The life of man upon earth is a continual warfare. Our enemy is ever on the watch to surprise us, and he generally turns his battery against the weakest part of the citadel of our hearts, the place where he knows, by our frequent falls, the tendency of our perverse inclinations, our favourite passion, the one which does us the most injury, and yet the one which we least think of mastering, because it is agreeable to us, and because we flatter ourselves in the belief that our losses therein are slight: but it is by this that our enemy makes his advance, and tries to surprise us and capture us if he can. Each one of you, therefore, must watch well over this weakest part of her soul, and in order to begin to give you some instruction on this spiritual warfare, my very dear daughters, I am going to point out to each of you in particular the failing as to which you must watch yourselves, and the fine which you must pay when you fall: but I desire that, having paid this fine, you should take a new courage to fight more generously at the first attack, and that you should never lose heart in fighting, nor hope of conquering.

The general challenge.

The frequent thought of God's word to Abraham:

* Should this be 1613? Sister C. F. Roget (No. 6) is stated to have died 14th June 1613. [Tr.]

*Walk before me and be perfect.** And in order that the exterior action may not engross the interior attention and intention, my dear daughters will make six returnings to God at times not occupied by meditation, Office, or reading, when the attention is already bound to be actually applied. The fine for each failure will be the verse: *Et beata viscera Mariæ Virginis, quæ portaverunt, &c.*, and the protectors of the challenge, St. Antony, St. Bruno, and St. Francis of Paula.

Challenge for the particular examen.

1. Universal love for the worship of God, and specially preparation for and attention to the divine Office, vocal and mental prayers, readings, sermons, and devout discourses; against the remembrance of the world and attention to temporal things: the fine for each failure, the Psalm, *Laudate Dominum, omnes gentes,* for the re-establishment of ecclesiastical perfection; with my Mother Jeanne-Françoise Fremiot de Chantal, Our Lady, my Angel Guardian, and St. Francis of Assisi.

2. Interior recollection with our particular Saints and our Angel Guardian, in the time of silence, in solitude, in our cell, or other place unfilled by exercises which already require the mind's attention; against natural weariness and importunate distractions: as a fine for each failure, the antiphon, *Sancti Dei omnes,* for all prelates and pastors of the Church, with my Sister Marie-Jacqueline Favre, St. Joseph and St. Michael.

3. Serious attention to ourselves and our charges;

* Gen. xvii. 1.

against the superfluous care of others' charges, and the looking after their affairs: as a fine for each failure, the *Salve Regina*, for all Christian kings and princes: with my Sister Jeanne-Charlotte de Brechard, St. Augustine and St. Catharine.

4. Commiseration for the faults of others when we cannot justly excuse them: but we must not reveal them, nor ever speak of them, except to our superiors —the confessor or our Mother—for the amendment of them; against facility in speaking ill of our neighbour: as a fine for each failure, the antiphon, *Sancta Maria:* with my Sister Anne-Jacqueline (Coste), out-sister, St. John Baptist and St. Paul.

5. Sweetness and condescension towards all; against ill-humour and thought of self: as a fine for each failure, the verse: *Virgo singularis, inter omnes mitis*, &c., for all those who are aspiring to Christian perfection: with my Sister Peronne-Marie de Chastel, St. John and St. Jerome.

6. Indifference about the quality and quantity of food, as about everything else opposed to our sensuality; against softness and care of ourselves: as a fine for each failure, the *Sub tuum præsidium*, for all the necessitous, vicious, and ill-living poor: with my Sister Claude-Françoise Roget, St. Anne and St. Joachim.

7. The frequent recollection of the presence of God at recreations and everywhere else; against exterior unquiet and interior wandering thoughts: as a fine, *Dominus pars hæreditatis meæ*, &c., for all those who are consecrated to God: with my Sister Marie-Marguerite Milletot, St. Bernard and St. Agnes.

8. The renouncing of our own will in everything

and as to everything that we can, with promptitude of obedience to those who have authority over us; against self-will and our carnal liberty: as a fine for each failure, the prayer, *Respice quæsumus Domine*, for all captives and prisoners: with my Sister Marie-Adrienne Fichet, St. Peter and St. Magdalen.

9. Loving acceptance of all sorts of corporal discomforts and spiritual troubles, rejoicing in them; against immortification of the senses and false liberty: as a fine for each failure, a *Pater* and *Ave*, for all pilgrims and strangers: with my Sister Claude-Marie Tiollier, St. Gregory and St. Clare.

10. Fidelity and promptitude in working out our perfection; against irresolution and pusillanimity: as a fine for each failure, the antiphon, *Beata Dei Genitrix Maria*, for the conversion of pagans, Turks, and infidels: with my Sister Claude-Agnes Joly de la Roche, St. Alexis and St. Elizabeth.

11. Mortification of the senses, both interior and exterior; against every sort of eagerness and curiosity of spirit: as a fine for each fault, the *Ave Maria*, for the extirpation of heresy: with my Sister Marie-Aimée de Blonay, St. Charles and St. Frances.

12. Simplicity, truthfulness, and candour; against envy, jealousy, and unstraightforwardness: as a fine for each failure, the verse: *Monstra te esse matrem*, &c., for the re-establishment of Christian perfection: with my Sister Marie-Marthe le Gros, St. Martha and St. Bernardine.

13. Humiliation, lowliness, and contempt of self; against self-confidence and self-conceit: as a fine for each failure, the verse: *Vitam præsta puram*, &c., for courtiers, that they may enter into themselves in their

life of vanity: with my Sister Marie-Françoise-Avoie Humbert, St. Bonaventure and St. Catharine, Martyr.

14. Affability and sociability amongst people of the world, with evenness of temper; against self-esteem and too great taciturnity: as a fine for each failure, the verse, *Solve vincla reis,* &c.: with my Sister Anne-Marie Rosset, St. Ambrose and St. Antony of Padua.

15. Watchfulness over one's actions, good active use of time, and abstaining from speaking of self or what belongs to self; against idleness and indulgence in vain and useless conversation (*caqueterie*): as a fine for each failure, the prayer, *Respice quæsumus,* for all the wanderers of the earth: with my Sister Marie-Antoine Tiollier, St. Bridget and St. Barbara.

16. A perfect desire to please God and our superiors in our actions; against our inclination to seek self and to please the world: as a fine for each failure, the *Regi sæculorum immortali,* &c., for the exaltation of the holy name of God amongst all that live: with my Sister Anne-Françoise Chardon, St. Catharine of Genoa and St. Onuphrius.

17. Not to complain of anything that may happen to us, such as sickness, discomfort, want of some temporal thing, nor even of our imperfections or slowness in perfection; not to be continually accusing ourselves, through humility, or rather through levity, and not to keep correcting our neighbour: as a fine, a *De profundis* for the souls in Purgatory: with my Sister De Gouffier, St. Antony and St. Reparatus.

LETTER XI.

To Mother de Chantal.

Reason for having the change of rooms, &c., made at the end of the year.

Last day of 1613.

Yes, my very dear daughter, my mother, we must love the most holy will of God in little and in great changes. That which hinders me from going to see you to-day is little and great; I will tell it you at our first meeting. Meantime, make your little and great changes with all the perfection that you can. After having well thought it over before God, I am decided that we must confirm our congregation in making its changes on the day on which God makes his, who causes us all to pass from one year to another, giving us an annual lesson on our instability, on our mutations, on the removal and annihilation of the years which lead us to eternity.

LETTER XII.

To a Lady.

Detachment and littleness the spirit of the Visitation.

15*th October* 1614.

If divine Providence make use of you, my dear daughter, you ought to humble yourself greatly, and to rejoice, but to rejoice in this sovereign goodness, which, as you know, has made it clear to you that it wishes to have you vile and abject in your own eyes, by the consolations which it has given you in the attempts which you have made to lower and abase yourself. No, indeed, my dear daughter, I shall not be in anxiety about your direction if you walk by that path, for God will be your guide, and, moreover, you will not be without persons to give you counsel in this, according to your desire. I am writing to Father Grangier, whom also I ask you to salute very affectionately from me, assuring him of my humble service.

You do extremely well to testify a very absolute indifference, the more so because it is the true spirit of our poor Visitation to keep oneself very abject and little, and to esteem oneself as nothing except in so far as it shall please God to look upon our abjection, and hence to have in esteem and honour all other forms of living in God, and, as I have said, to be amongst other congregations what the violet is among flowers—low, little, of unpretending colour. And let it suffice such a one that God has created her for his service, and that she may yield some little good odour in the Church, so that all which is most to the glory of God may be followed, loved, and persevered in. This is the rule of all true servants of God.

It is without doubt to the great glóry of God that there is a Congregation of the Visitation in the world, for it is useful unto some particular effects which are special to it; wherefore, my dear daughter, we ought to love it. But if there are more exalted people, who also have grander aims, we ought to serve and reverence them very heartily when occasion presents itself.

I shall then await more particular news from you about the service which you can render to this new plant. If God wills it to be a plant of the Visitation, and a second Visitation, may his goodness be ever glorified for it.

I am very glad that you lodge at the Ursulines; it is one of the congregations which my spirit loves. Salute them again from me, and assure them of my affection for their service as to all that lies in my power, which, however, will never be anything, because of what I am.

Keep closely, my dear daughter, within the enclosure of our sacred resolutions. They will keep your heart if your heart keeps them with humility, simplicity, and confidence in God.—Your most humble and affectionate brother and servant.

LETTER XIII.

To Mother de Chastel.

Consolation and remedies in temptations to impatience: the struggle between the spirit and the flesh.

SS. Simon and Jude, *28th October* 1614.

Truly, my very dear daughter, you give me great pleasure in calling me your father, for I have indeed a heart lovingly paternal towards yours, which I see still a little weak in these ordinary light contradictions which occur, but I do not cease to love it. For although it seems to itself sometimes that it is about to lose courage over the little words of reprehension which are said to it, still it has never yet lost its courage, this poor heart; for its God has held it with his strong hand, and, according to his mercy, he has never abandoned his miserable creature. O my dear daughter, he will never abandon it; for although we are troubled and tormented by these troublesome temptations to sadness and impatience, still we never wish to quit God, nor Our Lady, nor our congregation, which is his, nor our rules, which are his will.

You say in good truth, my poor dear daughter Peronne-Marie, that there are two men or two women that you have in you. The one is a certain Peronne-Marie, who, like S. Peter at first, is a little touchy, sensitive, and ready to be put out and vexed when she is contradicted: that is the Peronne who is a daughter of Eve, and therefore of evil humour. The other is a certain Peronne-Marie who has a very good will to be all God's, and, in order to be all God's, to be very simply humble and humbly sweet towards all her neighbours; and this one it is who would like to imitate St. Peter, who was so good after Our Lord had converted him: it is this Peronne-Marie who is a daughter of the glorious Virgin Mary, and consequently is of good affection. And these two daughters of these different mothers fight; and the good-for-nothing one is so bad that sometimes the good one has much ado to defend herself, and then it seems to this poor good one that she has been conquered, and that the bad one is the braver. But no, indeed, my poor dear Peronne-Marie, that bad one is not braver than you, she is only more persistent, perverse, overbearing, and self-willed; and when you begin crying she is very glad, because this is always so much time lost, and she is glad to make you lose time when she cannot make you lose eternity.

My dear daughter, raise high your courage, arm yourself with the patience which we ought to have with ourselves; often arouse your heart that it may be enough on its guard not to let itself be surprised; give some little attention to this enemy; think of her if you like wherever you go; for this bad daughter is everywhere with you, and if you do not think of her she will think of something against you. But when it happens that she attacks you on a sudden, although she make you tremble a little and give you a little wrench, be not troubled, but call upon Our Lord and Our Lady; they will extend to you the holy hand of their help; and if they sometimes leave you in trouble, it will be in order to make you cry out again, and more loudly, for help.

Have no shame about this, my dear daughter, any more than St. Paul had, who confesses that he had two men in him, one of whom was rebellious to God and the other obedient. Be very simple, do not get angry, humble yourself without discouragement, encourage yourself without presumption; recognise that Our Lord and Our Lady, having laid upon you the distraction of the house, know well and see that you are disturbed therein; but they do not cease to love you provided that you are humble and trustful. But, my, daughter, be not ashamed to be a little dusty and dirty; dust is better than blemishes; and provided that you humble yourself, all will turn unto good. Pray earnestly to God for me, my dear daughter, truly well-beloved: and may God be for ever your love and protection. Amen. Day of SS. Simon and Jude, 1614.

LETTER XIV.

TO MOTHER DE CHANTAL.

The Saint wishes her God-speed in her journey to Lyons to make there the first branch of the Visitation.

26th January 1615.

WELL now, my dear daughter, since God is the unity of our heart, who shall ever separate us? No, neither death, nor life, nor things present, nor things future, shall ever separate us or divide our unity. Let us go, then, my dear daughter, with one sole heart, where God calls us; for the diversity of paths makes no diversity in ourselves, as it is for one single object and for a single subject that we go. O God of my heart! hold my dearest daughter by your hand, may her Angel be ever at her right hand to protect her; may the Blessed Virgin Our Lady ever cheer her with the look of her sweet eyes.

My dear daughter, heavenly Providence will aid you; invoke it with confidence in all the difficulties with which you will find yourself surrounded. In proportion as you go on, my dear mother, my daughter, you must take courage, and rejoice that you please Our Saviour, whose pleasure alone pleases all Paradise. As for me, I am there where you are yourself, since the divine Majesty has so willed it eternally. Let us go, then, my dear daughter, let us go sweetly and joyously to do the work which our Master has appointed us.

My very dear mother, my daughter, it comes to my memory that the great St. Ignatius, who bore Jesus

Christ in his heart, went joyously to serve as food for the *lions*, and to suffer martyrdom from their teeth; and here you go and we go, if it please this great Saviour, to *Lyons*, to do many services for Our Lord, and to prepare for him many souls of whom he will make himself the Bridegroom. Why shall not we go joyously in the name of Our Saviour when this Saint went so cheerfully to the martyrdom of Our Saviour? How happy are those spirits which move according to the will of this divine Spirit, and seek him with all their heart, leaving all, and the very father whom he has given them, in order to follow his divine Majesty!

Go, my dear mother, my daughter; your Angels here keep their eyes upon you and your little flock, and cannot abandon you, since you do not leave the place of their protection nor the persons over whom they watch, except for the purpose of not leaving the will of him to do whose will they very often think themselves happy to leave heaven. The Angels there, who await you, will send their benedictions to meet you, and as you go towards their districts, they lovingly regard you, because it is to co-operate in their holy ministry.

Keep your hearts in courage; for since your heart is God's he will be your courage. Go, then, my daughter, go with a thousand thousand benedictions which your father gives you; and be sure that he will never fail to breathe forth with every breath of his soul holy wishes for you. It will be his first exercise at his awakening in the morning, his last when he lies down in the evening, and his chief intention at holy Mass. *Vive Jésus, et Marie!* Amen.

LETTER XV.

To the Same, at Lyons.

Encouragement in the difficulties of her enterprise: exhortation to charity and forbearance.

February 1615.*

I HAVE received none of your letters, my most dear daughter, since your departure. What does this mean? I pray. Now I know well all the same that your charity is invariable, but I learn by letters from Lyons that you are ill, and also a little disappointed to find things not on so good a footing as our desire made me imagine. These, my dear daughter, are true signs of the goodness of the work: the approach is always difficult, progress a little less so, and the end happy.

Do not lose courage, for God will never lose the care of your heart, and of your flock, so long as you confide in him. The gate of consolations is narrow; the after-way makes up. Do not be disheartened, my dear daughter, nor let your spirit sink amid contradictions. When was the service of God ever exempt from them, particularly at its birth?

But I must tell you frankly what I fear more than all on this occasion; it is the temptation of aversion and repugnance between you and our N.; for it is the temptation which ordinarily occurs in matters which depend on the co-operation of two persons; it is the temptation of earthly angels, since it arose between the greatest saints, and it is the weakness

* The French says, "End of January;" but the house at Lyons was only founded on 2nd February. [Tr.]

of all of us who are children of Adam, and ruins us unless charity deliver us from it. When I see two Apostles separate from one another * through disagreeing about a third companion, I find these little repugnances very bearable, provided that they spoil nothing, as that separation did not disturb the Apostolic mission. If something of the kind happened between you two who are women, it would not be very bad, supposing it did not last. But still, my dear daughter, lift up your spirit, and be assured that your action is of great consequence; suffer, do not get impatient, soften everything; bear in mind that it is God's work in which this lady acts according to her ideas, and you according to yours, and that both of you ought to bear and forbear with one another for love of Our Saviour: two or three years soon pass, and eternity remains.

Your corporal malady is an extra burden, but the help promised to the afflicted ought to strengthen you greatly. Above all, keep from discouragement. Believe me, you must sow in labour, in perplexity, in anguish, to gather with joy, with consolation, with happiness; holy confidence in God sweetens all, obtains all, and establishes all. I am entirely yours, in truth, my dearest daughter, and I cease not to beg God to make you holy, strong, constant, and perfect in his service.

I salute very cordially our dear sisters and conjure them to pray to God for my soul, inseparable from yours and theirs in the love which is according to Jesus Our Saviour.

* Acts xv.

LETTER XVI.

To the Same.

In the spiritual life we must be ever beginning again, with courage always increasing: it is a maxim of the Saints to speak little of self: congratulations on having the Blessed Sacrament in the new house.

February 1615.

Believe me, my dear mother, as yourself. God wants unknown great things from us. I saw the tears of my poor sister N., and methinks all our childishness proceeds from no fault but this, that we forget the maxim of the Saints, who have warned us that every day we should consider we begin our course of perfection; and if we thought properly of this we should not be disturbed at finding miseries in ourselves, or things to amend. We have never done; we must always begin again and again with a good heart. *When a man hath done, then shall he begin.** What we have done up to now is good, but what we are going to begin shall be better; and when we have finished it we will begin another thing which shall be better still, and then another, till we depart out of this world to begin another life, which will have no end, because nothing better can come to us. Go and see, then, my dear mother, whether we are to weep when we find some work to be done in our souls, and whether we must have courage to go ever forward, since we must never stop, and whether we need to have resolution in our renunciations, since we must

* Ecclus. xviii. 6.

bring the razor *to the division of the soul and the spirit,** of the nerves and the sinews.

Truly, my dear mother, you see that my heart, which is your own, is full of this sentiment, since it pours out these words, though without leisure and without having thought over them. But now, my dear mother, observe well the precept of the Saints, which all have regarded who want to become so, to speak little or not at all of oneself or of what belongs to self. Do not think that because you are at Lyons you are dispensed from the compact which we made, that you should be moderate in speaking of me, as also of yourself. If the glory of the Master do not require it, be brief, and exactly observe simplicity. The love of ourself often dazzles us; eyes must be very true to avoid being deceived when we look at ourself. This is why the great Apostle cries out: *For not he who commendeth himself is approved, but he whom God commendeth.* †

The good Father Granger said right, and the Holy Spirit will be pleased with him for it. I am very glad that in your hive and in the midst of this new swarm you have your King, your honey, and your all. The presence of this sacred Humanity will fill all your house with sweetness; and it is a great consolation to souls who are attentive to faith to have this treasure of life near. I have prayed this morning with a special ardour for our advancement in the holy love of God, and feel greater desires than ever for the good of your soul. Ah! I say, O Saviour of our heart, since we are every day at your table to eat not your bread only but yourself, who are our living and supersubstantial bread,

* Heb. iv. 12. † 2 Cor. x. 18.

grant that we may every day make a good and perfect digestion of this most perfect food, and that we may perpetually live by your sacred sweetness, goodness, and love. Well, now, God does not give so much desire to this our one heart without willing to favour it with some corresponding effect. Let us hope, then, my one sole mother, that the Holy Spirit will crown us one day with his holy love; and while waiting let us perpetually remain in hope, and make space for this sacred fire, emptying our heart of ourselves as far as shall be possible to us. How happy shall we be, my dear mother, if one day we change our ownself into this love, which, making us more one, will perfectly empty us of all multiplicity, to have in our heart only the sovereign unity of his most holy Trinity! May this be ever blessed, world without end. Amen.

LETTER XVII.

To the Same.

The pigeons and little birds at Sales: thoughts on charity and simplicity. Her manner of prayer is good: his own prayer. Reference to the Treatise on the Love of God.

The second day of Lent (5*th March*) 1615.*

I WROTE to you when going to Sales, my dearest mother, and now I write to you on my return. I have had three consolations, and you will be very glad to know them, for what consoles me consoles you also.

* The French says, "Second day of Lent, or 26th February 1615." In this year Ash Wednesday was 4th March. [Tr.]

First, my dear little sister,* whom I find ever more amiable, and desirous to become greatly devout.

Secondly, yesterday, Ash Wednesday, I had my morning all alone in the gallery and in the chapel, where I had a sweet memory of our dear and desirable conferences at the time of your general confession: and I cannot describe what good thoughts and affections God gave me on this subject.

Thirdly, there had been a heavy snow, and the courtyard was covered with a good foot of snow. John came in and swept a small space clear of snow and threw down corn there for the pigeons to eat, who all came together into that refectory to take their refection, with an admirable peace and decorum; and I watched them with interest. You would not believe what great edification these little creatures gave me; for they never said one single little word, and those who had finished their meal first flew to one side to wait for the others. And when they had left half the space free there came round them a number of smaller birds who had been watching them; and all the pigeons who were still eating retired into a corner, leaving the greatest part of the place to the little birds, who came in their turn to the table to eat, the pigeons not minding them at all.

I admired the charity: for the poor pigeons had such great fear of distressing these little birds to whom they were giving alms, that they kept all by themselves at one end of the table. I admired the discretion of these beggars, who did not come for alms till they saw that the pigeons were near the end of their

* His brother's wife, Madame de Thorens, daughter of Mother de Chantal.

repast, and that there was sufficient left. At last, I could not keep from tears, to see the charitable simplicity of the doves, and the confidence of the little birds in their charity. I do not know whether a preacher would have touched me so sensibly. This image of virtue did me great good all the day.

But they have come to hasten me, my dear mother: my heart entertains you with its thoughts, and my thoughts most frequently entertain themselves with your heart, which is, without doubt, one same heart with mine.

Your prayer of simply committing yourself to God is extremely holy and wholesome. You must never have a doubt of it: it has been so closely examined, and always been found to be the manner of prayer in which Our Saviour wished you. So there is nothing more to be done than quietly continue in it.

God favours me with many consolations and holy affections, by lights and sentiments which he diffuses in the superior part of my soul; the inferior has no part therein. May he be blessed for it eternally. May God, who is the soul of our heart, my dear mother, deign ever to fill you with his holy love. Amen.

I do what I can for the book. Be sure that it is a great martyrdom to be unable to gain the time required; still I get on well, and I think that I shall keep my word to my dear mother. You are, my very dear mother, all precious to my heart. May God make you ever more and more entirely his. I salute our dear sisters.

LETTER XVIII.

To the Same.

Consolations under calumny: holy indifference to be cultivated: liberty as to spiritual communications: imperfect souls to be received and borne with.

13*th May* 1615.

I praise God, my dear mother, because this poor little congregation of servants of the divine Majesty is much calumniated. Alas! I regret the sins of the calumniators, but this injury received is one of the best marks of the approbation of Heaven; and in order that we may be able to understand this secret, Our Lord himself was calumniated—in how many fashions! Oh! *blessed are they who suffer persecution for justice sake.**

Your interior affliction is also a persecution for justice, for it tends to adjust your will exactly to the resignation and indifference which we love and praise so much. The more Our Lord subtracts his sensible consolations, the more perfections he prepares for us, provided that we humble ourselves before him, and cast all our hope upon him.

We must cultivate the most holy indifference, to which Our Lord calls us. Whether you are here or there, what can separate us from the unity which is in Our Lord Jesus Christ? † In fact, it is a thing which henceforth makes no difference to our souls, this being in one place or two, since our most precious unity subsists everywhere, thanks to him who has effected it.

* Matt. v. 10. † Rom. viii. 35.

How many times have I said it to you, my dear mother, that heaven and earth are not distant enough to separate the hearts which our Lord has joined! Let us remain at peace in this assurance.

I much prefer that the house should confide entirely in you, for so things will go very smoothly and sweetly, provided you are left at liberty, and they rest upon your word: but I fear that they may want to keep you there; this would be an unjust thought, and one I could not listen to. I say thought, because the thing itself must not be spoken of. You must, then, on this subject speak sweetly and justly, and declare that you will have a very sufficient care of that house.

It is necessary to guard like the apple of one's eye the holy liberty which the Institute gives as to spiritual communications and conferences. Experience tells me that nothing is so useful to the servants of God, when it is practised according to our rules.

I answer that the self-assertion of these souls nourished in their own judgment would not prevent their being received, if there had been explained to them the general maxims of sweetness, charity, and simplicity, and the throwing off of natural humours, inclinations, and aversions which ought to reign in our Congregation: for, after all, if we would only receive souls with whom there was no trouble, Orders of religion would be of scarcely any service to our neighbour, since these souls would almost everywhere do well.

My dear mother, live joyful, courageous, peaceful, united to Our Saviour; and may it please his goodness to bless the most holy oneness which he has made of us, and to sanctify it more and more. I salute our dear sisters. Ah! how much perfection do I wish them!

This 13th day of May—on which I commence the twenty-third year of my life in the ecclesiastical state, full of confusion at having done so little towards living in the perfection of this state.

LETTER XIX.

TO THE SAME.

The Saint consoles her by telling her that she is united to Christ though she does not feel his presence: "Hallowed be thy name."

21st July 1615.

MY VERY DEAR DAUGHTER—Upon a time * Magdalen was speaking to Our Lord, and thinking herself separated from him, she wept and begged for him, and was so overcome that while seeing him she saw him not. Well, now—courage! Let us not anxiously trouble ourselves; we have our sweet Jesus with us, we are not separated from him; at least so I firmly believe. *Woman, why weepest thou?* No, we must no longer be woman, we must have a man's heart; and provided that we have our soul steady in the will of living and dying in the service of God, let us not trouble ourselves about darkness, or powerlessness, or barriers. And speaking of barriers, Magdalen wanted to embrace Our Lord, and this sweet Master puts a barrier. No, he says, *Touch me not; for I have not yet ascended to the Father.* There on high will be no barriers; here we must endure them. Let it suffice us that God is our God, and that our heart is his home.

* John xx.

Shall I tell you a thought which I lately formed in the hour of the morning which I reserve for my poor weak soul? My point was the petition of the Lord's Prayer: *Hallowed be thy name.* O God, I said, who will give me the happiness of one day seeing the name of Jesus graven at the very bottom of the heart of her who already bears it marked on her breast? I called to mind also the palaces in Paris, on the front of which is written the name of the princes to whom they belong; and I rejoiced to think how the palace of your heart is "*Jesus Christ's.*" May he deign to live there eternally. Pray earnestly for me, who am so greatly and so paternally yours.

LETTER XX.

TO MOTHER FAVRE, SUPERIORESS AT LYONS.

The excellence of her vocation: advice in temptation: care for observance of rule and for encouraging generosity of spirit. Various salutations.

ANNECY, 13*th December* 1615.

IT is true, my dear daughter, we have long delayed writing to you; moreover, on my part, for three weeks I am dragging on between health and sickness; but it is not that which has hindered me from writing; the fact is, no opportunity, either slight or great, has presented itself. In future when there is none here we will send to Chambery, for there it is never wanting. But do not you, my dear daughter, write so many letters each time; it will suffice when you have written all to our dear mother, to put one single little note for the poor father, who says nothing except that he is all yours.

I am pleased beyond what can be expressed to see that you ardently love your vocation ; that alone can sanctify you, and nothing without that. Thanks to God, we see that his divine Providence wills to use it for the good of many souls in various places where they want this Congregation, which by miracle seems to be fertile in the very instant of its birth.

I certainly think that of those young persons who want to see the practice and nature of the rules you must make a part come here, that you may not be overcharged with an excessive care, nor similarly our dear Sister Marie-Aimée, whom I see already, methinks, tottering a little under the burden: but you will increase her courage, and will give her the strength of a generous zeal on the foundation of a profound humility.

I have seen the temptation. Alas! my dearest daughter, we must have some; this one sometimes harasses the heart, but never terrifies it, if it be somewhat on its guard and remain brave. Humble yourself profoundly, and be not alarmed. Lilies which grow among thorns are whiter, and roses by the waterside smell sweeter and become musky: *He who has not been tempted, what does he know?* *

If your trouble lie in some sensible feeling, as you seem to give me to think, change your corporal exercises when you are attacked by it; if you cannot well change your exercises, change your place and posture. It is driven away by these various changes. If it lie

* Eccles. xxxiv. 9.

in your imagination, sing, keep with the others, change your spiritual exercises, that is, pass from one to the other, and the changing of place will help you here again.

Above all, be not discouraged; but often renew your vows, and humble yourself before God. Promise victory to your heart on the part of the Blessed Virgin. If anything be a scruple to you, say it boldly and bravely, without making any reflection on it, when you approach the Sacrament of Penance. But I hope in God that with a noble spirit you will keep yourself exempt from all that can cause scruple.

I am quite willing that you should wear the hair-shirt once a week, unless you recognise that this makes you too slothful in other more important exercises, as sometimes happens.

Keep firmly, my dear daughter, to the strict observance of the rules, and the religious behaviour of yourself and the whole house. Cause great respect to be shown to sacred places and things. The care which you will take in all this will be very agreeable to Our Lord, above all if it be taken with humility, sweetness, and tranquillity.

Our sisters will tell you all the news here, and of the reception of the good Madame de Chatelar, and Mlle. d'Avise. This disgusts the world a little; but it cannot be helped, Our Lord must be served.

I told our Sister de Gouffier that I wanted henceforward to give generosity to the devotion of our sisters, and to take away the sensitiveness which one often has for oneself—that little softness which disturbs our peace, makes us desire spiritual and interior privileges, makes us excuse our humours and flatter our inclinations. But, my dear daughter, we have not yet got to it, though truly all make progress towards it. Well, I doubt not that God gives you the same sentiments, since you are one same spirit with all of us.

I approve your continuing to call our mother, mother, since this is a consolation to you, and your calling me father, for I have towards you a heart far more than paternal. Know this, my dear daughter, that since you are in office you are always so present to me, that I seem to myself to be perpetually with you, not without making a thousand thousand wishes about your dear soul.

Be most careful to offer a little salutation to my Lord the Archbishop sometimes on my part. You could not think what I owe to him, or how God blessed the little visit which he made here. I salute M. de Saint Nizier, of whom you think so much; may God increase blessings upon him and upon our reverend chaplain. Also, I salute Madame the wife of President Le Blanc, when you see her, and M. Colin and M. Vulliat, not to mention my dear Sister Marie-Peronne, to whom I belong entirely, as to all our good sisters. Lastly, I salute your heart, which mine cherishes with all its strength, wishing it the blessing of Our Saviour's—to which be glory eternally, Amen, as to that of his holy Mother, Our Lady.

Your renewal of vows not having been made on the Presentation, you can make it on New Year's day, or on the day of the Kings, or when my Lord Archbishop chooses; for I have no doubt you wish that it should be he who will receive them. Our sisters here said before Mass, while I was vesting, the *Veni Creator;* and after the renewal, the *Laudate Dominum omnes gentes*, and pronounced their vows very solemnly.

My dear daughter, I am all yours.

LETTER XXI.

TO THE SAME.

Consolation and encouragement.

18*th December* 1615. [Tr.]

IT is assuredly true, my dear daughter, your consolations console me greatly, but above all when they are founded on so firm a rock as is that of the presence of God. Walk ever thus near to God, for his shadow is more healthful than the sun.

There is no harm in trembling sometimes before him in whose presence the Angels themselves tremble; on condition, however, that holy love, which is over all his works, remain ever the higher part, the beginning and the end of your considerations.

See, then, how well things go, since these little sallies of your spirit do not flash out so suddenly, and your heart is a little gentler. Be ever faithful to God and to your soul. Always be correcting yourself of something; do not do this good office by force, but try to take pleasure in it, as lovers of country occupations do in pruning the trees of their orchards.

Our Lord will, without doubt, supply all that is wanting from elsewhere, in order that you may make a more perfect retreat with him, provided it be he whom you love, whom you seek, whom you follow. And you do so, I know, my daughter; but do so then always, and recommend me to his mercy, since I am with all my heart your very affectionate servant, &c.

LETTER XXII.

TO THE SAME.*

The excellence of acknowledging one's imperfections.

18th December 1615. [?]

YES, yes, in God's name, my dear granddaughter; I know well what your heart has been towards me—but do you not want me to take the time and the season for planting therein the plants of most excellent virtues, whose fruit is everlasting? I have no leisure, but I tell you in truth that your letter has embalmed my soul with so sweet a perfume that for a long time I had read nothing which had given me so perfect a consolation. And I say again, my dear daughter, that this letter has given me fresh movements of love towards God, who is so good, and towards yourself whom he wants to make so good, for which I am truly obliged to render thanks to his divine Providence. It is thus, my daughter, that we must in good earnest put our hands into the folds of our hearts, in order to tear out the foul productions which our self-love breeds therein by means of our humours, inclinations, and aversions.

* The older editions of the French text put simply "To a Sister of the Visitation." Letter XXI. has the same date as this letter. [Tr.]

What a satisfaction to a most loving father's heart to hear that of his most beloved daughter confess that she has been envious and malicious! How blessed is this envy, since it is followed by so sincere a confession! Your hand, when it wrote your letter, performed a braver deed than ever did that of Alexander. Do then, by all means, what your heart has proposed. Do not distress yourself about what has happened; but simply, humbly, lovingly, confidently, reunite your spirit to that of this amiable soul, who, I am sure, will thereby receive a thousand consolations. O my daughter, it is a great part of our perfection to support one another in our imperfections; for in what can we practise love of our neighbour save in this support? My daughter, she will love you, and you will love her, and God will love you all. And as for me, my dear daughter, you will love me also, since God so wills, and consequently gives me a perfect love of your soul, which I conjure to go from good to better, and from better to better, in the acquiring of virtues. Walk courageously and with heart upraised. *Vive Jesus!* Amen.

LETTER XXIII.

TO A SUPERIOR OF THE VISITATION [MOTHER FAVRE].

Encouragement to renounce all for God, and to have no solicitude.

Early in 1616.*

TRULY I see with my own eyes, methinks, and feel with my own heart, that you have made an exercise

* The French has "about December 1615." [Tr.]

of very great renunciation. But, O how blessed are the naked of heart! For Our Lord will clothe them again with graces, with benedictions, and with his special protection. Poor and wretched creatures that we are in this mortal life, we can scarcely do anything good without suffering some evil for it; nay, we can hardly even serve him in one direction without leaving him in another; and often it is required to leave God for God, renouncing his sweetness to serve him in his sorrows and travails.

My very dear daughter—Ah! maidens who get married give up without difficulty the presence of their fathers and mothers, and of their country, to put themselves under husbands who are very often unknown to them—at least their dispositions are unknown—with the object of bearing to them children for this world. Surely a greater courage than this God's daughters must have, to form in purity and sanctity of life children for his divine Majesty. But all the same, my dear daughter, we can never quit one another, we whom the very blood of Our Lord, I mean his love by merit of his blood, holds glued and joined together. Certainly, for my part, I am in truth so perfectly yours that in proportion as these two or three days of distance seem to separate us corporally, I join myself with stronger and fuller affection spiritually to you, as to my daughter most dear. You will be the first with our mother in my prayers and in my solicitudes—sweet solicitudes, however, because of the extreme confidence which I have in this celestial care of divine Providence over your soul, which will be blessed if it cast also all its apprehensions into this bosom of infinite love.

So then, my dear daughter, have your eyes lifted up high to God; increase your courage in most holy humility, strengthen it with sweetness, confirm it in equality of mind; make your spirit perpetually mistress of your inclinations and humours; allow no fears to take possession of your heart: *one day will give you the knowledge of what you shall do the next.** You have so far got through many hazards, and this by God's grace; the same grace will deliver you from the difficulties and perils of the way, one after the other, even if he have to send an angel to bear you up in the more dangerous passages.

Do not turn back your eyes upon your infirmities and weaknesses, unless to humble yourself; never to discourage yourself. Often behold God on your right hand, and the two Angels whom he has appointed you, one for your person, the other for your little family. Say often to them, to these holy angels: My Lords, how shall I act? Beseech them to impart habitually to you that knowledge of the divine Will which they contemplate, and the inspirations which Our Lady desires that you should receive from her own breasts of love. Do not take notice of that variety of imperfections which exist in yourself and in all the daughters whom Our Lord and Our Lady have put under your charge, except to keep yourself in the holy fear of offending God; never to alarm yourself; for we must not marvel that each herb and each flower in a garden requires its special care.

I have learnt one or two of the graces which God gave to our very dear Sister Marie-Renée at her decease. She was most truly my daughter; for when I

* *Day to day uttereth the word,* Ps. xviii. 2.

was there she made a review of her whole life, to give me a knowledge of what she had been, with incredible humility and confidence, and without great necessity, to my extreme edification, when I think of it again. Now she is there praying for us, and for you in particular, since she passed away as your daughter and with your assistance.

Give me the consolation, my dear daughter, of often writing to me and always telling me the things which you think I may profitably know of the state of your heart, which I bless with all mine in the name of Our Lord, and am in God all yours.

LETTER XXIV.

TO THE SAME.

On good and on useless desires : advice in temptation.

ANNECY, *17th April* 1616.

I RETURNED yesterday from the Chablais, my dear daughter, where, thanks to God, I have left the Barnabite Fathers established, according to the command of His Highness and the Cardinal Prince ; to-morrow I am going to console Madame the Countess of Tournon on the death of her husband, to which I am bound by the relationship which is between us, and the obligations which I have to the memory of the deceased. This is by way of telling you, my dear daughter, that I am writing to you without leisure, and yet I want to answer the two questions which you put to me some time back ; for I see clearly that it is of no use to wait for convenience to do better, since I am destined to continual pressure of troublesome affairs.

My dear daughter, there are two kinds of good desires; one, those which increase the grace and glory of God's servants; the other, which effect nothing. Desires of the former kind are thus expressed: I should like, say, to give alms, but I do not, because I have not the wherewithal; and these desires greatly increase charity and sanctify the soul: thus devout souls desire martyrdom, reproaches and the cross, which yet they cannot obtain. Desires of the second kind are expressed thus: I should like to give alms, but I do not will to do so; and these desires are not hindered from effect by impossibility, but by meanness of spirit, timidity, and want of earnestness, whence they are useless and do not sanctify the soul, nor give any increase of grace, and of them, St. Bernard says, hell is full.

It is true that for the entire resolution of your difficulty you must note that there are desires which seem to be of the second sort, and yet all the same are of the first; as, on the contrary, there are some which appear to be of the first, and are really of the second. For example, no servant of God can be without this desire: Oh how greatly I would wish to serve God better! Alas! when shall I serve him as I desire? And because we can always go from better to better, it seems that the effects of these desires are only hindered by want of resolution. But this is not true, for they are hindered by the condition of this mortal life, in which it is not so easy for us to do as to desire. For which reason these desires in general are good, and make the soul better, giving it fervour, and persuading it to progress. But when, in particular, some occasion of making progress presents itself, and a person instead of coming to deed stops short at desire—as, for example, an occasion presents itself of pardoning an injury, of renouncing my own will on some particular subject, and instead of granting this pardon, making the renunciation, I simply say: I would much desire to pardon, but I am not able; I would like to make this renouncement, but it cannot be—who does not see that this desire is a mere occupation of the fancy, yea, that it makes me more guilty in having so strong an inclination towards good and not putting it into act? And these desires made thus seem to be of the first sort and are of the second. Well, it will now be easy for you to settle your doubt, I think. But if there yet remain some difficulty write it to me, and sooner or later I will answer you with all my heart, which is indeed wholly yours, my very dear daughter.

Those who are tempted with unbecoming imaginations in meditations on the life and death of the Saviour should, as far as possible, represent the mysteries to themselves simply by faith, without using the imagination. For example: My Saviour was crucified; it is a proposition of faith; enough that I simply apprehend it, without imagining to myself how his body hung on the cross. And when the improper imaginations arise, you must turn upon them, and drive them back by affections proceeding from faith. O Jesus crucified, I adore you; I adore your torments, your pains, your travail; you are my salvation. For, my dear daughter, to want to leave off meditating on the death or life of Our Lord, on account of these filthy representations, would be to play the enemy's game, who tries by this means to deprive us of our greatest blessing.

Truly I am out of breath, but you will supply by your goodness. I will write at another time to Sister G. M., and then to Sister M. A., and meanwhile I salute their love, which I pray to recommend me earnestly to Our Lord; as also Sister Frances Teresa, and all the other sisters, whom I greatly love in the faith of Our Saviour. I salute the reverend chaplain, and am his entirely. Adieu! my dear daughter, À Dieu (to God) may we be eternally, to love and bless him without ceasing.

I humbly salute M. de Saint Nizier, and the Rev. Father Philip, and beg you, when you see the Rev. Father Rector, to assure him of my very humble and sincere affection. I salute Mesdames Vulliat and Colin.

LETTER XXV.

To Mother de Brechard, about to Found the House at Moulins.

Discouragement is the temptation of temptations: it is no fruit of humility, neither does corporal infirmity justify it. She is to rule on supernatural principles.

About August 1616.*

The service which you are going to render to Our Lord and his glorious Mother is apostolic; for you are going to collect, my dear daughter, many souls in a congregation, to lead them as a band to the spiritual warfare against the world, the devil, and the flesh, for

* The French says "about the end of 1615." [Tr.]

the glory of God; or, rather, you are going to make a new swarm of bees, which in a new hive will work in divine love, more delicious than honey. Well, then, walk courageously with perfect confidence in the goodness of him who calls you to this holy duty. When did any one hope in God and was confounded? The distrust which you ought to have of yourself is good so long as it serves as a base to the confidence you should have in God; but if ever it lead you to any discouragement, disquiet, sadness, or melancholy, I beseech you to reject it as the temptation of temptations, and never permit your spirit to argue and reply in favour of the disquiet or depression of heart to which you may feel yourself tending. For it is a simple and entirely certain truth that God permits many difficulties to arise in the way of those who undertake his service, but still that he never lets them fall under the burden so long as they rest in him. It is, in a word, the great point in your case, never to employ your spirit to defend and support the temptation to discouragement under any pretext whatever, not even if it should be under the specious pretext of humility. Humility, my dear daughter, refuses offices; but it is not obstinate in its refusal, and when employed by those who have the right, it no longer reasons upon its unworthiness as to that thing, but believes all things, hopes all things, bears all things with charity; it is always simple, is holy humility, and a great follower of obedience; and, as it never dares to think itself can do anything, so it always thinks that obedience can do everything, and as true simplicity humbly refuses charges, true humility exercises them simply.

Your body is a mass of weakness, but charity which is its clothing will cover all. A weakly person excites to a holy considerateness all who know her, and even causes a tenderness of special predilection, provided that she be seen to bear her cross devoutly and sweetly; one must be just as frank in taking and asking remedies as gentle and courageous in bearing the illness. He who can preserve sweetness amid pains and feebleness, and peace amid the worry and multitude of affairs, is almost perfect; and although one finds few, even Religious, who attain to this degree of blessedness, yet there are some, and have been at all times, and we must aspire to this height. Almost everybody finds it easy to practise certain virtues and hard to practise others, and every one argues in favour of the virtue which he practises easily, and tries to exaggerate the difficulties of the virtues which are contrary to it. There were ten virgins, and only five of them had the oil of sweet mercy and mildness. This equableness of humour, this gentleness and sweetness of heart, is rarer than perfect chastity; but it is all the more desirable for that. I recommend it to you, my dear daughter, because to it as to the oil of the lamp is attached the flame of good example, nothing giving so much edification as sweetness of charity.

Hold the balance duly amongst your daughters, so that natural gifts may not make you distribute your affections and kindness unjustly. How many disagreeable persons are there who are very agreeable in the eyes of God. Beauty, gracefulness, the gift of speaking well, often present great attractions to those who live according to their inclinations; charity regards true virtue, and the beauty of the heart, and spreads itself over all without distinction.

Go, then, my daughter, to the work for which God has raised you up; he will be on your right hand, so that no difficulty may shake you; he will henceforth hold you, so that you may follow his way. Have a courage not only great, but one that will hold out and endure; and to have it, ask it often of him who alone can give it; he will give it you if in simplicity of heart you correspond with grace. Love and peace, and the consolation of the Holy Spirit, be for ever in your soul. Amen.

P.S.—You are my daughter, and with paternal dilection I give you the holy benediction of God. Blessed may you be in going, in staying, in serving God, in serving your neighbour, in humbling yourself down to your nothingness, in keeping yourself within yourself; may God be entirely your all.

LETTER XXVI.

To Mother Favre, at Lyons.

Exhortation to charity and union.

10*th September* 1616.

This dear granddaughter who does not write, does she not deserve to be herself left in silence? But my affection does not allow it. And what shall I say to you then, my dear daughter? I recommend to you confidence in God, perfect simplicity and sincere dilection.

You have there those poor sisters, who are under your responsibility, and depend on your help in the advancement of your undertaking, for which they have come to you; unite your hearts and feeble strength, for by union you will get invincible strength.

Our mother will tell you, perhaps, if she has leisure for it, my fear lest the little foxes enter the vineyard to destroy it;* I mean aversions and repugnances which are the temptations of the Saints. Suffocate them in their birth. Make yours a united charity, and suspect all that shall be contrary to union, to support of one another, to the mutual esteem which you should have together.

Beware of human prudence, which Our Saviour reckons foolishness, and work in peace, in sweetness, in confidence, in simplicity. As soon as you have done what you have to do, it will be well to finish off your own private business. Live all of you in the bowels of divine charity, my dearest daughter, to whom I am with all my heart yours, &c.

LETTER XXVII.

To a Religious Priest.

Reasons why the Saint prefers the little Office to the great Office for the Visitation: he desires to be commanded to establish a seminary.

1617. [?]

My Reverend Father—The case of the Ladies of the Visitation at Rome consists in this point, that it would

* Cant. ii. 15.

please His Holiness to allow them not to be obliged to say the great Office, for the following reasons:

(1.) There is no nation in the world in which women pronounce Latin so badly as in France, and especially here; and it would be impossible to make them properly learn the pronunciation of the whole great Office, whereas it would be easy to teach it them for the little Office of Our Lady, and, in fact, they pronounce it very well already.

(2.) In this congregation it is desired to receive sisters of delicate constitution, and those who for lack of bodily strength cannot be received into more austere religious Orders. Now those who are obliged to the great Office, if they want to say it distinctly and deliberately, cannot do so without effort, and if they say it quickly and fluently, make themselves ridiculous and lose devotion. Wherefore, it is more becoming that those who for want of corporal strength could not say it composedly, should say only the little Office.

(3.) There is an example at Paris, where the Sisters of St. Ursula, Religious of the three solemn vows, say only the little Office.

(4.) The Sisters of the Visitation have many spiritual exercises which they could not do if they said the great Office.

I had thought of naming to you the other points, but I remember that the Father Procurator General has them at great length. I must tell you that the rules for which approbation is asked are all according to the rule of St. Augustine, except as to absolute enclosure, which St. Augustine had not established, but to which the sisters wish to bind themselves, according to the sacred Council of Trent. Perhaps the Holy See will appoint some one here, some Regular prelates and other theologians, to revise, correct, and approve them.

I do not see that there is need to inform you of anything else on the subject, except that as to the monastery of this city, seeing that its Church is consecrated under the title of the Visitation of Our Lady and of the glorious St. Joseph, it would be desirable to get a plenary indulgence for this last day, and for the title days of the other houses and monasteries of this Congregation, besides the indulgence of the day of the Visitation, which is the general title of the Congregation.

My Lord of Lyons is there, who, if he pleases, has power to favour the business; and I think it will please him to do so, because he has in his metropolitan city a house of the Visitation where God is greatly honoured.

But, my reverend Father, we must treat all things quietly and with circumspection; which I say because some ecclesiastics who are austere and exact in their own practice, have given certain signs that they were not satisfied that there should be in this congregation so little austerity and penitential rigour: but the end must always be kept in view, which is to be able to receive maidens and women who are weakly, whether by age or in constitution.

I also desire to obtain a letter from the Congregation of Bishops, addressed to me and to the clergy of this diocese, by which it should be enjoined upon me to erect a seminary for those who aspire to the ecclesiastical state, where they can be trained in the ceremonies, to catechise and preach, to sing, and to other such clerical qualifications; for we have some, besides little children, who want to be ecclesiastics, and who study for no other end. I want the clergy to be included in the letter in order to be able to impose some little tax on the benefices for the purpose. The Council of Trent would suffice, but to apply it more efficaciously the above letter would be required. I am, your &c.

LETTER XXVIII.

To Mother Favre, at Lyons.

On the change of the Visitation from a Congregation into an Order: entire detachment of the Saint.

October 1617 [?].

My very dear Daughter—If my Lord Archbishop says to you what he has written to me, you must answer him that you have been left there to serve in the establishing of your Congregation with all your poor strength, that you will try to guide your sisters well according to the rules of the Congregation, that if it please God after this that the Congregation change its name, state, and condition you will refer yourself to his good pleasure, to which the whole Congregation is entirely consecrated; add that in whatever way God may be served in the society in which you now serve him you will be content.

And in effect, my dear daughter, there must be that spirit in our Congregation; for it is the perfect and apostolic spirit. And if it could be useful for establishing some other Congregations of good servants of God, without ever establishing itself, it would only be all the more agreeable to God, for it would have less ground of self-love. On the points which he proposes to me, without which he does not will to establish our poor Congregation in his diocese, I leave him the choice without any reserve. It is entirely indifferent whether the good of this Congregation be done in this way or in that other, although I should have found a special sweetness in the title of simple Congregation, where charity alone and fear of the Beloved would serve as enclosure.

I agree, then, that we should make a formal Religious Order; and, my dear daughter—I speak to you with the entire simplicity and confidence of my heart—I make this acquiescence with quietness and tranquillity, yea, with an unparalleled sweetness; and not only my will but my judgment is very glad to render the homage which it owes to that of this great and worthy prelate.

For, my daughter, what do I aim at in all this save that God may be glorified, and that his holy love may be spread abroad more plentifully in the heart of those souls who are so happy as to dedicate themselves entirely to God? Be sure, my dear daughter, that I have a perfect love for our poor little Congregation; but without anxiety. Without anxiety, indeed, love does not ordinarily subsist, but mine, which is not ordinary, lives, I assure you, entirely without it, through a particular confidence which I have in the grace of Our Lord. His sovereign hand will do more for this little Institute than men can think. And I am, more than you could believe, yours.

For the rest, what will you say about our domestic afflictions? It is not the dear sister-in-law de Thorens that you saw, it is quite another sister whom we have seen dying lately. For from about a year ago she became so perfect that she could no longer be recognised, but, above all, since her widowhcod, when she vowed herself to the Visitation. And, Oh! what an end she made! Certainly the most holy, most sweet, and most dear that could be imagined. I loved her with a love far greater than fraternal; but as it has pleased the Lord so be it done: may his holy name be blessed. Amen.

LETTER XXIX.

TO THE SISTERS OF THE VISITATION AT ANNECY.

Excellence of the religious state as compared with a secular life: they are to be spiritual bees.

GRENOBLE, *5th March* 1617.*

COULD my soul ever forget the dear children of its womb? No, my very dear daughters, my dear joy and my crown, you know it well, I am certain; and your hearts will well have answered for me that if I have not written to you till now, it is only because writing to our good mother, the mother of all, I knew well that I wrote to you no less than to her, by that sweet and salutary union which your souls have with hers; and because, moreover, the holy love which we reciprocally bear one another is written, methinks, in

* The French has "1st April 1616." The year is certainly wrong. The Saint preached the Lent at Grenoble in 1617. He speaks of the feeding the multitude as the Gospel of "to-day." This Gospel is read on fourth Sunday of Lent, which in 1617 was 5th March. [Tr.]

such great characters in our hearts that one can very nearly read our thoughts here from Annecy.

I am with rather more people than when I am in my ordinary dwelling near you; and the more I see of this miserable world the more displeasing it is to me, and I think that I could not live in it if the serving some good souls in the advancement of their salvation did not give me some relief.

Oh! my dear daughters, how much more happy I find the bees, who leave not their hive except for gathering honey, and are only collected together to compose it, who have no striving but for that, and whose striving is according to order, and who do nothing in their houses and monasteries save the sweet-smelling work of honey and of wax.

How much more happy are they than those libertine wasps and insects, which flying so aimlessly and more readily to unclean things than to clean, seem to live only to annoy other animals and give them pain, while giving themselves a perpetual disquiet and useless solicitude. They fly everywhere buzzing, sucking, and stinging while their summer and their autumn last; and come winter, they find themselves without a refuge, without provision, and without life;—while our chaste bees, which have as the object of their sight, of their smell, of their taste, only the beauty, perfume, and sweetness of the flowers spread out for them, have, besides the nobleness of their occupation, a very delightful retreat, an agreeable provision, and a contented life, amidst the stores of their past labour.

And those souls in love with our Saviour, who follow him in the Gospel as far as the desert heights, make there on the grass and flowers a more delicious feast than ever those did who enjoyed the sumptuous service of Ahasuerus, where abundance choked enjoyment, because it was an abundance of meats and of men.

Live joyous, my dear daughters, amongst your holy occupations. When the air is cloudy, amid dryness and aridities, work within your heart by the practice of holy humility and abjection; when it is fine, bright, and clear, go make your spiritual expeditions on to the hills of Calvary, of Olivet, of Sion, and of Thabor. From the desert mountain where our Saviour feeds his dear flock to-day, fly up to the summit of the eternal mount of heaven, and see the immortal delights which are there prepared for your hearts.

Ah! how happy are these well-beloved hearts of my daughters, in having given up some years of the false liberty of the world in order to enjoy eternally that desirable slavery in which no liberty is taken away save that which hinders us from being truly free.

May God bless you, my dear daughters, and make you advance more and more in the love of his divine eternity, in which we hope to enjoy the infinitude of his favours in return for this little but true fidelity which in so slight a thing as is this present life, we will observe, by help of his grace. May the dilection of the Father, of the Son, and of the Holy Ghost be for ever in the midst of your hearts, and may the bosom of Our Lady be our refuge for ever. Amen. 1st April 1610.*

God has done me the favour of having been able to write all at one breath, though almost without breath-

* So the printed text, clearly by mistake. The Visitation was not then founded. See previous note. [Tr.]

ing, these four little words to my dear daughters, who, placed together like flowers in a bouquet, are delicious to the Mother of the "Flower of Jesse," and flower of mothers. Ah! Lord, may it be unto an odour of sweetness. Amen, Amen. *Vive Jesus,* in whom I am your most affectionate servant.

LETTER XXX.

TO A RELIGIOUS OF THE VISITATION.

On the obligation of her vows, and on expulsion from religious Orders.

About 1618.*

YOUR vows, my dear daughter, are as strong as the vows of all Orders of religion in the obligation by which they bind the conscience of the sisters to their observance. It is true, however, that a sister who desires to lose her soul and her honour can marry after the vows, and so could the most-strictly professed one in France if she wanted to be lost, and to make use of the *Edict of pacification.* The formulary of your vows is made according to those of like congregations in Italy, and much more expresses the force of the obligation than do most of the formularies of the Rule of St. Benedict.

The vow of chastity is fundamental, according to the ancient Fathers, in monasteries of women, and the others are not less essential.

It is true, one can be dispensed from simple vows, and from the others also—though more easily from

* The French has no date. [Tr.].

those than from these—but not without grave occasion, and when it is expedient. Here the Jesuit Fathers are in an extremely good position, and maintain the lustre of their most illustrious Company by this means, which the world does not approve, but God and the Church do highly: and all religious Orders in ancient times were of that kind, solemnity of vows having been established but a few hundreds of years.

Expulsion has always existed among the ancient religious; it is a necessary rigour. To expel a sister because she would not observe silence would not be done for not observing silence, but for an obstinate will of troubling and overthrowing the order of the Congregation, and contemning the Holy Spirit, who has ordained silence in religious houses. And if one expel not for obstinate disobedience and conscious contempt of the Order, I do not know what one will expel for. In a word, religious, even those most solemnly so, expel; at any rate, we see religious expelled from the Order of St. Francis, even from the Capuchins; and the Jesuit Fathers, who are so cautious and prudent, expel for disobediences, if these are even a little cherished and clung to.

The extension of the novitiate for a good reason is not contrary to the Council [of Trent], as those have declared who have the office of explaining it; and theologians also so understand the case. In fact the Carmelites do it as seems expedient.

If these good gentlemen had studied and thought as much before censuring as we have in establishing, we should not have so many objections. Well, God be praised; I hope that everybody will soon be pacified, through the conclusion that will be made at Rome.

My dear daughter, for God's sake have good courage; it is for him also that you live and labour. May he be ever blessed and glorified. Amen. If those who make this objection are persons of study, they can read Leonard Lessius, Jesuit, where they will find what is wanted.

LETTER XXXI.

TO A SUPERIORESS OF THE VISITATION.

The Visitation not founded for the education of young girls.

23rd January 1618.

MY DEAR DAUGHTER—We must remain at peace in what God disposes and ordains; we on our part have done so to-day; at seven in the morning we lost for this life the good Father Dom Simplician, and at three the good M. de Sainte Catherine, two great servants of God, while there was scarcely a single person ill in this city. O heavenly Providence! without scrutinising the effects you cause, I adore and embrace them with all my heart, and acquiesce in all the events which proceed from them by your will.

My dear daughter, you must entirely avoid receiving girls before the age; because God has not chosen your institute for the education of little girls, but for the perfection of matrons and maidens who at such an age as to be able to discern what they are doing are called thereto; and not only experience but reason teaches us that such young girls placed under the discipline of a monastery, too much out of proportion with their childishness, dislike it and receive it reluctantly; and if they afterwards desire to take the habit it is not from the true and pure motive which the sanctity of the institute requires. And it does not follow that what is done for one time must be done at other times, any more than it follows that when a man has burdened himself with a just charge for one friend, he must overburden himself with a second charge for a second friend; and those who would be friends of our institute will have patience till their children are of suitable age.

O my dear daughter, how inconsistent are the thoughts of men! How many cry out when we take their children grown up, mature and settled, and how many would wish to give them from the cradle!

LETTER XXXII.

To a Superioress of the Visitation.

A Superior must be weak with the weak: consolation to be drawn from the thought of God's providence and of heavenly rewards.

19*th February* 1618.

I SEE you, my dear daughter, quite ill and suffering over the illnesses and pains of your daughters. One cannot be a mother without pangs. *Who is weak*, says the Apostle,* *and I am not weak* with him? And our ancient Fathers say upon this, that hens are always in distress while they are rearing their chickens, and

* 2 Cor. xi. 29.

that it is this which makes them continually utter their cries, and that it was so with the Apostle.

My dear daughter, who are also my grand-daughter, the Apostle also said * that when he was weak then he was strong, *for that the power of God is made perfect in infirmity.* And you then, my daughter, be very strong amid the afflictions of your house. These long maladies are good schools of charity for those who help in them, and of loving patience for those who have them; for the first are at the foot of the cross with Our Lady and St. John, whose compassion they imitate, and the others are on the cross with Our Lord, whose Passion they imitate.

As to the sister of whom you write to me, God will make you take the proper course. This sweetness in suffering is a sort of presage of future abundant favours of Our Lord in this soul, wherever she may go or dwell. Salute, I beg you, these two daughters tenderly from me, for it is so I love them.

Meanwhile, if it is found proper to send back this novice, it must be done with all the charity possible, and God will bring everything to his glory. God keeps † and blesses the goings out as well as the comings in of those who do all things for him, and who do not occasion their own goings out by their ill conduct. His Providence thus makes us will the sacrifice which it afterwards does not let us make, as we see in Abraham. And methinks I say something about this in the book of "The Love of God," but I do not call to mind where.‡

So enlarge your heart, my dear daughter, amid tribulations; increase your courage, and see the great Saviour bending down from high heaven towards you,

* II Cor. xii. 9, 10. † Ps. cxx. 8. ‡ Bk. ix. 6. [Tr.]

watching how you walk in these tempests, and by a thread of his invisible Providence holding your heart and steadying it, so that he may ever keep it to himself. My dear daughter, you are a spouse, not as yet of Jesus Christ glorified, but of Jesus Christ crucified; for which cause the rings, the rich chains and the ornaments which he gives you, and which he wants you to wear, are crosses, nails, and thorns, and the marriage-feast is gall, hyssop, and vinegar. In heaven above we shall have the rubies, diamonds, and emeralds, the wine, manna, and honey. I do not say this, no indeed, my dear granddaughter, as if I thought you to be discouraged, but because I think you are suffering, and I feel I ought to mingle my sighs with yours, as I feel my soul to be mingled with yours. Do not tell me that you abuse my kindness when you write me long letters; for truly I always love them and find them sweet.

This good Father says that I am a flower, a vase of flowers, and a phœnix; but in reality I am but a corruptible man, a crow, a dunghill. And still love me well, my dear daughter, for God ceases not to love me or to give me extraordinary desires of serving and loving him purely and holily. In fact, after all, we are too blessed in being able to aspire to an eternity of glory by the merits of the Passion of Our Lord, who makes a trophy of our misery to convert it into his mercy, to which be honour and glory for ever and ever. Amen. I am yours, my dear daughter, you know it well; I say yours, after an incomparable manner.

LETTER XXXIII.

To Mother de Chantal.

The Saint's extreme affection for her. The only aim of a Christian's life should be to give it more and more entirely to his Saviour.

March 1618 [*Grenoble?*].

My dear Daughter—This night during my wakeful times I have had a thousand good thoughts for my sermons; but strength has failed me to bring them forth. God knows all, and I direct all to his greater glory, and adoring his Providence I remain at peace. There is no help for it: I must do what I will not, *and the good which I will I do not.** I am here in the midst of preachings and of a large audience, larger than I thought; but if I do nothing here it will be little consolation to me.

Believe that meantime I think at every moment of you and of your soul, for which I incessantly express my desires before God and his Angels, that it may be more filled with the abundance of his graces. My dearest daughter, what ardour do I seem to have for your advancement in most holy celestial love, to which, while celebrating this morning, I have again dedicated and offered you, mentally lifting you up in my arms as one does little children, and big ones, too, when one is strong enough to lift them. Behold something of what imaginations our heart makes on these occasions. Truly I am pleased with it, that it should thus employ all things for the sweetness of its incomparable affection, referring them to holy things.

* Rom. vii. 19.

I have not failed to make a special memento of your dear husband deceased. Ah! what a happy exchange you made that day, embracing the state of perfect resignation, in which with such consolation I found you! And your soul, taking a Spouse of so high a condition, has reason indeed to find an extreme joy in the commemoration of the hour of your betrothal to him. And so it is true, my dear daughter, that our unity is wholly consecrated to the sovereign unity; and I feel with ever increasing force the reality of the union of our hearts, which will truly keep me from ever forgetting you until after, and long after, I have forgotten myself to fasten myself so much the better to the cross. I am going to try to keep you ever exalted permanently on the throne which God has given you in my heart, a throne based upon the cross.

For the rest, my dear daughter, go on establishing ever more and more your good purposes, your holy resolutions; deepen more and more your consideration of the wounds of Our Lord, where you will find an abyss of reasons which will confirm you in your generous undertaking, and will make you feel how vain and low is the heart which makes elsewhere its dwelling, or which builds on other tree than that of the cross. O my God! how happy shall we be if we live and die in this holy tabernacle! No, nothing, nothing of the world is worthy of our love: it is all due to this Saviour who has given us all his own.

In truth, I have had great sentiments, these last days, of the infinite obligations which I have to God; and with a thousand emotions of sweetness I have again resolved to serve him with the greatest fidelity I can, and to keep my soul more continually in his divine presence; and with all this I feel in myself a certain joyfulness, not impetuous, but methinks efficacious, at undertaking this mine amendment. Shall you not be very glad, my dear daughter, if one day you see me well fitted for the service of Our Lord? Yes, my dear daughter, because our interior goods are inseparably and wholly united. You wish me perpetually many graces; and as for me, with incomparable ardour I pray God to make you quite absolutely his own.

God knows, most dear daughter of my soul, how gladly I would wish to die for the love of my Saviour! But, at least, if I cannot die for it, may I live for it alone. My daughter, I am greatly pressed; what more can I say to you save—may this same God bless you with his great benediction.

Adieu, my dear daughter; press closely this dear Crucified One to your bosom. I beseech him to clasp and unite you more and more to himself. Adieu, again, my dear daughter: behold I am far advanced into the night, but still further in the consolation which I have in imagining sweet Jesus seated on your heart. I pray him to stay there for ever and for ever. Adieu, yet once more, my good, my dear daughter, whom I cherish beyond compare in Our Lord, who liveth and reigneth world without end. Amen. *Vive Jésus!*

LETTER XXXIV.

TO A RELIGIOUS PRIEST.

Religious exercises by which the Sisters of the Visitation supply for not saying the great Office.

26th April 1618.

MY REVEREND FATHER—As to the question which that good gentleman of whom you write to me asks, about the occupations of the Sisters of the Visitation, in case they do not say the great Office, there are two things to say.

(1.) Since they say the little Office solemnly and with pauses, they employ as much time as most other religious women give to saying the great Office, with this difference only, that they say it with more edification and better pronunciation than the latter.

Certainly, a week ago in a monastery near this city, I saw things which might well make the Huguenots laugh; and some of the nuns told me they never had less devotion than at Office, where they managed always to commit plenty of faults, partly from not knowing the accents and quantities, partly from not knowing the rubrics, or again from the haste with which they were obliged to say it; and they declared it to be impossible for them, amid so many distracting things, to keep their attention. I do not, however, mean to say that they are to be dispensed, unless when the Holy See, taking compassion on them, shall think it good. But, at the same time, I do mean to say that there is no impropriety but much advantage in leaving to the Visitation the little Office alone. In fact, my Reverend

Father, this little Office is the life of devotion in the Visitation.

(2.) The second answer is that in the Visitation there is not a single moment which is not most usefully employed in prayer, examination of conscience, spiritual reading, and other exercises. I am sure that the Holy See will favour this work, which is against neither the law nor the religious state, and which acquires it so many houses of obedience at a time and in a kingdom where it has lost so many; and since also there is not so much to be considered with regard to houses of women, inasmuch as they are of no consequence to the other Orders, nor can be occasion of complaint to nuns founded under other statutes. Solely the consideration of the greater glory of God gives me this desire, and the advantage of many souls capable of excellently serving his divine Majesty in this congregation, if charged only with the little Office, while incapable of following the great Office. Will it not be a thing worthy of Christianity that there should be a place whither these poor daughters can retire, who have the heart strong but the eyes and constitution weak? For the rest, my Reverend Father, labour diligently to make the work of your seminary succeed, for in my opinion it will be necessary in the future. Your friend and servant, &c.

LETTER XXXV.

TO A SUPERIORESS OF THE VISITATION.

On longanimity and resignation. The excellence of founding a religious house: privileges of founders.

ANNECY, 19*th August* 1618.

TELL me, my dear daughter, what is your heart doing? It is, I assure myself, more brave than usual in this holy Octave, in which we celebrate the triumphs of our Queen, in whose protection our spirit reposes and our little congregation breathes. O my daughter, we must keep this heart uplifted, nor suffer that any accident of dryness, anxiety, or weariness cast it down, for although such may separate it from the sensible consolation of charity, yet can they not separate it from real charity, which is God's sovereign grace to us during this mortal life. Our imperfections in treating affairs, whether interior or exterior, are a great subject of humility, and humility produces and nourishes generosity.

But what privilege have founders before God? Their privileges are great, because they share after a special way in all the good things done in the monastery and by occasion of the monastery. It is a work of charity almost the most excellent that one can do; much greater, without doubt, than to build a hospital, receive pilgrims, support orphans. But before men there is no further privilege than that of being supported and assisted and honoured in the monastery, in which secular foundresses generally obtain the right of entrance, and after death particular benefits.

But this daughter, desirous to be a religious, will, I am sure, assert her privilege, as far as she is concerned, by obeying better than the rest, and by making the best progress she can in humility, purity of heart, sweetness, modesty, and obedience; since the privilege of true religious is to abound in the love of the heavenly Beloved.

For the rest, I rejoice that this daughter makes so good an election, and that quitting men's love, so little lovely, she consecrates herself to the most lovely love of her God, the true Spouse of noble souls.

LETTER XXXVI.

To a Superioress of the Visitation.

On the freedom of spiritual communications.

PARIS, 21*st January* 1619.

MY DEAR DAUGHTER—As to the matters which you name to me, the rule as to the extraordinary confessor must not be altered, nor must any one trouble weak sisters who want to communicate with the extraordinary more than four times a year; but it behoves that if the sisters have not the confidence to ask to speak to him, he himself should have it to speak to them sometimes; and if he have it not you must give it him, if he be a father who can receive it.

For as a just liberty of communication must be provided for the sisters, so must they be kept in the rule of simplicity and humility; and it is not reasonable that the weakness of some should cause extraordinary confessions to be multiplied for all the congregation, and should put the poor ordinary confessor in grief and distress.

In short, if each sister is to be free to believe in her interior inclinations, submission and union will cease, and with it the congregation—which God forbid. Those, then, who want to confer extraordinarily let them do so in the spirit of a sweet liberty; let them confess if they like while making their communication, without urging the rest to the same desire, and without artfully leading them to imitate themselves.

Here, we are trying to overcome the temptations aroused against the introduction of the Visitation, and hope that we shall do so. May God bless you! Your very affectionate father and servant in Jesus Christ, &c.

LETTER XXXVII.

To Mother de Chantal.

The weak to be corrected with mildness.

How glad I am, my dear mother, of the good news of your health! May the great God, whom my poor soul and yours will to serve for ever, be blessed and praised, and may he deign to fortify more and more this dear health, which we have dedicated to his infinite holiness. But meantime the heart, how is it in you? Ah! my dear mother, what blessings do I desire it! When will our love, triumphing above all our affections and thoughts, make us wholly united to the sovereign love of Our Saviour, to which ours incessantly aspires? Yes, my dearest mother, it aspires incessantly, though for the greater part of the time insensibly. I was truly much disappointed this morning that I had to leave my work just as there had come to me a certain fulness of the sentiments which we shall have on the sight of God in Paradise—for I was going to write on that in our little book *—and now I have them no more. Still, as I only turned from them to go and receive the pledges of this same sight in the holy Mass, I hope they will come back to me when the time requires. O my dear and sole mother, may we perfectly love this divine object, who prepares for us so much sweetness in heaven! Let us be indeed all his, and walk night and day amongst thorns and roses till we arrive at that heavenly Jerusalem.

The granddaughter walks by a very safe way, provided that its roughness does not discourage her. The easiest ways do not always lead us the most directly nor the most safely; one is so occupied sometimes with the pleasure that one finds there, and with looking on one side and the other at the pleasing prospects, that one forgets in this to be diligent in the journey. I must be brief. Look at this note which was sent me this morning; and as I have not seen this poor creature, and you will see her before me, I thought I should do well to send it to you. Alas! my dear mother, what harm does vanity do to these poor little

* The *Treatise on the Love of God.* [Tr.]

souls, who do not know themselves, and place themselves in risks! But still, as you know, while remonstrating earnestly you must use love and sweetness; for admonitions have a better effect so, and otherwise one might drive away these somewhat feeble hearts. Only I do not know how you will be able to say that you do not know of the quarrel. Well, God will inspire into our heart what to say on this point, as I beg him to do, as likewise to inspire me what to preach to-night. I write amid many distractions. Good night, my dear mother. I am, your very affectionate servant in Jesus Christ.

BOOK III.

Later Letters to Sisters of the Visitation.

[This later series opens with a set of letters which passed between St. Francis and St. Jane Frances during a retreat which the latter made shortly after the establishment of the Paris Visitation. St. Francis was too ill to conduct this retreat personally as he had intended. These letters, with the last part of Book IX. of the *Treatise on the Love of God*, contain his sublimest teachings for perfect souls. The remainder of the book consists of various instructions and exhortations to St. Jane and his other daughters. The institute was now rapidly spreading. We find allusions to the seven other houses which were founded during St. Francis's life after the founding of the first House of Paris. These were in 1620, Montferrand, Nevers, Orleans; in 1621, Valence; in 1622, Dijon, Belley, and S. Estienne en Forez.]

LETTER I.

To Mother de Chantal, Superioress at Paris.

St. Francis exhorts her to the practice of self-renouncement: it consists in a perfect indifference to all things and an entire acquiescence in the will of God.

Paris, *8th August* 1619.*

My dearest Mother—I am sure that I shall have to spend to-day again in solitude and silence, and perhaps to-morrow: if not, I will prepare my own soul with yours, as I told you before.

* Thus the French: 1616 seems the true date. [Tr.]

I entirely wish you to continue the exercise of renouncing self, submitting yourself to Our Lord and to me. But, my dear mother, I want you to mingle with this some acts of your own, in the form of ejaculatory prayers, approving of this renouncement; as for example: I will it indeed, Lord; take away, freely take away all that clings to my heart. No, O Lord, let me except nothing, tear me from myself. O self, I quit thee for ever, until my Lord command me to take thee again. This ought to be gently but firmly declared.

Further, you must please, my dear mother, take no foster-father; yea, as you see, you must quit the one whom you will still have, and must stay as a poor little wretched creature before the throne of the divine mercy, and remain quite denuded of all things, without demanding any act or affection whatever for creatures: on the contrary, making yourself indifferent as to the acts and affections it may please God to ordain, not dwelling upon the thought that it is I who will act as your foster-father. Otherwise, taking a father at your own liking, you would not go out of self, but would be ever finding your own interest, which is the very thing we must above all avoid.

Admirable are the renunciations of our self-esteem, and of what we were according to the world (which was, in truth, nothing, save in comparison with the poor); of our own will, of complacency in creatures and in natural affection; in a word, of all self, which we must bury in an eternal abandonment, to see and to know it no longer as we have seen and known it, but only when God so ordains for us, and as he ordains for us.

Write and tell me how much you approve this lesson.

May God deign to possess me for ever, Amen: for I am his here, and I am his there, where I am in you, as you know, very perfectly; for you are indivisible from me except in the exercise and practice of the renunciation of all ourself for God.

LETTER II.

FROM MOTHER DE CHANTAL TO THE SAINT.

Answer to the Preceding.

9th August 1619.

AH! my only father, what good does this dear letter do me! Blessed be he who inspired you with it, and blessed be the heart of my father for ever and ever!

Truly I have an extreme desire, and, as I think, am in a firm resolution, to live in my self-renunciation, by the grace of my God: and I trust he will aid me. I feel my spirit quite free, and in a certain profound and infinite consolation to see itself thus in the hands of God. It is true that all the rest of my being remains ever in much distress: but if I do well what you told me, my sole father, as certainly I will do with God's help, all will constantly get better.

I must say this to you: if I were to let my heart go, it would seek to clothe itself again with the affections and desires which it fancies our Lord will give it; but this I by no means permit, so that these projects only appear in the distance; for, methinks, I must ponder, love, and will nothing except according to the orders of the foster-father who will be given me; and I am careful not to notice who this may be.

May my God fortify you by his sweet goodness, and make us perfectly accomplish what he desires from you, my dearest father; may Jesus make you a great saint, and I believe he will. Blessed be his goodness for your cure and good rest. Good-bye, my true father; to-night I will give you news of me.

LETTER III.

To Mother de Chantal.

Same Subject.

9th August 1619.

O my Jesus! what a blessing and consolation to my soul to know that my mother is quite stripped of self before God! For a long time I have had an incomparable sweetness when I chant these responses: *Naked came I out of my mother's womb, and naked shall I return thither: the Lord gave me* her, *and the Lord hath taken* her *away, blessed be the name of the Lord.**

What a happiness is that of St. Joseph and the glorious Virgin, on the journey into Egypt, when, most of the way, they see nothing except the sweet Jesus. It is the end of the Transfiguration, my dear mother, to see no longer Moses, nor Elias, but Jesus only. It is the glory of the sacred Sulamitess to be alone with her God only, so as to say to him: *My beloved to me, and I to him.*† We must then remain for ever all

* Job. i. 21. † Cant. ii. 16.

despoiled, in affection, although in effect we clothe ourselves; for we must have our affection united so absolutely and so simply to God that nothing may cling to us. Oh how blessed was that Joseph of old who had neither buttoned nor clasped his mantle, so that when they would hold him thereby, he let it go in an instant!

I admire with sweetness the Saviour of our souls, coming naked from the womb of his mother, dying all naked on the Cross, and then put back into his mother's bosom to be buried. I admire his glorious Mother, who was born without her maternity, and was stripped of that maternity at the foot of the Cross, and who might well say: naked was I of my greatest good when my son came into my womb, and naked am I when I receive him dead into my bosom. *The Lord gave him to me, the Lord took him away: blessed be the name of the Lord.* I say then to you, my dear mother: Blessed be the Lord who has despoiled you! Oh how content is my heart to know that you are in so desirable a state! And I say to you as it was said to Isaias:* *Walk and prophecy naked these three days:* persevere in keeping to this self-renunciation before our Lord; there is no longer need to make acts, unless they come naturally to your mind, but only softly to sing, as you can, the canticle of your renouncement: *Naked came I from the womb of my mother,* and the rest.

Make no further acts of effort, but, founded on yesterday's resolution, go, my dear daughter, *hearken and incline your ear; forget your people*—your other affections—*and your father's house, for the king* hath desired your free-heartedness and simplicity.† Remain

* Isa. xx. 2. † Ps. xliv. 11, 12.

at rest there, in a spirit of very simple confidence, without even looking where your garments are; I mean not looking with any attention or solicitude.

Good-bye, my dear mother. Glory to Jesus, deprived of father and of mother on the cross! Glory to Jesus, despoiled of all things! Glory to Mary, despoiled of her Son at the foot of the cross. Remain in the tranquil acceptance of your poverty of spirit; make no violent efforts; peacefully refresh the body. *Vive Jesus!* Amen.

LETTER IV.

FROM MOTHER DE CHANTAL TO THE SAINT.

Answer to the preceding.

9th August 1619.

MY ONLY FATHER—M. de Grandis told me to-day that we must still take great care of you; that you must no longer be so sparely dieted; that we must keep and nurse you very carefully, on account of the inflammation which threatens. I am very glad of these orders, and that you will keep your solitude, as it will be used for the further profit of your dear soul: I could not say *our* soul, because I seem no longer to have a part of it, so stripped and so despoiled do I see myself of all that was most precious to me.

Ah! my true father, how deep the knife has cut! Shall I be able long to remain in these sentiments? At least our good God will please to keep me in my resolutions, as I desire. Ah! what force have your words given to my soul! How they touched and consoled me when you said: "O my Jesus! What a blessing and a consolation to my soul to know that you are quite stripped of self before God!" May Jesus deign to continue to you, my father, this consolation, and to me this happiness.

I am full of good hope and of a very peaceful and tranquil courage. Thanks to God I am not urged to regard that which I am stripped of; I remain in a certain simplicity; I see it as a thing far away; it keeps coming up indeed and touching me, but I turn away immediately.

Blessed be he that has despoiled me! May his goodness confirm and strengthen me unto the effecting, when he wills me to come to it. When our Lord gave me that sweet thought of abandoning myself to him, which I manifested to you on Tuesday—ah! I never thought that he would begin to despoil me by means of myself, thus making me begin the work. May he be blessed for all, and deign to strengthen me!

I did not tell you that I had little interior light and consolation: I am only at peace about all. It even seems to me that our Lord, during these days past, has somewhat withdrawn from me that little sweetness which the sense of his dear presence gives; the same, more or less, to-day. There remains little to support or rest my spirit; perhaps it is that this good Lord would pass his hand throughout my whole heart, to take all and strip me of all. His most holy will be done!

My only father, to-day it came to my memory that one day you commanded me to despoil myself. I answered: I do not know what of; and you repeated:

Did I not clearly tell you, my daughter, that I would despoil you of all? Oh how easy it is to quit what is outside of ourselves! But to quit our skin, our flesh, our bone, and to pierce into the interior, and to the very marrow—which, meseems, is what we have done—this is a great, a difficult thing, and impossible to aught but the grace of God. To him then is the glory due, and to him be it given for ever.

My true father, am I not clothing myself in the consolation I take in conversing with you when I take it without your leave? It seems to me that in future I should do nothing, and that I should no longer have thought, affection, or will, save in so far as everything is commanded me.

I conclude then by wishing you a thousand good-nights, and by telling you what has come into my mind. I think I see the two portions of our united soul make one, abandoned and given over to God alone. Amen, my dearest father. And may Jesus live and reign for ever! Amen. Do not risk anything by rising too soon; I fear this holy feast may make you run into some excess. God guide you in everything.

LETTER V.

TO MOTHER DE CHANTAL.

Same subject.

9th August 1619.

MOST affectionately I give you good-night, my dear mother, beseeching God that as he has reduced you to the sweet holy purity and simplicity of children, he would henceforth take you in his arms like St. Martial,* to carry you as he chooses to the perfection of his love.

And take courage; for if he has stripped you of consolations and the sense of his presence, it is in order that even his presence may no longer occupy your heart, but himself and his good pleasure, as with her who wishing to embrace him and stay at his feet was sent elsewhere. *Touch me not,* he said to her, *but go, tell Simon and my brethren.*† Well—we will talk of it together. Blessed are the naked of heart, for Our Lord will clothe them. May his goodness deign not to leave me with so little sanctity, in a profession and at an age when I ought to have so much. My mother, live joyously before God and bless him with me for ever and ever. Amen.

LETTER VI.

TO THE SAME.

Same subject.

10*th August* 1619.

ALL goes well, my dearest mother: in good truth you must remain in this holy detachment till God reclothes you. *Stay there,* said Our Lord to his Apostles, *till you are endued with power from on high.*‡ Your solitude must not be interrupted until after Mass tomorrow.

My dear mother, your imagination is quite mistaken in representing to you that you have not put away and

* Ancient tradition gives this as the name of the child whom Jesus took in his arms (Matt. xviii.). He was the Apostle of Aquitaine. [Tr.]

† John xx. 17.

‡ Luke xxiv. 49.

abandoned the care of yourself and affection for spiritual things: for have you not quitted and forgotten *all?* Declare to-night that you renounce all virtues, only wanting them in the measure God will give them; and only trying to acquire them in so far as his goodness will employ you in them for his own good pleasure.

Our Lord loves you, my mother, he wishes to have you all his own: henceforth have no other arms to carry you than his, no other bosom to rest on than his and his Providence: cast not your eyes elsewhere, nor stay your spirit save on him alone: hold your will so simply united to his that nothing may intervene.

Think no more about the friendship, the unity, which God has made in us, think not of your children, nor your heart, nor your soul, nor indeed of anything whatsoever: for you have given up all to God. Clothe yourself with Our Lord crucified, love him in his sufferings, make ejaculatory prayers on this: what you have to do, you must no longer do because it is your inclination, but purely because it is the will of God.

I am very well, thank God. This morning I have begun my review, which I shall finish to-morrow.

I feel insensibly at the bottom of my heart a new hopeful determination to serve God better, *in holiness and justice all the days of* my *life;* and yes, I also find myself stripped of self, thanks to him who died naked in order to make us undertake to live naked. O my mother, how happy were Adam and Eve, while yet in their state of pure innocence! Live totally in happy peace, my dear mother, and be clothed with Jesus Christ our Lord. Amen.

LETTER VII.

TO A SUPERIORESS OF THE VISITATION.

How to act when criticised: how to secure the love and the respect of subjects.

2nd October 1619.

MY VERY DEAR DAUGHTER—Take good care not to fall into any discouragement when you are murmured at or criticised a little. No, my dear daughter; for I assure you that the business of finding fault is very easy, and that of doing better very difficult. There needs but very little ability to find fault, and something to talk about, in those who govern or in their government; and when some one reproves us, or points out to us the imperfections in our conduct, we ought to listen quietly to it all, then lay it before God, and take counsel about it with our assistant sisters; and after that do what is considered best, with a holy confidence that God will bring all to his glory.

Do not be quick to promise; but ask time to make up your mind in matters of any consequence. This is fitting in order to secure the good success of our affairs, and to nourish humility. St. Bernard writing to one of my predecessors, Arducius, Bishop of Geneva: "Do all things," he says, "with counsel, but the counsel of a few persons, who are peaceable, wise and good." Do this so sweetly that your inferiors may not take occasion to lose the respect which is due to your office, nor to think that you have need of them for governing; modestly let them know, without saying it, that you are acting so to follow the rule of modesty and humility, and what is prescribed by the constitutions. For you see, my dear daughter, it behoves as far as possible to act so that the respect of our inferiors for us may not diminish love, nor love diminish respect.

Do not trouble yourself at being a little governed by that good soul outside; but go on peacefully, either acting according to her advice in things where there lies no danger in contenting her, or acting otherwise when the greater glory of God requires it; and then you must, as cleverly as you can, gain her approval.

If there be some sister who does not show sufficient respect for you, let her know it through one of the others whom you may judge the most suitable for this, not as if from you but as if from this person herself. And in order that your gentleness may in no way resemble timidity or be regarded as such, if you were to see a sister who made a profession of not showing this respect, you would have yourself sweetly to show her, by herself, that she ought to honour your office and work with the rest to preserve in dignity the charge which binds together the whole congregation in one body and one spirit.

Well now, my dear daughter, keep yourself entirely in God, and be humbly courageous in his service, and often recommend to him my soul, which, with all its affection, cherishes yours most perfectly, and wishes it a thousand thousand benedictions. When I say to you: do not show this letter, I mean, do not show it indiscriminately; for if it be a satisfaction to you to show it to some one, I am very willing. Your very affectionate father and servant, &c.

LETTER VIII.

TO A SISTER OF THE VISITATION.

Abnegation of self-will is the best austerity.

1st January 1620.

I HAVE seen the suggestions which the enemy of your progress makes to your heart, my dear daughter, and I see likewise the grace which the most holy Spirit of God gives you to keep you strong and firm in the pursuit of the way in which he has placed you. My dear daughter, this evil one does not mind our wounding the body provided that he can make us always do our own will: he does not fear austerity but obedience. What greater austerity can there be than to keep one's will in subjection and continual obedience? Remain in peace; you are a lover of these voluntary penances, if, indeed, the works of self-love can be called penances.

When you took the habit, after many prayers and much consideration, it was decided that you should enter into the school of obedience and of abnegation of your own will, rather than remain given up to your own judgment and to yourself. Do not then let yourself be shaken, but remain where Our Lord has put you. It is true that you have there great mortifications of the heart, seeing yourself so imperfect and so worthy of being often corrected and reproved: but is not this what you ought to be seeking, this mortification of the heart and continual knowledge of your own abjection?

But, say you, you cannot do such penance as you

would. Oh tell me, my dearest daughter, what better penance can a heart do which commits faults than to submit to a continual cross and abnegation of self-will? But I say too much; God himself will uphold you with the same hand with which he placed you in this vocation; and the enemy shall have no victory over you, who, as the first daughter of that country, ought to be well proved by temptation and excellently crowned by perseverance. I am all yours, my dear daughter, &c.

LETTER IX.

To a Superioress of the Visitation.

On a difference as to ecclesiastical precedence. Monasteries to be content with moderate dowries. On self-love in austerities.

11th January 1620.

My dear Daughter—I confess that I cannot at all understand these considerations of ceremony, because I have never thought of them. Quite four times, at least, I have preached at Paris for the reception of nuns, and a simple priest has performed the service: once I made the reception and a Jesuit Father preached, and under both arrangements I did not cease to be what I am. Whoever preaches, the good M. N. takes the place and performs the function of the Bishop; wherefore if he perform the office I do not see that another person may not preach, whatever he may be. Neither my Lord the Bishop of Nantes, nor my Lord the Archbishop of Bourges, makes any difficulty about it at Paris, nor have I ever made any here at St. Clare's or St. Catherine's.

But all the same I also admit that it truly shows a little human nature in good M. N. to think that it affects his reputation whether he performs or does not perform the office, even though he has not the talent of preaching; and for my own part I think quite the contrary: but at last what can be done?—for to turn his mind away is to upset it altogether. It will then be well that if our good M. N. can persuade his relatives to be satisfied, he should give the exhortation, and I cannot imagine what reason they can have to be dissatisfied since it is so good and so honourable a thing; and at the same time there will be more distinction about the affair in this way than in any other. But if this cannot be done, you must ask some Religious Father; for what can one do with all these fancies? Time is short, and there seems no chance of inducing my Lord to act otherwise. I assure you, my daughter, that when a young person of quality entered the Carmelites, I gave the exhortation, and M. du Val, doctor of theology, performed the office; whereas he would have preached better than I and I better have performed the ceremony than he. Alas! what trifles are we tied to!

Well then, such is my advice. But if even this cannot be, then the office will have to be before dinner and the exhortation after dinner. Meantime, my dear daughter, this is true, that he who has his heart and his intention in God feels little, at least in the superior part, of the agitations of creatures; and he who has it in heaven, as St. Gregory said to two bishops, is not blown about by the storms of earth.

Not only do I consent, but I approve, yea with all my heart exhort, that when rich parents give reasonably, according to their condition and means, they should not be teased to give more. As, for example, with the daughter who is making her trial, I would a hundred times rather have a thousand crowns quietly, than twelve hundred with bitterness and long vexatious struggling. God's spirit is generous, sweet, and humble: one would perhaps gain two hundred crowns by disputing, but one would lose four hundred in reputation; and we take away from the rich the desire of letting their daughters come when we exact so avariciously all that we can. That is my opinion; that is what I have done here.

She is right, undoubtedly, this good daughter, in thinking that her fasting humour is a true temptation: it was, it is, and it will be, so long as she continues to practise these abstinences. It is true that by them she weakens her body and its sensuality; but by a poor exchange she strengthens her self-love and her self-will; she starves her body, and she overcharges her heart with the poisonous growth of self-esteem and self-pleasing. Abstinence which is practised against obedience takes away the sin from the body to put it in the heart. Let her give her attention to cutting off her own will, and she will soon quit these phantoms of sanctity in which she reposes so superstitiously. She has consecrated her corporal strength to God; it is not for her to break it down unless God so order it; and she will never learn what God orders save by obedience to the creatures whom the Creator has given her for her guidance. This is what is required, my dear daughter; you must help her against this temptation by the advice of some true servant of God; for more than one person is required to uproot this self-satisfaction in exterior sanctity, dearly esteemed by the prudence of self-love. Do this then, ask M. N. to instruct and fortify her against this temptation; and if he thinks well let it even be in your presence.

Is it in real earnest, my dear daughter, that you say: we are quite poor, thank God? Oh! if it be so, how gladly would I say: happy then are you, thank God! But I scarce dare to speak of a virtue which I only know by the infallible description of the king of the poor, Our Lord: for as to myself I have never seen poverty close.

Keep to what I told you as to Communion, and let your intention be to unite your heart with that of him whose body and heart you receive both together. Afterwards do not occupy yourself in thinking what are the thoughts of your mind about this, since of all these thoughts there is not one which is *your* thought, save that which you have deliberately and voluntarily accepted, which is to receive Communion for the union and as the union of your heart with that of the Beloved. Your very affectionate servant, &c.

LETTER X.

TO A SUPERIORESS OF THE VISITATION (*perhaps the same*).

She is not to dwell on her miseries, and is to commit to God the care of her reputation. Singularity and self-will in spiritual exercises a dangerous delusion. Virtue depends not on feeling but on the consent of the will. On change of confessors.

14*th January* 1620.

I WROTE to you the day before yesterday, my dear daughter, and replied to your two previous letters. O my daughter, the truly well-beloved of my heart, act just in this way. Do not permit your spirit to consider its miseries, let God work; he will make something good out of it. Have but little reflection upon what your nature may mingle with your actions. These sallies of self-love must be treated by neglect; having disavowed them twice or thrice a day you have finished with them. They must not be rejected with violence, it is enough to say a little *no*.

You are right; a daughter who belongs to God ought not to think of her reputation; it would be unbecoming. As for me, says David,* *I am very young and despised; but I forgot not thy justifications.* Let God do with our life, and our reputation, and our honour, as he chooses, for it is all his. If our abjection serve for his glory ought we not to glory in being abject? *I will glory in my infirmities,* said the Apostle,† *that the power of Christ may dwell in me.*

* Ps. cxviii. 141. † 2 Cor. xii. 9.

What power of Jesus Christ?—humility, consent to abjection.

I am writing to this poor dear daughter. I never saw a temptation more manifest or more patent than this: it is almost without cover or pretext. To break vows in order to fast! To pretend to be good in solitude and not good in the congregation! To want to live for self by way of living for God! To desire to have the entire control of one's own will in order better to follow the will of God—what chimeras! That a melancholy, strange, disagreeable, hard, sour, bitter, self-willed inclination, or rather fancy and imagination, can be an inspiration—what a contradiction! To give up praising God and to be silent through ill-humour in the offices which holy Church appoints, because one cannot give praise in a corner according to one's wish—what an extravagance! But still, I hope that God will draw glory from all this, since this poor dear daughter submits herself in everything that is commanded her and has a reverence for your presence. Often give commands to her, and impose upon her mortifications opposed to her inclinations: she will obey, and although it will seem to be by force it will still be profitably, and according to the grace of God.

Indeed, my dear daughter, you must truly make no difference between your soul and mine in the confidence which you must have in me; and take good courage to form the acts of union and of acquiescence in God's will by the superior portion and point of your spirit, without distressing yourself at all for not having feelings of devotion during your times of weakness, since consent to good and to evil can be given without feelings, and feelings can be without consent.

One ought not to be fickle in wanting to change a confessor without strong reason; but one ought not either to be altogether unchanging, because legitimate causes of changing may arise; and Bishops ought not to tie their hands so closely that they cannot make a change when necessary, above all when the sisters with common consent request it: the same of the spiritual father. I have no leisure. *Vive Jesus*, in all and everywhere, and above all in the midst of our hearts! Amen.

LETTER XI.

To a Sister of the Visitation.

[Apparently the one spoken of in preceding letter.]

Cautions against a spirit of self-seeking and self-will.

14*th January* 1620.

My dear Daughter—The thought of leaving your congregation has all the truest marks of temptation that could be found; but God be praised that in this assault the keep is not yet surrendered nor (as I think) ready to surrender. Oh! my daughter, beware, beware, of wanting to leave. There is no middle term between your leaving and your ruin; for do you not see that you will never leave save to live to yourself, of yourself, by yourself, and in yourself? And this so much the more dangerously for its being under pretext of union with God, who however neither desires nor ever will desire to have any union with those morose, self-seeking and singular solitaries, who leave their vocation, their vows, their congregations, through bitterness of heart, through vexation of spirit, and through a disgust with common life, with obedience, with rules and holy observance.

Do you not see Simeon Stylites so prompt to leave his pillar on the advice of the elders?—while you, my dear daughter, will not leave your abstinences on the advice of so many good people, who have no interest in wanting to make you leave them except to render you free and detached from love of self. Well then, my dear daughter, sing henceforth the canticle of love: *Behold how good and how pleasant it is for* sisters *to dwell together in unity!** Treat your temptation roughly; say to it: *Thou shalt not tempt the Lord thy God: Get thee behind me, Satan: Thou shalt adore the Lord thy God, and him only shalt thou serve.*†

I leave you to think for yourself, my dear daughter. To make genuflexions to the Blessed Sacrament, as if out of ill-humour, after the temptation—what greater mark of temptation can one have? The effect of inspirations is humble, sweet, tranquil and holy. How then can your inclination be an inspiration, when it is so ill-tempered, hard, sullen and disturbed? Withdraw yourself from it, my dear daughter; treat this temptation as one treats those of blasphemy, infidelity, heresy, despair: do not parley with it, do not come to terms with it, do not listen to it; contradict it, as far as ever you can, by frequent renewals of your vows, by frequent submissions to your superior. Often call upon your good Angel; and I hope, my dear sister,

* Ps. cxxxii. 1. † Matt. iv.

that you will find the peace and sweetness of the love of your neighbour. Amen. I am writing to you without leisure; but do what I tell you. Sing in the choir ever more constantly in proportion as the temptation says, keep silence, after the example of that holy blind man. The peace of the Holy Spirit be with you.

LETTER XII.

To a Sister of the Visitation.

Consolations in sickness: consideration for the sick a mark of the Visitation Order; confidence in God.

7th February 1620.

THIS paper goes to find your eyes, in order through them to salute your heart, most dear to mine, my very dear daughter. Oh that poor heart! I see it very ill, in the letter which you wrote me on the 12th December, which I received very late. But I speak wrongly, without meaning it, my dear daughter; it is not your heart which is sick, it is your body; and on account of the tie which there is between them it seems to the heart that it suffers the evil of the body. My dear daughter, do not think yourself to be burdened when you suffer what you have to suffer; you must do it for the most holy will of God, who has given this weight and this measure to your bodily state: but love knows all and does all; it seems to make me a physician.

I am a great favourer of the sick, and am always afraid lest the inconveniences which they cause should excite a spirit of prudence in the houses, and a tendency to desire to dismiss them without getting leave from the spirit of charity, under which our congregation has been founded, and for which there has been expressly made the distinction of sisters which is seen therein. I favour then the cause of your sick person, and provided that she is humble, and acknowledges herself indebted to charity, you must receive her, poor daughter. It will be a continual holy exercise for the charity of the sisters.

O my dear daughter, remain at peace; do not occupy yourself with your imperfections, but keep your eyes uplifted towards the infinite goodness of him who to keep us in his humility lets us live in our infirmities. Have every confidence in his goodness, and he will have a care of your soul and of all that concerns it, beyond what you could think.

I will help M. N. in all that I can; but I must confess that in the matter of business and affairs, particularly worldly ones, I am a poor priest more than ever I was, having learnt at court to be more simple and less worldly.

Remain in peace, my dear daughter, and live wholly in God. I salute very cordially our dear sisters, and am entirely yours, my dear daughter. Our mother has plenty of work cut out in France, in the multitude of houses which are asked for. *Vive Jesus*, and may his name be blessed for ever and ever! Amen. You are my very dear daughter, and God wills that I should have the consolation of saying so.

LETTER XIII.

To a Superioress of the Visitation.

Counsels to be interpreted with discretion; multiplicity of exercises chiefly intended for beginners.

22nd February 1620.

Well, my dear daughter, I tell you that if I have said in some conference, twelve hours in the house for one in the parlour, I said what would be desirable if it were practicable. One often says such things, which must be understood with allowance, that is, when the things can be done reasonably, according to places, times, and the affairs one has to transact. So remain at peace, and apply this principle wisely, prudently, not drawing a hard and fast line, nor rigorously nor word by word.

The Directory of the novitiate proposes a multitude of exercises, 'tis true; and further it is good and suitable in the commencement to keep spirits regulated and occupied: but when in progress of time souls are a little practised on this multiplicity of interior acts, and are shaped, broken in and made active, then the exercises unite in one exercise of greater simplicity, either the love of complacency, or the love of benevolence, or the love of confidence, or of uniting and reuniting the soul with God, insomuch that this multiplicity converts itself into unity.

And besides, if there be some souls, even in the novitiate, who are fearful of subjecting their spirit too closely to the appointed exercises, provided that this fear does not proceed from caprice, self-sufficiency, disdainfulness or melancholy, it is for the prudent mistress to conduct them by another way, although this one is ordinarily useful, as experience shows. Live wholly in God, in peace, in sweetness, courageously and holily, my dear daughter. I am in him entirely yours.

LETTER XIV.

TO MOTHER ANNE-MARIE ROSSET, SUPERIORESS AT BOURGES.

On the reception of a certain sister, and on the Constitutions.

27th March 1620.

MY VERY DEAR DAUGHTER—This note which I can only get out by force from amidst an overload of affairs is only to tell you that as this good daughter about whom you write to me was one of the first of this house, and was of such great consideration as you tell me, I think that, to content this good lady and various persons of respectability, she must be received to profession, since, moreover, there is no obstacle of consequence, and I think that this womanish tenderness about herself will gradually pass away. She can be of the number of associated sisters, who are, I think, the objects of the greatest charity that can be exercised, while waiting for her courage to rise, so that she may be able to bring herself round somewhat to choir. In a word, she must exercise a generous and sweet charity towards her spirit, and consider that God wanted her there for that purpose.

I am looking over the rules and constitutions, and

the formularies; in which I have found great mistakes both in the printing and the writing. These I am correcting, and will put the blessed vows so expressly that everybody may be satisfied, and so there may be peace. My dear daughter, I will write again to you soon, but I thought I ought not to delay any longer to write this note.

I salute your heart with all the affection of mine, and am entirely yours. I salute our dear sisters. Blessed be God. Amen.

LETTER XV.

To Mother de Chastel, at Grenoble.

On receiving young postulants or aspirants, and the way of treating them: also on the rules for Associated Sisters.

16th May 1620.

My very dear Daughter—The girl of whom you write to me, as she is of such great consequence, can very well be received, provided that she is about twelve years old. It is true that these young people give trouble, but what of that? I find no blessing without burden in this world. We must so adjust our will that it should either not aim at things that please, or if it do aim at them and desire them, that it should also willingly accommodate itself to things that displease, which are inseparably joined with those that please. We have no wine without dregs in this world. So you must choose: is it better that there should be thorns in our garden in order to have roses, or that there should be no roses in order to have no thorns? If this girl bring more good than harm, it will be good to receive her; if she bring more harm than good, you should not receive her.

And speaking of young girls, Sister N. (Jeanne-Marie, daughter of the woman who keeps the gate), who was received so young, is ill with a malady which is painful, and, according to M. Grandis, mortal; for she is consumptive. I went to see her the other day, and I had an unspeakable consolation in seeing so quiet an indifference as to death or life, so sweet a patience, and a smiling countenance under a burning fever and amid many sufferings, she asking as her only consolation to be allowed to make her profession before her death.

Now, if you receive the one whom you speak of, you must certainly not oblige her to the exercises, for this might disgust her at such a tender age, which cannot ordinarily relish that which is of the spirit. As to the habit, you must not give it to her before the age, but you will do well to provide her a very simple dress, and a little kerchief to wear on her head, so that she may in some way resemble a religious, and it will be good to have it black or dark, without ornament, as I saw at Saint Paul's at Milan, where there were about a hundred and fifty sisters, and twenty or twenty-five novices, and quite as many postulants (*prétendantes*), who were there at school and waiting: these last were all clothed alike in blue, and wore a uniform dress. I say the same of the little girl, Lambert; and it will be a slight preparation for the habit; this latter can be given to girls of good disposition a few months before the time, but not the position of novice, as was done with Sister Jeanne-Marie; nor should this ever be done except for urgent causes. A little habit, dark or white, or of whatever colour you choose, with something of the shape of the religious dress, which would show that they are aspiring and waiting till the age, should satisfy them.

That subjects should go to Lyons or elsewhere does not matter at all; and do not trouble yourself about it. When you have got into our monastery, its advantages will have their attractions like the others, and maidens will come there as doves come to fresh white dove-cots. Meanwhile, my dear daughter, he who seeks only the glory of God finds it in poverty as in abundance. Those good daughters do not love a poverty that pinches, neither are we ourselves violently in love with it. Those then that want to go to Lyons, quietly and peaceably let them go; God takes better care of you than that all this should matter. You will excuse me, my dear daughter.

I hope that God will help us that the great Office may never be introduced into this congregation; and the Pope himself has given some instruction about it. It is good, moreover, that there should be Associated sisters, for the sake of those who could not say the Office, either from having weak or short sight, or from some weakness of chest or other infirmity. It is for this reason that the exercises which should be given them instead of the choir Office have not been marked; for these must be selected according to their infirmity. If their sight is bad they can say the Rosary. If they suffer from the chest and not from the eyes they can say their Hours, and the superior can put them to some duty not incompatible with their infirmity. I have lately been reading the 1st Constitution, where it is clearly enough stated that Associated sisters, like the domestic sisters, shall say *Paters* and *Aves* instead of the Office: this is at pages 118, 119. So there is no obligation to say the Hours, but it will be enough for them to do what is said in this article of the constitutions, the superior for the rest employing them according to what she sees they can do.

It will be good that our mother from Lyons [Favre] should call at Grenoble to see you; you will both receive consolation from it. And do not distress yourself about the little touch of joy which your heart feels at this; for it is nothing, and only serves to make us humble ourselves quietly, to discover the misery of our nature, and to make us wholly desire to live according to grace, according to the Gospel, according to the spirit of our Lord. Always speak freely to me, for I protest before God and his Saints that I am yours, my very dear and truly beloved daughter. I salute our sisters tenderly, and also those good ladies.

LETTER XVI.

TO A SUPERIORESS OF THE VISITATION (*probably the same*).

Directions as to the treatment of one of her daughters and as to points of the rule: advice and encouragement for herself, particularly as to simple confidence in God.

June 1620.*

WE have been engaged here since the day before yesterday in choosing the sisters to be sent into France,

* The French has no date. [Tr.]

my very dear daughter. And our mother writes to me that you will give her one and the house of Lyons another, which with the eight we shall supply will make the number she wants. But I do not yet know how we shall manage to go to fetch yours. Well, we will think about it, and meanwhile amid this confusion, I answer you, my dear daughter, in as little space as I can.

I see in this sister (Anne Marie) a certain something that is very good and that pleases me. There is somewhat of the extraordinary, which ought to be considered without excitement, in order that we may not be misled either on the side of nature, which often deludes itself by the imagination, or on the side of the enemy, who often diverts us from the exercises of solid virtue to occupy us in these actions of outside show. You must not be surprised that she is not so exact in doing what she does, for this often happens to persons who are attached to the interior, and cannot all at once give due attention to everything. The thing is, not to let her make much of these sights, these feelings or pains, but, making little reflection on all this, let her do in simplicity the things in which she is employed. You can take her away from the kitchen when she has served there yet some little time. Oh how excellent and to be loved is this kitchen, because it is humble and abject!

Choir sisters may be put into the class of Associates and Associates into that of choir sisters when reason requires, as is said concerning the domestic sisters in the 1st chapter of the Constitutions.

If I go to Rome I will try to serve Madame de Sautereau in her desire.

To know when it is required for contracts that the spiritual Father should be present, and when not, depends on the nature of the contracts; for there are some in which it is required and others where it is not, as the Bishop has need of the presence of his Chapter in some contracts, in others not. It is for instructed people to settle this as occasion arises; one cannot lay down a general rule. There is sometimes inconvenience, but one could scarcely remove it without falling into a greater. Whether M. Dutine calls himself spiritual Father or not in contracts neither makes nor mars, for this name can be understood in various ways.

The work *On the Will of God* can be read, except the last Book, which, being scarcely intelligible, might be improperly understood by the imagination of readers, who, desiring these unions, would easily imagine that they had them, without as much as knowing what they are. I have known religious women, not of the Visitation, who having read the books of the Mother [St.] Teresa, found on their own reckoning that they had as many perfections and spiritual acts as she had, though they were far indeed from it, so greatly does self-love deceive us.

This expression: Our Lord suffers in me such and such things, is altogether extraordinary; and although our Lord has sometimes said that he suffered in the person of his own, to honour them, yet we ought not to speak so advantageously of ourselves. For our Lord only suffers in the person of his faithful friends and servants, and to boast and proclaim ourselves to be such has a little presumption in it; self-love is often very glad to make its account thereby.

When the doctor has to enter the monastery, to see

some sick person, it is enough that he have permission in writing at the beginning, and it will last till the end of the illness; the carpenter or mason to the end of the work for which he enters.

Your way is good, my dear daughter, and there is nothing to object to, save that you go considering your steps too much, for fear of falling. You make too much reflection on the movements of your self-love, which are doubtless frequent, but which will never be dangerous so long as, tranquilly, not letting yourself be annoyed by their importunity nor alarmed by their multitude, you say no. Walk simply, do not desire repose of spirit too earnestly, and you will have the more of it. Why do you put yourself in trouble? God is good; he sees very well what you are; your inclinations cannot hurt you, bad as they may be, since they are only left to you to exercise your superior will in making a more profitable union with that of God. Keep your eyes uplifted, my dear daughter, by a perfect confidence in the goodness of God. Do not be anxiously solicitous for him, for he told Martha that he did not wish it, or at least that he was better pleased that there should be no solicitude, not even in doing good.

Do not examine your soul so much about its advancement. Do not want to be so perfect, but in simple earnest live your life in your exercises, and in the actions which come to be done in their time. *Be not solicitous for to-morrow.** As to your way, God who has guided you up to the present, will guide you to the end. Remain in entire peace, in the holy and loving confidence which you ought to have in the sweetness of heavenly Providence.

* Matt. vi. 34.

Ever pray devoutly to our Lord for me, who cease not to wish you the sweetness of his holy love, and in his love that of the blessed dilection of your neighbour, whom this sovereign Majesty loves so much. I picture you to myself high up in the beautiful air,* where you regard as from a holy hermitage the world which is below, and see displayed the heaven to which you are called. I assure you, my dear daughter, that I am greatly yours, and my faith tells me that you do well to live entirely in the bosom of divine Providence, outside of which all is but vain and useless affliction. May God be for ever in the midst of your heart. Amen.

LETTER XVII.

TO MOTHER DE BRÉCHARD, SUPERIORESS OF THE VISITATION AT MOULINS.

How she is to act in the difficulties which arose over the foundation at Nevers: the most painful unkindness is the unkindness of good people and friends: we must will God only.

26th July 1620.

I DID not suspect that this difficulty would ever arise over the foundation of Nevers, my very dear daughter—what reason is there for it? A young person is at Moulins; therefore she and her means must stay there. But those who make the difficulty are so worthy of great respect, and have so much claim on your house and on all the Congregation, and have so much holy

* The monastery at Grenoble was on the top of a hill. [Tr.]

zeal and piety, that although it is not in strictness very serious, we must, I think, let it be valid to some extent, according to the advice of the Rev. Father Rector, who, as Mlle. du Tertre writes to me, thinks that half will suffice to begin the foundation, and the other half to satisfy properly the house at Moulins.

There remains the difficulty of your person and that of this dear daughter; for I see also the strong desire which M. le Marechal and his lady have that you, and she as well, should stay at Moulins. And I must own that this affair is regarded in such a spirit that I am fearful of speaking my mind; yet I do it, and I say that it would be well for you, who have been acting and who are known, to take Sister P. Jerome to Nevers, and establish her there as well as you can in a stay of a month or two: and when I say that you should go I mean to speak also of Mlle. du Tertre, my daughter, whom I know to be inseparable from you.

Now, I am supposing that these gentlemen will put confidence in your plighted promise to return infallibly and bring back Mlle. du Tertre with you; but if they will not, you must send Sister P. Jerome with two or three whom she may choose, and do the best that can be done, provided that the division is made in writing: for Sister P. Jerome has courage and capacity enough, by God's grace, for succeeding in this enterprise.

I assure you, my dear daughter, that this difficulty has not troubled me except for the pain which I know you have had from it, concerning which I needs must ask you just to read the chapter on patience in *Philothea*, where you will see that the sting of honey-bees is more painful than that of other insects. The attacks of friends on our liberty are inexpressibly grievous; but, after all, we must tolerate them, then bear them, and finally love them as dear contradictions.

Undoubtedly, we must will only God, absolutely, invariably, inviolably; but the means of serving him we must only will quietly and lightly, so that if we are hindered in the employment of them we may not be greatly disturbed. We must will little, and with little will, all that is not God. So then, take courage; if the Father Rector and I are trusted, as I said above, all will only go the better for this. Do you remember the foundation of this monastery here? It was made, like the world, out of nothing at all, and now 16,000 ducats * have been spent in buildings, and not one single sister furnished a thousand except my Sister Favre.

Nevers will be a blessed house, and its foundation firm and solid, since it has been troubled. But if by good hap these gentlemen of Moulins will not consent to the terms which the Father Rector and I think right, what should be done? I cannot really imagine it, but in case it were so, you would have to take good care of Sister P. Jerome and her company, and let our Mother know, who perhaps has some other foundation on her hands where she could be employed. Otherwise she must be sent back to us when the weather is a little more favourable.

And in all events it behoves to remain at peace in the will of God, for which ours is made. I salute with all my heart this dear Sister P. Jerome, and Sister Françoise-Jacqueline, and all our dear sisters. At last,

* About £5000. [Tr.]

blessed are they who do not their own will on earth, for God will do it in Heaven above. I am totally yours, my dearest daughter, and wish you a thousand benedictions. Salute, I beg you, the Reverend Father Rector.

LETTER XVIII.

To Mother de Chantal.

Human prudence not to be followed in accepting subjects. His tender love for souls: he would have them strong.

Probably about 1620.*

My very dear Mother—In this matter of the reception of sisters which you write to me about, there is an extreme danger lest one should throw oneself too much on human prudence, lest one should rest too much on nature, and too little on God's grace. I have a difficulty in preventing people from considering weakness of constitution and corporal infirmities. One would have neither the one-eyed, nor the lame, nor the sickly enter into the marriage feast. In short, it is very hard to fight against the human spirit, for abjection and pure charity. I add then this word, my dear mother, to tell you that according to your order I have written to our Sister de N. lovingly; and I assure you, my dear mother, I do so with all my heart, for I love this poor daughter with a perfect heart. But it is a strange thing! There are no souls in the world, as I think, who love more cordially, tenderly, and (to speak in all sincerity) more lovingly than I; and I even somewhat abound in affectionateness, and words there-

* The French has no date. [Tr.]

of, particularly at the beginning. You know that it is according to the truth and the variety of this true love which I have for souls; for it has pleased God to make my heart so: but still I like souls that are independent, vigorous, and not feminine; for such great tenderness disturbs the heart, disquiets it, distracts it from loving prayer to God, hinders entire resignation and the perfect death of self-love. That which is not God is for us nothing. How can it be that I feel this, I who am the most affectionate person in the world, as you know, my dear mother? Yet in truth I do feel it; but it is a marvel how I reconcile it all together; for it is my idea that I love nothing at all but God, and all souls for God. Ah! Lord God, do yet this grace to my whole soul that it may be in you solely. My dear mother, this discourse is unending. Live joyously, wholly full of God and of his love. Good-night, my dearest mother. I feel this unity which God has made, with an extraordinary power.

LETTER XIX.

To a Religious of the Visitation.

Perfection to be gained by the continual practice of divine love: the gift of prayer will be given to the soul that is empty of self: an alms vowed but not bestowed may be transferred to an object equally good.

1620.

Oh how many benedictions will God pour out on your heart, and how many consolations on mine, if you go on increasing in the perfect practice of divine love, my dear daughter! The Holy Spirit sometimes follows the method of inspiring by degrees what he wants done as a whole, and his calls are wont to be very solid. That good man in the Gospel * who had two sons said to the one: My child, *go work in my vineyard; and he said: I will not; but afterwards*, on reflection and returning to himself, *he went*, and worked hard. Then the father said to the other: My child, go and work in my vineyard; *and he answered: I go, and yet he went not* at all. Now, said Our Lord, *which of the two did the father's will?* Undoubtedly the first, my dear daughter.

You have too good a heart not to do perfectly what has to be done, for the love of him who will only be loved entirely; walk then truly so, my dear daughter; your spirit upraised in God and regarding nothing but the face and eyes of the heavenly Spouse, to do all things according to his pleasure; and doubt not that he will pour out upon you his most holy grace, to give you strength equal to the spirit which he has breathed into you.

The sacred gift of prayer is all ready in the right hand of the Saviour. As soon as ever you shall have emptied yourself of self, that is, of the love of your body and of your own will, that is, when you are very humble, he will pour it into your heart. Have patience to walk with short steps till you have legs to run with, or rather wings to fly. Be content yet a while to be a little *nympha*, soon you will become a full-formed bee.

Humble yourself lovingly before God and men, for God speaks to ears bowed down. *Hearken*, says he to his spouse,† *and see, and incline thine ear, and forget*

* Matt. xxi. † Ps. xliv. 11.

thy people and thy father's house. So the well-beloved Son prostrates himself on his face when he speaks to his eternal Father, and awaits the answer of his oracle. God will fill your vessel with his balm when he sees it empty of the perfumes of this world, and when you are humble he will exalt you. But, my dear daughter, do not say like the younger son of that man, I will go and work, save with a firm desire of going.

Well now, it is the truth that I have written, once only, to N. to say, that an alms vowed but not bestowed was to some extent capable of being transferred to another work of equal piety; but that being vowed, given over, completed, it could no more be withdrawn; because an alms actually given is no longer his who gave it, but belongs of full right and most certainly to him who has received it, and particularly when he has received it without condition, or under a condition which on his side he is ready to execute.

But as to complaining of you, certainly I have never done it, nor in any way compromised my opinion, which is that of all theologians. But, moreover, it is the best in the world for applying to the case, if you will but follow it, in spite of what the world may say. Moreover, it is the same thing whether you give here or there, since the God of the monastery of N. is God of the monastery of N., as both houses are equally the most holy Virgin's, and your own, my dear daughter, whom I conjure to persevere in loving me constantly in Our Lord, as I am for ever and without reserve invariably yours, not ceasing to beseech the most holy Virgin, most beloved Lady of heaven and earth, to love you and to make you the entirely beloved one of her Son, by the continual inspirations which she will obtain for you from his divine Majesty. Your most humble father and servant, &c.

LETTER XX.

To Mother de Chastel, at Grenoble.

On the difference which had arisen between the Countess de Dalet and her mother: vows of chastity: duties of daughters to parents: how religious superiors should act as between mother and daughter.*

25th April 1621.

After all, my very dear daughter, it is true, as I have often said to you, that discretion is a virtue without which no virtue is virtue, not even devotion, if true devotion can be without true discretion.

This good lady, of whose fine and rare qualities you were the first to make me an admirer, sadly complains of her daughter for that having found a swarm of bees with their honey she occupies herself too much with them and eats too much honey, contrary to the advice of the Wise Man, who said: *Thou hast found honey; eat what is sufficient for thee.*† She will have told you all her reasons better than I could lay them before you, except this perhaps, that your religious house has great obligations to her, as you yourself have written to me. Take care, my dear daughter, to contribute all you can to the satisfaction of this mother as regards this her daughter, who is indeed obliged to give up, I do not say a few, but many of her consolations,

* See *Letters to Persons in the World.* Bk. III. 8, 9.
† Prov. xxv. 16.

however spiritual they may be, in order to leave many to her mother.

I confess that I do not understand how a mother of so much sense, perfection, and piety, and a daughter of such great virtue and devotion, do not remain entirely united in that great God, who is the God of union and conjunction: but still I know that this does happen, and that even Angels, without ceasing to be Angels, have contrary wills on the same subject, without, however, any division or dissension, because they perfectly love the will of God, which as soon as it appears is embraced and adored by all. Ah! is there no way to make these two ladies love it, this holy will? For I am sure they would both yield themselves to its obedience.

This good lady, the mother, speaks to me of a vow of chastity made by her daughter, and says that it is rashly taken. This I do not touch; for many things must be considered before it can be decided that a vow of chastity can or should be dispensed from, or is capable of dispensation, since there is nothing to be esteemed like the chaste soul. But this mother speaks of another thing, which is that she would rather have her daughter altogether a religious, since in that case they will no longer ask her to be security, and the administration of the children's fortunes will be confided to her. But here again I do not know what to say, as I do not know what is the vocation of Heaven, and I see this good lady's children so young: this is the thing which gives me more concern than the rest.

All that the lady complains of is that her daughter keeps her purse to herself, amidst the many troubles and trials in which she sees her mother to be, and does not give her any assistance. Now this, my dear daughter, is quite against my sentiments. St. Francis could not approve the ants' hoarding, but it seems to me that a daughter who has means should never spare them for her mother, and I speak of what is wanted for her peace of mind and just satisfaction.

I write to you with my head full of business, and amid much confusion. And further, I am writing to you by guess-work; for I am sure that to speak rightly on this occasion I should have to hear the parties at full length. But so long as this cannot be, the mother's side must be taken; there is always a just presumption in her favour.

At the same time, she only asks you to use your influence to moderate the zeal which this good daughter has for her retreats; and this is a thing which cannot and should not be refused, as moderation is always good in all exercises, except in that of loving God, whom one ought not to love by measure. Use then your efforts for this moderation, to which it will be easy to bring this good daughter, since her good mother permits her to go and enjoy her devotion in peace at all the great feasts of the year, and also for three days every six weeks, which is a good deal.

I have said enough: I am sure, my dear daughter, that after having invoked the Holy Spirit he will give you light to properly effect or advise this moderation. I am in Our Lord entirely yours. I beseech him ever to reign in your soul, in your dear congregation, and to inspire all of you to pray often for me. Amen.

LETTER XXI.

To Mother de Chantal.

She is not to appeal to law in order to retain the dowry of a sister who is going to leave the convent. Vanity of earthly things and of human prudence.

1621.

This is what I am writing to my very dear daughter, according to my real sentiments. The truth is, one talks continually of being a child of the gospel, and scarcely any one holds its maxims in such entire esteem as is due. We have too many aims and designs; we would have the merits of Calvary and the consolations of Thabor both together, have the favours of God and the favours of the world. Go to law! no indeed, I will not: *To him that would take away thy cloak give thy coat also.** What is she thinking of? Four lives like hers would not suffice to terminate her affair by way of law. Let her die of hunger and thirst after justice; for blessed will she be. Is it possible that her sisters are unwilling to give her anything? But if it be so, is it possible that the children of God insist on having all that belongs to them, when their Father Jesus Christ willed to have nothing of this world belonging to him?

Ah! how greatly I desire her good—but above all, the sweetness of the peace of the Holy Spirit, and the assurance which she ought to have as to my sentiments towards her: for I can say that I know they are according to God, and not only that, but they are from

* Luke vi. 29.

God. What is the good of so much concern for so transitory a life, and of making a gilded frame for a paper picture? I tell her paternally my sentiments; for I certainly love her beyond belief: but I say it before Our Lord, who knows that I lie not.

O my mother, I fear natural prudence extremely in the discernment of the things of grace; and if the prudence of the serpent be not diluted with the simplicity of the dove of the Holy Spirit, it is altogether poisonous.

What more shall I say to you? Nothing else, my dear mother, save that I cherish your heart incomparably, and as mine own, if mine and thine can be said between us, where God has established a most unchangeable and indissoluble unity, for which may he be blessed for ever. Amen.

LETTER XXII.

FROM MOTHER DE CHASTEL, SUPERIORESS AT GRENOBLE, TO THE SAINT.

She asks to be allowed to resign her charge.

About May 1621.

MY LORD—The infirmity under which I suffer oppresses me to such an extent that it sometimes brings me down to a tedium and disgust of my life. God having given me a great natural aversion for Offices, sufficiently teaches me by this chastisement that he has not destined me for them. I do not think I can any longer in conscience hold a place which I do not merit. It is doing an injustice to my sisters, who are the spouses of Jesus Christ, to leave them any longer a superior incapable of serving them on account of her infirmities, incapable of instructing them, and unworthy to govern them for want of virtue. This reproach continually gnaws my heart; and when the worm attacks this first and chief part, all the rest of my body gives way to sadness, and remains without strength or courage.

LETTER XXIII.

To Mother de Chastel.

Answer to the Preceding.

I well believe, my very dear daughter, that you think we ought to relieve you of the charge and quality of Mother, but we do not think so at all. Oh! my dear daughter, do you think Our Lady was less the Mother of Our Lord when she appeared all beside herself with sorrow, and when loaded with distress, and quite overwhelmed with affliction, she breathed out that word, Yes, my Son, because so it hath pleased thee—than when with exalted voice and heart thrilling with joy she sang the heavenly song of her *Magnificat?* Do not fear to disedify the sisters; God will take care of that. Your heart is simple, frank, and sincere, your way is good, and I find nothing in it to object to except that you consider your steps too scrupulously through fear of falling. About what do you trouble yourself so much? God is so good! Do not be so solicitous for him; he reproved Martha for it; do not want to be so perfect.* St. Paul warns you *not to be wiser than it behoveth to be wise.*† Examine not so much your soul on its progress; it is useful for you not to know your graces and the riches which you have acquired before God; comfort your poor heart, which I paternally cherish before God, and it is God who wills that I should have the consolation of saying so. Remain at peace then, my dear daughter; be a mother, and a good mother, as long as God shall so ordain.

LETTER XXIV.

To Mother de Chantal.

On the gifts of understanding and of counsel, which had fallen respectively to the two saints at the annual drawing of lots.

Whitsuntide 1621.‡

Oh that I might, my dearest mother, receive and employ well the gift of holy Understanding, to penetrate more deeply into the holy mysteries of our faith! For this penetration marvellously subjects the will to the service of him whom Understanding so admirably acknowledges to be all good, within whom it is all absorbed and occupied; in so far that as it no longer thinks anything can be good compared with this goodness, so it cannot will to love any good in comparison: like as an eye which should be planted deep within the sun could behold no other brightness.

* That is, do not anxiously want to see yourself so perfect. [Tr.]
† Rom. xii. 3.
‡ The French has "29th May 1621." [Tr.]

But because while we are in the world we can only love in well-doing, because our love here must be active, as I shall say to-morrow in the sermon, God helping, we have need of Counsel in order to discern what we ought to practise and do for this love which urges us; for there is nothing which so much urges us to the practice of good as heavenly love. And in order that we may know how we should do good, what good ought to be preferred, to what we should apply the activity of love, the Holy Spirit gives us his gift of Counsel.

So then, here is our soul well dowered with a good portion of the sacred gifts of heaven. May the Holy Spirit who favours us be for ever your consolation. My soul and my spirit adore him eternally. I beseech him ever to be our wisdom and our understanding, our counsel and our fortitude, our knowledge and our piety, and to fill us with the spirit of the fear of the eternal Father. It was not without you that we celebrated this feast of Pentecost, for I well remember the holy devotion which you have for this solemnity.

LETTER XXV.

To a Superioress of the Visitation (*probably M. de Bréchard*).

We are not to trust to human providence but to divine, and we should be as willing for God to be served by others as by ourselves.

24th July 1621.

O my dear daughter, how sad to consider the effects of human prudence in these souls about whom you write to me, the mine and thine reigning so much the more powerfully in spiritual things because they seem to be a spiritual mine and thine; whereas they were not simply unspiritual but carnal. Oh how far is all this removed from that pure charity, which has not jealousy nor envy, and *which seeketh not her own.** My daughter, this prudence is opposed to that sweet repose which the children of God should have in heavenly Providence.

One would think that the erection of religious houses and the vocation of souls were effected by the contrivances of natural wisdom; and I am willing to believe that for the construction of the walls and wood-work nature will suffice: but the vocation, the union of called souls, their multiplication, is either supernatural or is good for nothing. Things which God does by a peculiar grace we make too much an affair of state, and put too much worldly policy into. It is always the poor rejected ones who have had blessing and increase, as Anna, Lia, and the rest.

But, my dear daughter, we must remain in peace, in sweetness, in humility, in charity unfeigned, without complaining, without moving the lips. Oh! if we can have a spirit of entire dependence on the paternal care of our God in our congregation, we shall with sweetness see the flowers multiply in other gardens, and shall bless God for it as if it were in ours. What matters it to a truly loving soul whether the heavenly Spouse be served by this means or by another? He who seeks only the contentment of the Beloved is content with all that contents him.

Believe me, the good which is true good fears not

* 1 Cor. xiii.

to be lessened by the increase of other true good. Let us serve God well, and not say: *What shall we eat, what shall we drink,** whence will sisters come to us? It is for the master of the house to have this solicitude, and for the lady of the apartments to furnish them; and our houses belong to God and to his holy Mother. Give, as far as you can, the spirit of a true and most humble generosity to our dear sisters, whom I salute with all my soul. You are ever more and more my dearest daughter, entirely well-beloved, and I am your most affectionate servant, &c.

LETTER XXVI.

To an Out-Sister of the Visitation.

Nothing is little in God's service; but her office has a peculiar importance.

2nd August 1621.

My very dear Daughter—I am extremely glad to know that you have stayed in the more particular service of Our Lord, in the house of his most holy Mother, in a condition that I consider one of great profit. *I have chosen to be abject*, says the prophet,† *in the house of my God, rather than to dwell in the tabernacles* of the great, who are often not so good. You have been happy in having hitherto served God in the person of a mistress of whom God is master, and with whom you have had all kinds of opportunities of spiritual profit; but you are still more happy to go and serve this same

* Matt. vi. 31. † Ps. lxxxiii. 11.

Lord in the person of those who, to serve him better, have quitted all things.

It is a great honour, my dear daughter, to be charged with the protection of a house wholly composed of spouses of Our Lord ; for whoever guards the doors, "turns," and parlours of monasteries, guards the peace, tranquillity, and devotion of the house, and moreover can greatly edify those who have need to go to the monastery. There is nothing small in the service of God ; but it seems to me that this charge of the turn is of very great importance and exceedingly useful to those who exercise it with humility and spiritual-mindedness.

I thank you for the communication which you have made to me of your contentment, and pray you to salute Mesdames de Moignon, and, when you see her, Madame de Villeneuve. Your humble brother and servant, &c.

LETTER XXVII.

To a Superioress of the Visitation (*Mother Claude Agnes Joly de la Roche*).

God gives strength to effect all that he orders.

4th August 1621.

I know you sufficiently, my very dear sister, my daughter, to cherish you with all my heart in the love of Our Lord, who, having disposed you for the charge in which you are, has consequently obliged himself to give you his most holy hand in all the actions of your office, provided that you correspond on your part by a holy and most humble, but most courageous, confidence in his goodness. *God calls* to his service *the things that are not as the things that are,** and uses nothingness for the glory of his name equally as abundance.

Remain in your abjection as in the robes of your superiorship, and be valiantly humble and humbly valiant in him who struck the master-stroke of his power in the humility of his cross.

A maiden or matron who is called to the government of a monastery is called to a great work and one of high importance, above all when it is to found or establish; but God extends his all-powerful arm in the measure of the work he gives us to do. Keep your eyes fixed on this great Saviour, and he will deliver you *from pusillanimity of spirit and a storm.*†

The sisters who are with you are blessed to be serving there, by their good example and humble observance, as foundation to this spiritual edifice. I am for ever your most humble and affectionate servant in Our Lord, &c.

LETTER XXVIII.

To Mother de Chantal.

Thoughts of the greatness of God: directions as to her stay in Paris and the reciting of the Office: for many things there is no need to obtain express leave from Rome; the Saint's wishes as to the grille and the plan of his monasteries.

24th August 1621.

O my dear mother, God knows how joyful I was this morning to find my God so great that I could not even

* Rom. iv. 17. † Ps. liv. 9.

imagine his greatness! But since I am able neither to magnify it nor to increase it, I greatly desire, by God's help, to proclaim everywhere his grandeur and his immensity. Meantime let us sweetly hide our littleness in this greatness; and as a little chicken, covered over with the wings of its mother, lies so warm and safe, let us lay our hearts to rest under the sweet and love-full Providence of Our Lord, and warmly shelter ourselves under his holy protection. I have had many other good thoughts, but rather by manner of outflowing of heart into Eternity and the Eternal One than by manner of reasoning.

God be praised that you are in your house. The difficulties that you have had over getting in, will confirm your staying there, according to the method which it pleases God to employ in his service.

I judge that it is expedient you should come back, with a sincere resignation to return to where you now are when the service of God shall require it; for it behoves thus to live a life exposed to trouble, since we are children of the trouble and death of Our Saviour. But you must not hurry yourself; because, as you say, the winter will not hinder your journey, as it is necessary that you should stay a little amongst your daughters who are in France.

Alas! how do I affectionately deplore this absolute separation which takes this poor girl away from us, to remain at the mercy of the world. I can, however, do no more.

As to the Office, I am told that objection was made because for the chief feasts there were appointed the Psalms of Our Lady, with the chapter, verses, and prayer of the day. How subtle these objections are!

The Fathers of the Oratory do far more; and in Italy many bishops have entirely composed the Offices of the Saints of their Churches. But it cannot be helped; we must let people talk as they choose; and to make all as smooth as we can, we must therefore simply say the Office of the Blessed Virgin, and at the end add a commemoration of the day; for against this there is nothing to be said.

We have obtained from Rome the continuation of the Little Office for a further ten years, after the expiry of the seven which we had already. My agent says that it is wrong to apply to Rome for things in which it can be avoided, and some Cardinals have said the same: for, say they, there are things which have no need of authorisation, because they are lawful, which when authorisation is asked for are examined in a different way. And the Pope is very glad that custom should authorise many things which he does not wish to authorise himself on account of consequences. But of this we will talk on your return.

I have had made here a beautiful plan for a monastery, which I will send you on the first chance; he who drew it is a very good artist, and has made it from the descriptions of monasteries which St. Charles got made, though accommodating himself to the Visitation. I think we must make as soon as we can, according to the convenience of places, all the monasteries so; and the lattice work always very close, and the wooden bars distant from the *grilles;* for it is a great satisfaction to talk in the parlours without anxiety. A rail must also be put behind the *grille* of the choir in the same way as in the parlour.

I am expecting M. Crichant, whom I will embrace

with all my heart. May God bless you, my dear mother, and sanctify you ever more and more! I am for ever, my dear mother, yours, as you know.

LETTER XXIX.

TO THE SAME.

On charity to candidates who suffer under some corporal infirmity: superiors to be able to change their officers as they think best.

20th September 1621.

WHAT do we will, my dear Mother, except what God wills? Let us allow him to guide our soul, which is his bark; he will make it arrive at safe port. I am very glad, my dear Mother, that you love the lame, the deformed, the one-eyed, and even the blind, provided that they wish to be of upright intention; for they will not fail to be fair and perfect in heaven; and if one persevere in doing charity to those who have their corporal imperfections, God will cause to come, contrarily to human prudence, a number of those who are beautiful and agreeable even in the eyes of the world.

Here are the Constitutions. No doubt if these unauthorised examiners and censors, who make so many questions about everything, can give themselves a little patience, they will see that all is of God.

Our sisters here are still doing well; we have good and amiable novices, whom I confessed with the others as "extraordinary" in August, and I find them to my liking.

It seemed good to put in the Constitutions that the

superior can change the officers as she pleases during the year. Put this, I pray you, in the most proper place. May God fill you ever more and more with his most holy love! Amen.

LETTER XXX.

To a Religious Sister of the Visitation (*probably M. de Chastel.*)

Mothers should aim at the eternal good of their children. The chief qualification for the religious life is not strength of mind, but innocence and humility.

13th December 1621.

I HAVE extreme compassion for this good lady. Her disposition is only too good; or at least her good disposition is not sufficiently overcome by the supernatural in her. Alas! these poor temporal mothers do not sufficiently regard their children as works of God, but regard them too much as children of their womb; they do not sufficiently consider them as children of eternal Providence, and souls destined for eternity, but consider them too much as children of temporal bringing forth, and proper for the service of the temporal commonwealth. Well, if possible, I will write to her now, if I have ever so little leisure.

Since you are now settled in your new house, I have confidence in God that you say: Ah! my soul, fly *to the mountain like a sparrow.** But you look too closely at your thoughts. What does it matter if your heart receives attacks of your ancient fears about

* Ps. x. 1.

temporal means? Laugh at these fears, and remain firm in the word of our Master: * *seek first the kingdom of God and his justice, and all these things*, necessary for this poor life, *shall be added unto you.* This is our port of safety: and allow no reflections and no *buts* about this.

What do you call a great spirit, my dear daughter, and a little spirit? There is no great spirit except that of God, who is so good that he willingly dwells in our little spirits; he loves the spirits of little children, and subjects them to his pleasure better than older spirits. If the lawyer's daughter of whom you write to me is gentle, docile, innocent, and pure, as you tell me, take very good care not to send her away; for in whom dwelleth the Spirit of the Lord if not in the poor and innocent who love and fear his word? † We have here associated sisters of the black veil who do very well: but what does it matter if this one be not associated until she be capable of choir duties? It is for such persons that this rank of sisters has been arranged in the Constitutions.

When sisters have a good heart and a good desire, it matters not if they have not that great ardour of resolution; ardour sometimes comes from the natural disposition of the soul, as sometimes indifference does also; and God well knows how to engraft his grace on both one and the other in the orchards of religion.

But for all such occasions, *you have Moses and the Prophets:* ‡ you have your very good spiritual father. Hear him, listen to him, and salute him affectionately from me. Live, my dear daughter, with that divine

* Matt. vi. 33. † Is. lxvi. 2. ‡ Luke xvi. 29.

life, wholly commended into the hands of Our Lord. I am more and more entirely all yours.

LETTER XXXI.*

TO A SUPERIORESS OF THE VISITATION.

Directions how to behave towards a postulant whose parents had insisted on her entering into the convent: also of another postulant whose dispositions were not perfect.

About 1621.†

. . . Now as to the vocation of this young person,‡ I consider it good, though mingled with many imperfections as far as her spirit is concerned, and though it would be desirable that she should have come to God simply and purely, and because it is so good a thing to be entirely his. But God does not draw with equal motives all those whom he calls to himself; indeed few are found who come to his service solely and entirely to be his, and to serve him. Amongst the women whose conversion is illustrious in the Gospel, there was only Magdalen who came by love and with love: the adulterous woman came through public confusion, as the Samaritan woman by private shame; the Chananæan came to be relieved in her temporal necessity. St. Paul, the first hermit, at the age of fifteen, retired into his cave to avoid persecution; St. Ignatius of Loyola came through tribulation, and so with a hundred others.

* Part of this letter is given in *Letters to Persons in the World.* Bk. V. 17.

† The French has no date. [Tr.]

‡ Not the same that is spoken of in the first half of the letter. [Tr.]

We must not want to have all begin with perfection: it matters little how one begins, provided that one is quite resolved to proceed well or to finish well. Lia certainly entered unfairly into Rachel's place with Jacob, but she behaved so well, so chastely, and so lovingly, that she had the blessing of being an ancestress of Our Lord. Those who were compelled to go in to the nuptial feast of the Gospel none the less ate and drank well.

The dispositions of those who come to Religion are chiefly to be judged by subsequent perseverance; for there are souls which would not enter if the world looked favourably on them, and which, however, are found well disposed to despise sincerely the vanity of the world. It is quite certain, as the history of the case tells us, that this poor girl of whom we speak had not generosity enough to quit the love of him who sought her in marriage, and only the contradiction of her parents compelled her to it; but it does not matter if she has enough right understanding of things to know that the necessity which is imposed upon her by her parents is worth a hundred thousand times more than the free use of her own will and fancy (read in Platus, *On the Religious State*, Chap. 36, the answer which he has given to those who say they cannot tell whether they are called by God), and if she can truly say: I had lost my liberty had I not lost my liberty.

Now, my dear daughter, the way to help this soul, so as to make her know her good fortune, is to lead her as sweetly as one can to the exercise of prayer and the virtues; to display a great love for her on your own part and on that of all our sisters (taking no notice of the imperfection of the motive with which she entered); not to speak slightingly of the person whom she loved; and if she speak of him you must refer the matter to God, for instance by saying to her: God will lead him in the way which he knows to be best.

You ask me if an interview between the two can be permitted. I say that in my opinion it must not be altogether refused if it is much desired: but in the beginning you must give a sort of indirect refusal, and then when you see that the young person is quite determined to the blessed choice of God's love, you can permit two or three interviews, provided that they consent to the presence of two or three witnesses. If you are one of these you must dexterously help them to say adieu, praising their past intentions, leading them in a different direction, telling them they are happy to have stayed in the path to which reason has brought them, and that an ounce of the pure divine love which they will bear to one another in future is worth more than a hundred thousand pounds of the love with which they had begun their affection.

There is a good history on this subject in the *Confessions* of St. Augustine, of two gentlemen who had entered into espousals with two maidens, who all four, in imitation of one another, having given up the idea of marriage, became Religious.

And thus, without making a show of fearing their interviews too much, you must little by little conduct them from the way of love into that of a holy and pure dilection. If this young person has a reasonable spirit, as you have sent me word she has, I am sure that she will soon find herself quite transformed, and that she will admire the sweetness with which Our Lord draws her to his nuptials, with their all heaven-scented flowers and fruits.

As to what the world will say of this vocation, there is no need to make any sort of reflection; for this is in no way the ground of her being received. I answer about this soul according to my sentiments; you will guide her as you will see best.

As to Mlle. N., I likewise say that you should let her come, although the choice of place shows some imperfection of human feeling or motive mingled with her vocation; as on the other side there may be some in the dislike which Sister de N. has to her coming away from there: but take good care not to tell her this disparaging thought of her which comes to my mind, for all the same she is a very good sister, whom I love very much, because, as I am sure, she does not live according to her feelings, aversions, and inclinations, which make her desire the greatness and glory of her monastery, but rather according to the cross of Our Lord, which makes her perpetually disown the movements of self-love. . . .

LETTER XXXII.

To Sister M. A. Humbert.

Remedies against evil thoughts.

20th January [1622?].

To my very dear Daughter, my Sister Marie-Augustine Humbert—Do not trouble yourself at all about these extraordinary or terrible imaginations and thoughts which come to you; for according to the true knowledge which I have of your heart, I assure you before Our Lord that you can incur no sin by them. And to strengthen yourself in this belief, at the end of your morning exercise renounce by a short and simple disavowal all sorts of thoughts contrary to heavenly love; saying, for instance: I renounce all thoughts which are not for you, O my God; I disown and reject them for ever. Then when they attack you, you will have nothing to do but say occasionally: O Lord, I have renounced them, you know it. Sometimes you may kiss your cross or give some other sign that you confirm your disavowal; and do not vex yourself, do not worry yourself, since all this does not only not separate you from Our Lord, but gives you occasion to unite yourself more and more to his mercy. Go on then gently and sweetly serving God and Our Lady where you are called by their will. And may the grace and consolation of his Holy Spirit be ever with you. Amen. My dear daughter, live in God sweetly and simply, with a continual love of your own abjection, and a great courage to serve him who to save you died on the cross.

LETTER XXXIII.

To a Novice of the Visitation.

Congratulations upon her profession.

ANNECY, *24th January* 1622.

AND so, my very dear daughter, you are now at last on the sacred altar in spirit, to be sacrificed and immolated, yea consumed as a holocaust, before the face of the living God. Oh may this day be counted amongst "the days that the Lord hath made!" May this hour be an hour amongst the hours which God has blessed from all eternity, and which he has appointed for honour from all eternity! May this hour be founded in the holy humility of his cross, and end in the most sacred immortality of glory! How many desires will my soul make on this dear day for the soul of my dear daughter! How many holy exclamations of joy and happy omens upon that beloved heart! How many invocations to the most holy Virgin Mother, to the Saints and Angels, that they would honour with their special favour and presence this consecration of the spirit of my dear daughter, whose vocation they have obtained and whose obedience to vocation they have inspired!

I do not disjoin from your spirit, my dear daughter, that of dear Sister N., my well-beloved daughter. I unite it with yours in the same action: for as you know she found herself united with you in affection and love on the day of your Visitation, and it would seem that she then already immolated in resolution her heart with yours. How glad I am when I picture to myself that according to my hope they will announce to you in all truth that word of life-giving death: *Ye are dead, and your life is hidden with Christ in God:* * for, my dear daughter, on the truth of this word depends the truth of the event which afterwards they declare: *But when Christ shall appear, who is your life,* and the rest.†

I salute your dear soul and that of Sister N., and am ever in union of spirit according to God most singularly all yours.

* Col. iii. † Words used in the ceremony of Profession. [Tr.]

LETTER XXXIV.

TO MOTHER DE BEAUMONT, SUPERIORESS AT PARIS.

She is to have an entire trust in God, and to be a loving mother and nurse to her daughters.

25th January 1622.

MY VERY DEAR DAUGHTER—I wish you with all my heart a great humility within a great courage, that your courage may be altogether in God, who by his goodness holds you up, and in you holds up the sacred charge which obedience has imposed upon you. I hope this, my dear daughter, and that you will be like Anna of old, who before she was a mother often changed her countenance, as being touched with a diversity of thoughts and fears, but having become a mother, says the Sacred Scripture, *her countenance was no more changed*,* because, as I think, she was at rest in God, who had given her to know his love, his protection, and his care for her. For thus, my dear daughter, up to now the anxiety about direction and the apprehension of your future superiorship have agitated you a little, and have often made you vary in thoughts; now that you are mother of so many daughters, you should remain quiet, serene, and always equal, reposing upon divine Providence, which would never have placed all these daughters within your arms and in your bosom without having in some measure destined you an assistance, a help, a grace, most sufficient and abundant, for your upholding and support.

The Lord, said Anna,† *killeth and maketh alive;*

* 1 Kings i. 18.

* *Ibid.* ii.

he bringeth *down to hell and bringeth back again: the Lord maketh poor and maketh rich, he humbleth and he exalteth.* O let us say, my dear daughter, like another Anna: the Lord chargeth and dischargeth. 'Tis true; for when he imposes anything on one of his daughters, he so strengthens her that he bears the burden with her, and she is as it were discharged of it. Do you think that a Father so good as God is would make you nurse of his daughters without giving you an abundance of milk, of butter, and of honey? On this point there can be no doubt; only take notice of two or three words which my heart is going to say to yours.

Nothing makes the milk dry up like sadness, fretting, melancholy, bitterness, sourness. Live in holy joy amidst your children; show them a spiritual breast of kind looks and gracious welcome, that they may joyfully run thereto. It is this that the Canticles signify in the praise of the Beloved's breast: *Thy breasts are better than wine, smelling sweet of the best ointments.* Milk, butter, and honey are under thy tongue.*†

I do not say, my daughter, that you are to be a flatterer, a talker, or always laughing, but gentle, sweet, amiable, affable. In a word, love your daughters with a cordial, maternal love, a nurse's and a shepherd's love, and you will have done everything; you will be all to all, mother to each one and the refuge of all. It is the condition which alone suffices, and without it nothing suffices. My daughter, I trust that God who has chosen you for the good of many will give you the spirit, the strength, the courage, and the love for many. To him be honour, glory, and benediction for ever and ever. Amen.

* i. 1, 2. † iv. 11.

I am unchangingly yours, and I trust that you in no way doubt it. *Vive Jesus!*

LETTER XXXV.

To Mother Favre.

On unity of spirit amongst the houses of the Visitation: the soul that truly loves God must have no attachment to any particular work or plan.

2nd February 1622.*

I cannot think, my dearest daughter, that my Lord Archbishop will introduce any further laws into your house, since he has seen that those which have been laid down are, thanks to God, well observed. But if it please him to make some notable change, you must beseech him that he would deign to make his ordinances compatible with the holy uniformity which these houses ought to have in their form of living; in which those gentlemen whom you know will help you with their explanations and intercession. For, in truth, it would in my opinion be a thing far from edifying to separate and make different the spirit which God has meant to be one in all the houses. But I hope in Our Lord that he will give you *the mouth and the wisdom* † needed for this occasion, to answer holily, humbly, and sweetly. Live all of you in this sacred confidence, my dear daughter.

I wrote the other day to our sisters of Valence, and the dear, gentle little foundress is happy indeed to have to suffer something for Our Lord, who having founded

* The French has no date. [Tr.]

† Luke xxi. 15.

the Church militant and triumphant on the cross, always favours those who endure the cross: and as this little being is to remain but a short time in this world, it is good that her leisure should be employed in suffering.

I am astonished at these good sisters being so fond of their charges. What a pity, my dear daughter! She who loves the Master alone, serves him cheerfully and almost alike in all charges. Daughters with such dispositions would certainly not have been good for celebrating the mystery of to-day; for if Our Lady had put Our Lord into their arms they would never have been willing to give him back; but St. Simeon clearly shows that according to his name * he had perfect obedience, receiving this sweet charge so sweetly and giving it up so joyously.

I also wonder much at that other sister who cannot be satisfied where she is. Those who have strong health do not depend upon the air, but there are some who cannot exist save by changing climate. When shall we seek only God? O how happy shall we be when we have reached that point!—for everywhere shall we have what we seek, and seek what we have. May God make you progress ever more and more in his pure love, my very dear daughter, with all your dear sisters, whom I salute, &c.

* Which signifies, obedient.

LETTER XXXVI.

To Mother de Chantal.

Questions and instructions as to the visiting of the houses and the foundation of Dijon. His opinion on the case of the Abbess of Port Royal. Description of the sisters whom he is going to send.

Early in 1622.*

The thought has come to me while writing to M. Berger, that perhaps my Lord Cardinal will make him your spiritual Father at Paris, since he is going to be made a cleric at the Ash Wednesday Ember days, and I think that the House would be well and willingly served by him. I beg you to take occasion when you enter or leave Orleans to see the Mother Prioress of the Carmelites, eldest daughter of Sister Mary of the Incarnation. When I was in Paris, twenty years ago, she was not only my spiritual daughter, but my favourite; aged about thirteen, of a good, open, ingenuous disposition, as was also the mother superior,† who at that time made her first vow of virginity and her general confession to me. I am mistaken if you do not find at Moulins some sort of temptation on account of the singularity of Sister Marie-Aymée, but still I think it will only be a human temptation and requiring charity. M. Boucher, chancellor and theologian of Orleans, is my old schoolfellow, and has always had a great love for me.

Since the course of your journey from Paris to

* The French has "1614," an obvious error. [Tr.]

† The word "superior" seems to be a French editor's mistake. [Tr.]

Dijon, passing through the monasteries, requires that you go to Moulins, and that the sisters drawn from here and from Grenoble meet you there, it is necessary to know exactly the time when we must send them, and what arrangements will be made; that is, where the notice which we shall require will come from; but all the same it seems to me that as it is only forty leagues from here to Dijon it will greatly lengthen the journey to go to Moulins. I do not quite know how far it is from Moulins to Montferrand, but if it be convenient enough I think that it would be a consolation to these daughters that you should go to receive from them their superior [Mother Favre] for Dijon, whom, as I foresee, there will be a difficulty in taking away, as you will see by the letter which she has written to me, and which I send with this. I have already given notice to Sister Marguerite Milletot, besides whom it perhaps would be good to send there also Sister Bernard Margaret, who has improved so much that at last she has been received to profession.

I am of the opinion of M. de Marillac that our sisters when going through the country should carry their crucifix with them.

I have seen the account of the consultation held about our very dear daughter, Madame de Port Royal, upon which there is nothing to say except that I think it marvellously punctilious to determine that on account of length of time and of superiorship, despite an interior protest and increasing distaste, this daughter is so strictly obliged to stay that she cannot do otherwise; for although this may be probable as a matter of conscience, yet it is not acknowledged by all, and besides, the Pope can dispense from it. I also consider the comparison of the perfection of the rule of St. Benedict with that of the Visitation somewhat narrow and unfair; for the comparison should be made between the rule of St. Benedict and the rule of St. Augustine, and although perhaps the rule of St. Benedict might still remain superior in perfection, yet the comparison would remove all contempt for the Visitation, that is, all temptation to contempt. But all this that I tell you about this consultation is by no means to be brought forward, but simply to be considered with humility, and the decision to be left with sincerity to Rome. Hence you must take care to tell this good daughter that she must not with her impulsive spirit defend herself or answer back, but in this at least she must follow the institute of the Visitation, and in any case she will be able from time to time to console her spirit, since she has leave to go to the Visitation; and I also hope that when she accommodates herself sweetly to the good pleasure of God, he will comfort her at last.

If you knew, my dear mother, how much I am occupied and distracted in this town through the departure of M. Rolland, you would not be surprised that I do not write to the dear souls whom my soul and yours love so much. President Amelot's lady knows well, I am sure, that my heart is all hers before God and his Angels; I rejoice with her for the honour and happiness which her dear daughter Mary will have at this feast of Easter in making her first Communion. If I were there I should take it as a great favour to be her instructor in this action, which in truth is very important; the little book of Father Fulvius Androce on Confession and Communion contains many little points suitable for this, but since, as I think, the Rev. Father Suffren is at Paris, nothing can be wanting.

We will send then, when you tell us and when you so direct, sisters to accompany you to Dijon, according to the number which you may tell us to be necessary. We have thought for this purpose of Sister Marie-Adrienne Fichet, who has a good head and a good heart, as you know; of Sister Françoise-Augustine, from Moyran near Saint-Claude, whom I confess to be a daughter much to my liking, and if I mistake not entirely irreprehensible as to the interior and the exterior; of Sister Margaret Scholastica, of Burgundy, who is gentle, tractable, and sensible, a cousin-german of your assistant; of Sister Margaret-Agnes, who is from near Vienne, of good family, of good observance, and of an agreeable simplicity; of Sister Peronne-Marie Benod, a serving sister (*sœur domestique*), very gentle and willing, besides Sister Mary-Marguerite Milletot, who is to come from Grenoble, whom you know, and Sister Bernard Marguerite, the one from Dijon whom you sent us, about whose capacity there was indeed a doubt for some months, but who has since given full satisfaction. It must be considered whether you will think it better to have her professed here, or to have her sent to Dijon to be professed on the guarantee which would be given as to her capacity; for we thought that perhaps it would give satisfaction to have this done in the presence of her parents and friends, and so make her the first daughter of that monastery. So it will be for you, my very dear mother, to give us notice whether you want more or fewer sisters, and when they ought to start.

LETTER XXXVII.

To a Superioress of the Visitation.

On allowing benefactresses to stay in houses of the Visitation, and on receiving penitents: progress of the Institute: we must not defend ourselves or judge others.

1622.*

I SEE no objection to receiving Madame de N. or other benefactress of the kind, particularly when they want to leave the monastery no more, or at least want to leave it but seldom; for in this there is nothing contrary to good order.

I do not consider that monasteries of the Visitation must refuse all repentant women. Prudence must be tempered with sweetness, and sweetness with prudence. There is sometimes so much to be gained in penitent souls that nothing must be refused them.

It seems to me that the upright rods should be in the *grille* of the choir as in that of the parlour.

I think so, my dear mother—that it should be stated that we can with a little leisure provide for Marseilles. Our sisters will have written to you that sisters have been sent to Belley, and I tell you that in a little time some will be wanted for Chambery. Madame the Duchess of Mantua has strong desires for the advancement of our Institute; she is a very worthy princess, and so are her sisters.

Our Sister N. writes to me that some nuns, good servants of God, openly oppose her. I have written her a note to tell her to remain at peace. I will, with God's help, never let this maxim leave my mind, that

* The French has no date. [Tr.]

we must in no wise live according to human prudence, but according to the faith of the Gospel: *Defend not yourselves, my dearly beloved*, says St. Paul.* We must *overcome evil with good*, bitterness by sweetness, and remain in peace.

And never commit the fault of contemning the sanctity of an Order or of a person for a fault committed by them in the error of an immoderate zeal. My dear mother, may God be for ever your one love.

LETTER XXXVIII.

To Mother de Chantal.

Directions about her journeys. Total abandonment to the divine will.

Annecy, *22nd October* 1622 [21 ?].

Examine for yourself, my best and dearest Mother, I pray you, the letters sent herewith, and see whether there is a probability that you can without greatly incommoding yourself give this so much desired satisfaction to these dear souls; for if it can well be done, I for my part not only consent to it, but should most earnestly wish it, particularly if it is true that coming from Dijon to Montferrand you would be able to see your dear daughter on your way; and still more if coming from Montferrand to Lyons it were on your way to visit St. Estienne de Forez; and I own that it would be a consolation to me to have news of these new plants, which

* Rom. xii. 19. The Douay translation has *Revenge not:* the Latin is *non defendentes.* [Tr.]

God methinks has planted with his hand for his greater honour and service.

I must tell you, my dear mother, that this morning, having a little solitude, I have made an incomparable act of resignation, but one which I cannot write, and which I reserve to tell you by word of mouth when God gives me the grace of seeing you. O how blessed are the souls which live by the will of God alone! Ah! if from the mere tasting a very little of it by a passing consideration one have so much spiritual sweetness in the depths of that heart which accepts this holy will, with all the crosses which it presents, what shall it be with souls all steeped in the union of this will? O God, what a blessing to make all our affections humbly and exactly subject to those of purest divine love! Thus have we spoken, thus have we determined; and our heart has for its sovereign law the greater glory of the love of God. Now the glory of this holy love consists in burning and consuming all that is not itself, to reduce and convert everything to and into itself. It exalts itself on our annihilation, and reigns on the throne of our servitude. Oh! my dearest mother, how my will expanded in this sentiment! May it please his divine goodness to continue in me this abundance of high courage for his honour and glory, and for the perfection and excellence of this most incomparable unity of heart which it has pleased him to give us. Amen. *Vive Jesus!*

I beseech the Virgin Mary that she may keep you under the protection of her tender maternity, and your good Angel and mine that they may be your conductors, to make you arrive prosperously as far as the welcome of the poor father so specially yours, and of your dear daughters, who will all await you with a thousand desires, and particularly myself, who am to you in Our Lord neither more nor less than yourself. May God be ever our all. I am in him more yours than I could say in this world: for there are no words for this love there.

Well then, I think that a good month, or five weeks, will give an account of all these journeys (but I am supposing all the time that there is no peril from soldiers on the roads of those countries): after which I will tell you why, and how, I have at present no chance of writing more, though I am well, thanks to God. On the one hand, this bearer urges me extremely, that he may be able to catch you at Dijon; on the other hand, I am pressed for other good affairs, which I cannot give up. All goes well here, and I am more and more your most humble, &c.

LETTER XXXIX.

To a Superioress of the Visitation, his Cousin.

On the excellence of helping souls to advance in divine charity.

Annecy, *2nd November* 1622.

I BLESS with all my heart the sacred name of Our Lord, for the consolation which his divine Providence gives to your soul in the place where you are, and for the constancy which it establishes in your affection. Doubtless, my dearest cousin, my daughter, he who wills to please only this heavenly lover, is everywhere well, for he has what he wants. Oh how happy you are, and will be ever more and more, if you persevere in walking in this path! And how perfectly agreeable will you make yourself to the Beloved of those souls whom he draws into your bosom to make them his spouses, if you teach them to look only into the eyes of their Saviour, to lose little by little the thoughts which nature of itself would suggest to them, making them think altogether of him.

O my dear cousin! what blessings for your soul that God has destined you to cultivate and manage his sacred seed-plot. You are the mother, the nurse, and the waiting-woman of these daughters and spouses of the King. What a dignity! For that dignity what a reward, if you carry this out with the love and the breasts of a mother! Keep your courage strong and firm in this undertaking, and believe very unchangeably that I cherish and love you without condition or reserve as my dearest cousin and well-beloved daughter.

I saw, only a month ago, our Sister N., but I saw very little of her; and yet I saw within her soul, and found that she was all full of good affections. Oh how well situated are the daughters of St. Marie of the Visitation, amid so many means and occasions of greatly loving and serving Our Lord! It is grievous to see the good sisters in these monasteries, exposed to so many distractions of arrivals and visits. My dearest cousin, my daughter, praised be God. Amen. And I am, yours, &c.

LETTER XL.

To Mother de Chantal.

Superiors not to be guided by the human spirit, and not to be too eager to escape temporal anxieties.

1622, *about June.**

I am back and in health, my dearest Mother, but without leisure to make you a long narration; it will suffice if I answer the principal questions which you have asked me. I believe, my dear mother, because I see, that all superiors want to have troublesome and eccentric sisters removed from their monasteries, for it is the nature of the human spirit only to be pleased with pleasing things; but I am entirely of your opinion that one should not open the door for a change of monasteries to those sisters who desire it, but only to those who without desiring it are for some other reason sent by superiors; otherwise the slightest unpleasantness which happened to a sister would be capable of disquieting her and making her change; and instead of changing themselves they would think they had sufficiently cured their trouble when they changed their monastery.

I am glad that you are lodged as you desire. I have answered Madame de Monfan's and Madame de Dalet's letters, written to me while I was at Turin; I have seen how these two ladies exercise our superioress at Paris, but I see no remedy except patience and confidence in God.

M. Sanguin wrote me a long letter, and got the

* The French has no date. [Tr.]

Duke de Nemours to write to me, on the difficulties made about his daughter, but I have nothing to answer except that superiors on the spot must decide the matter, and not I, who can only get information from the statements of the parties, and who, moreover, am not a competent judge. I am much more scandalised with the contests which are going on between our sisters, the superiors of Moulins and of Nevers, for a certain thousand crowns which I would rather have at the bottom of the sea than in the minds of these daughters. Is it possible that persons brought up in the school of the folly of the cross are so attached to the prudence of the world that neither one nor other will yield, and that each can appeal to so many points of law? You must, however, try to stop the one who has the less right, provided that the spirit of the world still permit her to let herself be judged wrong; but I do not think this can be done before your arrival. The one at Nevers has not written to me about it, but the complaints of the one at Moulins prove that the idea of strict justice is deeply fixed in the mind of both one and the other.

I have almost the same aversion to the great desire which superiors have that their houses should be relieved by means of foundations; for all this springs from the human sense and the difficulty which each one has to carry her burden. It seems then to me to matter very little whether the house of Montferrand or that of Moulins be relieved by the foundation of Riom.

I am very glad of the satisfaction which you find in our Sister Françoise Augustine, and our Sister Parise, as also I am very sorry that the spirit of our Sister Valeret could not accommodate itself to the Institute.

God grant her the grace of attraction to a vocation conducive to her salvation.

I have already written to you on the subject of the benefactresses, whom I would not, as you would not, like to be in great numbers; but still this must be arranged with charity and discretion. As to Mlle. de Vigny, since she is such a good soul as you say, she may be granted what she wants, but in future you must not receive benefactresses who want to make so many conditions.

The number of sick in the house at Paris is a great presage of the blessing which God desires to give there, although the flesh is averse to it. I should indeed have liked a longer life for Madame the first president's lady, my dear daughter, but we must stop short and without a word before the decree of the heavenly will, which disposes of its own according to its greater glory. I am consoled by the sweet edification which she has left in the good example of her life: it was indeed wholly dedicated to the service of God, as I have known ever since I had the advantage of knowing her. I think the pious houses of Dijon and Burgundy will have lost much by this death, but it rarely happens that one profits without another's loss. . . .

LETTER XLI.

To a Superioress of the Visitation (*Mother de Chantal ?*).

It is best for nuns to be subject to the Ordinaries.

My very dear Mother—I find persons of consideration who strongly think and judge that convents should be under the Ordinaries, according to the old way restored throughout all Italy, or under the authority of religious men, according to the usage introduced four or five hundred years ago, observed throughout almost the whole of France. As for me, my dear mother, I frankly own to you that I cannot at present follow the opinion of those who would have the monasteries of women subject to religious men, in particular if of the same Order, as I follow in this the instinct of the Holy See, which when it can well do so hinders this subjection. Not that it has not laudably been so or still is so in some places; but that it would be still more laudably done otherwise; on this, however, there would be many things to say.

Further, it seems to me that it is no more unsuitable for the Pope to exempt the sisters of an Institute from the jurisdiction of the Fathers of the same Institute, than it was to exempt the monasteries from the ordinary jurisdiction, which had so excellent an origin and so long a possession.

And in the last place, I think that as a matter of fact it is the Pope who has subjected those good Religious women of France to the government of religious; but it seems to me that these good sisters of yours do not know what they are wanting when they would in the same way bring upon themselves the authority of the religious men. These are indeed excellent servants of God, but it is always a hard thing for sisters to be governed by Orders, which usually take from them holy liberty of spirit. My dear mother, I salute your heart, which is precious to me as my own. *Vive Jesus!*

LETTER XLII.

To a Superioress of the Visitation.

Candidates are to be judged not according to nature, but according to grace. Remarks on the form of profession.

My very dear Mother—At last God has willed that Sister N. should remain assistant by the majority of the votes, and he always wills the best; for she is a good, wise, steady person, and a true servant of Our Lord: a little hard and cold in countenance, but of good heart, brief in speech but to the point. We make but few prefaces, she and I, and little appendix either.

But to speak of our Sister N., I must tell you that she is a sister altogether admirable in words, in behaviour, in act, for in all things she breathes virtue and piety.

I am entirely of your opinion and that of our good Father N., as to our Sister N. Let a sister be of as bad a natural disposition as you like, but let her only act in essential matters by grace and not by nature, according to grace and not to nature, and she deserves to be received with love and respect, as a temple of the Holy Spirit, a wolf by nature but a sheep by grace. O my mother, I supremely fear natural prudence in the discernment of the things of grace; and if the prudence of the serpent be not tempered with the simplicity of the dove of the Holy Spirit, it is altogether poisonous.

I am astonished at those good Fathers who think that a person is bound to add that he or she is taking vows to superiors. If they looked at the form of profession of the Benedictines, which is the profession of the most ancient and numerous monasteries, they would have plenty of objections to make; for there is no mention at all made there either of superiors or of vows of chastity, poverty, and obedience, but only of stability in the monastery, and of conversion of manners according to the rule of St. Benedict. Whosoever promises obedience according to the Constitutions of Saint Mary, promises obedience and observance of vows to the Church and to the superiors of the Congregation or monastery. In a word, one must remain in peace; for he who wants to listen any longer to all that is said will have plenty to do.

LETTER XLIII.

To a Superioress of the Visitation.

One religious Order is not to despise another: the excellence of littleness.

My Daughter—Take good care not to respond in any way to those good sisters or their foundress, save by a quite invariable humility, sweetness, and simplicity of heart. *Defend not yourselves, my dearly beloved*:—these are the very words of the Holy Spirit, written by St. Paul.* There are sometimes human temptations amongst the servants of God; if we are animated by love we shall support them in peace.

If these good souls despise our Institute, because it seems to them less than their own, they go against charity, in which the strong do not despise the weak

* Rom. xii. 19. So the French, and the Vulgate. [Tr.]

nor the great the little. It is true they are more than you; but do the Seraphim despise the little Angels? And in heaven, wherein is the image on which we should form ourselves, do the great Saints despise the less? But apart from all this, in brief, he who most loves will be most loved, and he who shall have most loved shall be the most glorified. Love God dearly, and for God's sake love all creatures, particularly those who despise you; and then trouble yourself not.

The evil spirit exerts his efforts, because he sees that this little Institute is useful to the service and glory of God, and he specially hates it because it is little and the least of all; for he is an arrogant spirit and hates littleness, because it serves towards humility—he who has always loved pride, haughtiness, and arrogance, and who, because he would not stay in his littleness, lost his greatness. Labour in humility, in abjection; let people talk and act as they will. *Unless the Lord build the house, they labour in vain that build it,** and if God build it, they labour in vain that would destroy it. God knows when and with what souls he will fill your monastery. Remain at peace; and I am your, &c.

LETTER XLIV.

TO A SUPERIORESS OF THE VISITATION.

A Monastery is a school of perfection: obedience is the chief virtue required; even prayer must be regulated by this.

MY DEAR DAUGHTER—I will tell you, as to the difficulty which this good sister has, that she greatly deceives

* Ps. cxxvi. 1.

herself if she thinks that prayer perfects her without obedience, which is the dear virtue of the Spouse, in which, by which, and for which he willed to die. We know by history and experience that many religious and others have been holy without mental prayer, but without obedience, not one.

You are right, my dear daughter; there must be no reserve or condition; for should we receive souls in that way the congregation would find itself quite full of the subtlest and consequently most dangerous self-love in the world. One would stipulate for communicating daily, another for hearing three masses, another for attending the sick every day; and by this means each one would follow her humour or her own object, instead of following Our Saviour crucified.

It behoves that those who enter should know that the congregation is only founded to serve as a school and guide to perfection, and that all the sisters will be advanced towards it by the most suitable ways, and that those ways will be most suitable which they do not choose themselves. "He who is his own master," says St. Bernard, "is a scholar under a fool." Let her then remain in peace in the arms of her mother, who will carry and guide her in a good path.

Prayer must be loved, but it must be loved for love of God. Now she who loves it for God's love only wants as much of it as God wills to give her; and God wills to give only as much as obedience permits. If then this daughter (whom, however, I greatly love on account of the good that you tell me of her) wants to perfect herself after her own fashion she must be handed over to herself; but I doubt not, if she is really devout, and has the true spirit of prayer, that she will submit to simple obedience. She looks too far in advance when she says that she will accommodate herself for a short time to having only half an hour's prayer, but that she could not promise it for ever. The true servant of God is not solicitous for the morrow; she executes faithfully what he wants to-day, and to-morrow what he then wants; and after to-morrow what he shall want then, without stipulating either for this or for that. It is thus that we should unite our will, not to the means of serving God, but to the serving him and to his good pleasure. *Be not therefore solicitous for the morrow; saying, what shall we eat, or what shall we drink, or wherewith shall we be clothed? . . . For your Father knoweth that you have need of all these things. Seek ye therefore the kingdom of God . . . and all these things shall be added unto you.** This is to be understood of the spiritual as of the temporal.

Let then this daughter take a child's heart, a will of wax, and a spirit stripped and despoiled of all sorts of affections save that of loving God; and as to the means of loving him, they should be indifferent to her. Live sweetly and holily amid the pains which you suffer under your charge, my dear and well-beloved daughter, and I beseech God to be the life of your soul. Amen.

* Matt. vi.

LETTER XLV.

TO MOTHER FAVRE.

She is to conduct her daughters variously according to the Spirit of God: they must resist the tendency to over-emulation.

MY VERY DEAR GRAND-DAUGHTER—In my opinion there will be no harm in letting this good sister communicate; indeed you must if possible take from the sisters of the congregation that imperfection, ordinary with women, of vain and jealous imitation. They must be confirmed if possible in not wanting to do all that others do, but in simply willing what others will —that is to say, not all to do the same exercises, except those of the rule.

Yes, let each one walk according to the gift of God; but let all have that one and simple design of serving God, all having one same will, one same undertaking, one same project, with great resignation about fulfilling it, each one according to the means which the superior and the spiritual father shall deem expedient; in such sort that those who communicate more often may esteem others no less than themselves—since we oftentimes approach closer to Our Lord by withdrawing through humility than by approaching at our own choice —and those who do not communicate so often must not let themselves be carried away by a vain emulation.

It is true that we must not permit the rule to be exceeded save rarely, and for reasons like to these. My dear daughter, how happy shall we be if we are faithful! My soul cordially salutes your spirit, which may God bless with his holy hand. Amen.

LETTER XLVI.

TO A MISTRESS OF NOVICES OF THE VISITATION.

She must do her best with simplicity, and confidently leave the rest to God.

GOD will inspire you, my dear daughter, as to all he wants from you, if in the innocence and simplicity of your heart, with an entire resigning of your inclinations, you often ask him in your heart: *Lord, what wouldst thou have me to do?** And I am glad that you have already heard his voice, and that you serve him in the feeding of these daughters.

Nor was it a good excuse to say: I have no breasts, I have no milk; for it is not with our own milk or our own breasts that we feed the children of God; it is with the milk and the breasts of the divine Spouse; and we do no more than point them out to the children, and say: take, suck, draw and live. Keep your heart thus then open and large, to do well all the service that shall be laid upon you.

In proportion as you undertake, in virtue of holy obedience, many things for God, he will assist you with his help, and will do your work with you if you will do yours with him; now his is the sanctification and perfection of souls. Labour humbly, simply and confidently at this; you will never receive from it any distraction which will be hurtful to you. That peace is not good which flies the labour required for the glorification of God's name.

Live wholly for this divine love, my dear daughter,

* Acts ix. 6.

and know that it is with all my heart that I cherish your well-beloved soul, and never cease to recommend it to the eternal mercy of our Saviour, to whom I conjure you reciprocally to recommend me very often. I am all yours, my very dear daughter, &c.

LETTER XLVII.

To a Sister of the Visitation.

What it is to live according to the spirit, and what according to the flesh.

How very reasonable is it, my dear daughter, that I should write to you a little, and with what good heart I do it! Would to God that I had the spirit necessary for your consolation. To live according to the spirit, my well-beloved daughter, is to think, speak, and act according to the virtues that are in the spirit, and not according to the sense and sentiments which are in the flesh. Of these latter we must make use, must reduce them to subjection, and not live according to them; but those spiritual virtues we must serve, and must subject to them all the rest.

What are these virtues of the spirit, my dear daughter? They are faith, which shows us truths entirely elevated above the senses; hope, which makes us aspire to things invisible; charity, which makes us love God above all things and our neighbour as ourselves, with a love not of sense, not of nature, not of self-interest, but with a love pure, solid, and unchangeable, having its foundation in God.

Look, my daughter: the human sense, stayed upon

the flesh, causes us many times to fail in abandoning ourselves into the hands of God; we think that since we are of no worth God will make no account of us, as men who live according to human prudence despise those who are of no use. On the contrary, the spirit, stayed upon faith, takes courage amid difficulties, because it knows well that God loves, supports, and succours the miserable, provided that they hope in him.

The human sense would be engaged in all that is going on; and it so loves itself that it fancies nothing is good unless it has part therein. The spirit, on the contrary, attaches itself to God, and often says that what is not of God is nothing to it; and as it takes part in the things which are communicated to it through charity, so also does it willingly yield its share in things which are kept back from it through abnegation and humility.

To live according to the spirit is to love according to the spirit; to live according to the flesh is to love according to the flesh; for love is the life of the soul, as the soul is the life of the body. A sister is very sweet, very agreeable, and I love her tenderly; she loves me greatly, she favours me much; I love her in return for this. Who sees not that I live according to the senses and the flesh?—for animals which have no mind, and have flesh and senses only, love their benefactors and those who are sweet and agreeable to them.

A sister is rough-mannered, sharp, and uncourteous; but all the same she is very pious, and also desirous of improving herself and making herself more sociable; wherefore, not for any pleasantness I find in her nor for any self-interest, but for God's good pleasure, I love her, I go to her, I serve her, I embrace her. This love is according to the spirit, for the flesh has no share in it.

I am distrustful of myself, and for this reason would greatly desire to be let live according to that inclination ; who sees not that this is not according to the spirit? No, undoubtedly, my dear daughter; for while I was still quite young, and had as yet no spirit, I already lived so. But although according to my natural disposition I am timid and fearful, still I desire to try and overcome those natural passions, and little by little to do properly all that belongs to the charge which obedience, coming from God, has laid upon me ; who sees not that this is to live according to the spirit? My dear daughter, to live according to the spirit is to do the actions, say the words, and think the thoughts, which the Spirit of God requires from us. And when I say thoughts I mean voluntary thoughts.

I am sad, and therefore will not speak; parrots and boorish carters act so. I am sad, but since charity requires me to talk I will do so; thus do spiritual persons act.

I am despised and get angry about it; just so do peacocks and monkeys. I am despised and rejoice; the Apostles acted so.

Hence to live according to the spirit is to do what faith, hope, and charity teach us, whether in temporal or in spiritual things.

Live then wholly according to the spirit, my dear daughter; remain sweetly at peace; be quite assured that God will help you; whenever trouble arises, lay yourself within the arms of his paternal mercy and goodness.

May God be for ever your all, and I am in him all yours; you know it well.

Your honoured father is well, and so are all that belong to you according to the flesh; thus be it with what belongs to you according to the spirit! Amen.

LETTER XLVIII.

To a Sister of the Visitation.

We can avoid sins, but must not expect to conquer every evil inclination: patience and perseverance required in the practice of charity and in the struggle against self-love.

I RECALL your letter, my very dear daughter, in which with so much sincerity you describe to me your imperfections and your troubles; and I should much like to be able to correspond with the desire which you have of learning some remedy from me; but neither does leisure permit, nor as I think does your necessity require it; for doubtless, my dear daughter, the chief part of what you describe to me has no other ordinary remedy than the course of time, and the exercises of the rule under which you live: there are in the same way corporal maladies of which the cure depends on a good order of life.

Self-love, the esteem of ourselves, false liberty of spirit, these are roots which one cannot fully eradicate from the human heart; one can only hinder the production of their fruits, which are sins; for their risings, their first shocks or movements, cannot be altogether prevented so long as we are in this mortal life; though we can moderate them and diminish their quantity and their ardour by the practice of the contrary virtues, and above all, of the love of God.

It behoves then to have patience, and little by little to amend and cut off our bad habits, suppress our aversions and surmount our inclinations and humours as occasion requires: for at last, my dear daughter, this life is a continual warfare, and there is no one who can say, I am not attacked.

Repose is reserved for heaven, where the palm of victory awaits us. On earth, it is necessary always to fight between fear and hope; but hope should always be stronger, on account of the omnipotence of him who aids us. Do not then get tired of continually working for your amendment and perfection. Notice that charity has three parts—the love of God, affection for self, and dilection for our neighbour. Your rule assists you to practise all this well.

Many times in the day cast your whole heart, your spirit, and your solicitude upon God, with a great confidence, and say to him with David: * *I am Thine, O Lord, save me.*

Do not occupy yourself much in thinking what sort of prayer God gives you, but simply and humbly follow his grace in the affection which you ought to have for yourself. Keep your eyes well fixed on your unruly inclinations to uproot them. Never be surprised to see yourself wretched and loaded with evil humours. Treat your heart with a great desire of perfecting it. Have an indefatigable care to put it right when it stumbles.

Above all, labour as much as you can to strengthen

* Ps. cxviii. 94.

the superior part of your spirit, not concerning yourself with feelings and consolations, but with resolutions, purposes and strivings, which faith, the rule, the superior and reason will inspire you with.

Be not tender with yourself: tender mothers spoil children. Be not tearful or complaining; be not alarmed at those importunities and violences which you feel, which you find it so painful to manifest: no, my daughter, be not alarmed, God permits them to make you humble with true humility, abject and vile in your own eyes. They ought not to be combated save by yearnings for God, turning of the spirit from the creature to the Creator, with continual affections for most holy humility and simplicity of heart.

Be kind to your neighbour, and in spite of the risings and sallies of anger, pronounce very often on occasion these divine words of our Saviour: * O Lord, eternal Father, I love these neighbours, because you love them, and have given them to me as brothers and sisters, and you will that as you love them I also love them. So above all, love these good sisters, with whom the very hand of divine Providence has associated and bound you by a heavenly bond: support them, cherish them and put them in your heart, my dear daughter. Know that I have a most particular affection for your progress, God having obliged me thereto.

* From John xvii.

LETTER XLIX.

TO A SISTER OF THE VISITATION.

On the renunciation of self in order to belong entirely to God.

IT is the truth, my dear daughter, that my soul cherishes you most perfectly; and it is impossible for me, when I think of you, which is not very rarely, not to feel a very particular movement of love.

Well, it was absolutely required that the serpent should thrust itself by force into the hardness of the stone in order to strip itself of its old skin, and happily to renew its youth so as to be transformed into a dove. God be praised, my dear daughter, that you have suffered such dreadful pangs in bringing yourself forth in Jesus Christ!

Walk now holily and carefully in this newness of spirit, and take good care not to look back, for there would be extreme danger in that; and bless divine Providence, which had prepared you so amiable a nurse. Oh how good and gracious is God, my dear daughter! Truly I have had an incredible satisfaction in seeing how he has conducted you in the abundance of his love. Ah! then, never abandon him, and give entire liberty to your heart to unite and clasp itself unchangeably to his pleasure; for it is made to that end.

That this dear mother be superior I consent without difficulty; but that this could be done absolutely in the way you speak of I cannot see the way to, nor will it depend on me, who am of very little account here and of none at all elsewhere: I only repeat that as to my consent I give it, and besides will contribute what I can properly do for your intention.

But, my dear daughter, are we not children, adorers and servers of Heavenly Providence, and of the loving and paternal heart of Our Saviour? Is it not upon this basis that we have built our hopes? Do what he has inspired you for his glory, and doubt not but that he will do for your good what shall be best. Do not make terms with him: he is our Master, our King, our Father, our All; think of serving him well, he will think of helping us well.

And so, my daughter, to conclude, I will do all I can to give you this little satisfaction, though it is not much I can do: where you are I am sure they will do the same; but in heaven all will be done: you will be filled with consolations, by means which the Supreme Wisdom knows and sees, and which we know not.

Remain at peace, feed lovingly, carefully and faithfully this new dear infant which your soul has newly brought forth into the Holy Spirit, that it may strengthen in sanctity and increase in blessings, to be for ever loved of the Beloved. What further can I desire you, my very dear daughter? I am entirely, I assure you, your very humble, &c.

LETTER L.

To a Superioress of the Visitation.

Humility and sweetness the two chief virtues of a superior: "to ask nothing and refuse nothing" is the sum of the Saint's teaching.

It is the truth, my very dear sister, my daughter, that you have greatly pleased me by the trouble which you have taken to write to me, since also, as I see, you are the one to whom God has disposed to have the charge of superior committed. You will be granted leisure to well prepare yourself, by an entire submission to heavenly Providence, and a perfect strengthening of heart to exercise yourself well in humility, and in sweetness or mildness of heart—the two dear wishes which Our Lord recommended to the Apostles whom he had destined to the superiorship of the universe.

Ask nothing and refuse nothing about all matters of the religious life; this is the holy indifference which will preserve you in the peace of your eternal Spouse, and it is the one only teaching that I want practised by all our sisters, whom my heart affectionately salutes, with yours, my dear daughter.

BOOK IV.

Further Letters to Religious outside the Visitation.

LETTER I.

TO THE ABBESS OF PUITS D'ORBE.

Consolation on losing Madame de Chantal: weakness is not to discourage her, if the will be good. Advice on certain points in the management of her community. Assurances of affection.

SALES, 20*th April* 1611.

WELL now, my dear sister, my daughter, I am going to write to you as fully as I can on the subject of your letter, which has been handed to me by the sister whom you love so much, and who reciprocally cherishes you with all her heart.

It is true we have her at last, this dear sister, but still it is not I who have taken her away from you, it is God who has given her to us, as the result will with God's help make clear. I have no doubt that that little conversation which you had together at Bourbilly was very sweet to you; for it is a happy thing when two souls meet who love one another only in order to love God better; but it was impossible that this sensible presence should last long, because our common Master wants the one there and the other here for his service. But we do not cease to be ever joined and united, for we keep with one another by the common aim or undertaking that we have.

I am very glad that you fail but little in the exercises which I have appointed you; for this shows that those faults which you commit do not come from unfaithfulness but from weakness; and weakness is not a great evil, provided that a faithful determination put it right little by little, as I conjure you to do, my dear daughter, as regards your own weakness; without at all distressing yourself because ordinarily you have neither feeling nor relish in any of your exercises: for Our Lord does not require this from us, nor does it depend on ourselves to have it or to have it not.

So we must build on solid ground, and consider whether our will is fully delivered from evil affections, such as hardness of heart towards our neighbour, impatience, contempt of others, too strong affection for creatures, and the like. And if we have no reserve as to being all God's, if we have the determination rather to die than offend him, so long as these are the resolutions of our hearts and we feel them ever stronger in us, there is nothing to fear, and no cause to be troubled at not having sweetness or devout feelings.

Now we have a good proof of the strengthening of these dear resolutions, in that by the grace of God you have persevered in keeping to what I told you in confession, as you assure me; for this is worth a hundred thousand spiritual sweetnesses. Thus then do always.

I will say the Mass that you ask me, though I never say one which is not very expressly yours; but I cannot recall to mind the subject which you say I know —there is no need to do so.

If Madame Theniée continues unwilling to submit, you will have no part in her fault; meantime I rejoice that the rest of our articles are kept. And as for the one who will not accommodate herself to the community, you must bear with her, and show kindness towards her, and God will bring her round to the way of the others.

And so, my dear daughter, the multitude of difficulties terrified you, and you had thoughts of giving it all up; meantime you have found that all is done: it will be the same with all the rest, perseverance will overcome everything.

As to the pensions, they are rightly in your hands, as no one else can look after them; but you may well get one of your daughters to keep account of them. You made me smile when you wrote that you would have given their pensions to each of the religious if you had not feared that I should be cross with you. Oh! my dear daughter, when did you ever see me cross with you? I am, however, very glad that there is some little fear of displeasing a poor miserable father, for truly you will never displease me, my dear daughter, save when you displease Our Lord, and withdraw yourself from his pure and holy love.

You really must go to Chapter, spite of all the repugnance you may feel, and after the reading of the rule you must say something, be it merely—May God give us the grace to observe what has been read.

At Corpus Christi I see no difficulty about having the procession round the cloister, for this does not create a precedent on account of the greatness of the solemnity.

Alas! my daughter, if nobody worked for souls except those who have no difficulty in their exercises and who are perfect, you would have no father in me; we are not to give up consoling others because we are in perplexity ourselves. How many good doctors are there who are far from being in good health, and how many beautiful paintings are made by ugly painters? When therefore your daughters come to you, tell them simply and with charity what God may inspire you with, and do not send them away from you empty.

You do well thus to get Fathers Minim to come from time to time, for that will enlarge the hearts of your daughters, and will comfort their souls. I am grieved, with you, at the dislike which they have for your ordinary chaplain, but the introduction of the Minims can supply for all this, since, as you say, it is hard to find priests properly qualified, and this one is fairly capable. And now, my dear sister, my very dear daughter, you must take up your former courage, and rather die than give in.

Keep as much as you can with your daughters; for your absence can only give them occasions for murmuring; and nothing can so much sweeten their subjection to rule as your own, nothing can so well keep them in the enclosure of observance as to see you there with them; and it is in this that we must crucify ourselves for him who was crucified for us. How happy will you be if you dearly love your little flock—for after the love of God that holds the first rank.

I will write to you whenever I can and as much as

I can; and changelessly will I persevere in the affection which I have once with such goodwill given to you. Remain firm in this belief, for it is, with God's help, infallible. No, neither death, nor things present, nor those to come, shall ever separate me from that love which I bear you in Jesus Our Lord, to whom be honour and glory. Your, &c.

But look, my dear daughter, what I say to you I recommend to you very decidedly, for your sister has told me you want me to speak so. My dear sister, assure all your good and well-beloved sisters and daughters that I honour and cherish them very greatly, particularly Madame your very dear sister, and I am grieved that I cannot write to them now. And to humble you yet a little, salute from me M. Lafon and those good daughters who are serving God in the person of his servants; for all this is dear to me.

LETTER II.

To a Benedictine Nun.

On trust in God and resignation to his will in our employments: how far rash judgment is a grievous sin: how to act when a venial sin is forgotten in confession.

20th January 1612.

It will never happen to me, my dear sister, my daughter, to forget your heart, which mine will perpetually love in Our Lord. I see by your letter that you do not sufficiently lean on holy divine Providence. My dear daughter, if it took away your good sister, which we may hope will not happen so soon, you would not on this account cease to be under the protection of this best eternal Father, who would cover you with his wings. We should be miserable, my daughter, if we only established our trust in God by means of the creatures whom we love; and moreover, my dear sister, we are not to form to ourselves useless fears. It will be quite enough to receive the evils which come upon us from time to time, without anticipating them by the imagination.

As for the office you hold, it is a temptation not to have for it the love which is required, for the time in which you fill it; on the contrary I should wish, and God would wish, that you should exercise it cheerfully and lovingly; and by this means he would take care of the desire which you have of being relieved, and would give it effect in its time. For take notice once for all that we must never be unsubmissive even with one of our wills, but when something happens against our inclination we must accept it heartily, although we would heartily desire that it were not so: and when Our Lord sees that we are thus yielding he condescends to our intentions. I will write to your sister that she must make you do the serving like the others, for that is good.

When thoughts arise in us to the disadvantage of others, and we do not put them away promptly, but delay some little upon them, provided that we do not make a complete judgment, saying within ourselves, *it is really so,* this is not a mortal sin; nor even if we should say absolutely, *it is so,* provided that it is not in a matter of importance. For when that for which we judge our neighbour is not a grave thing, or when we do not judge absolutely, it is only a venial sin; and the same for omitting some verse of the Office or some ceremony—there is only venial sin. And when the remembrance of such a fault comes to us after confession, it is not required to return to our confessor in order to approach communion; indeed it is good not to return, but to reserve the matter to be told in the next following confession, and to tell it if you remember it.

As long as your sister has not chosen to receive your pension there is no fault of yours; but it will be well that she should manage it. My dearest sister, you must not lose courage even if you do not so faithfully practise the resolutions you make: you must strengthen your heart and so come to the execution of them. Persevere then, my dear sister, my daughter, and cease not to call upon God or to trust in him, and he will make you abound in his benedictions; thus do I beg him to do, by the merit of his Passion,-and the intercession of his Mother and of St. Frances.* Our sweet Saviour be with you then, my dear sister, my daughter, and I am, entirely in him, your very humble servant.

The good Mother de Chantal, who is ill, but as I hope without danger, salutes you with all her heart. I recommend her to your prayers, and myself also, my dear sister, my daughter. Adieu.

* The sister of the Abbess of Puits d'Orbe (see p. 32) was named Françoise. It seems clear that this letter was written to her. [Tr.]

LETTER III.

TO M. CAMUS, BISHOP OF BELLEY.

On renouncing the office of Bishop.

ANNECY, 14*th August* 1613.

MY LORD—It is only about a month since I received the letter which it pleased you to write me on the second of July; since then I have always been either travelling or ill, and have not been able to send you the answer you desire—or rather the answer you do *not* desire, if I have rightly understood the inclination which you felt when you did me the favour of writing to me. Now you may judge whether I can give your question a very satisfactory answer, since to the ordinary feebleness of my mind the extraordinary of my body, oppressed with the lassitude which the fever has left me, brings a new addition of weakness. But so good an understanding as yours is will see my intention well enough though badly expressed.

* 1st Proposition. To desire to lay down the burden of the episcopate for reasonable causes is not only no sin but is even an act of virtue, either of modesty or humility, or justice, or charity.

2nd Proposition. He is considered to be moved by good reasons to lay down the episcopate who is ready to submit in good faith his opinion of himself, his desire of resigning the episcopal office, and these reasons on which he relies, either to the counsel of a prudent man or at least to the judgment of superiors, and is ready to follow out the one or the other with the same alacrity.

* The remainder of this letter is in Latin. [Tr.]

3rd Proposition. Although the thought or desire of resigning the episcopate in lawful way is not a sin, still such an idea is very often not free from grave temptation, and most frequently arises through the action of the devil: the reason is that during the time spent in procuring relief from the burden, rarely or never are sufficient pains taken to bear it properly; as he who is deliberating about putting away his wife is scarcely anxious about duly loving her meantime. Better would it be then for you to urge yourself to take more pains henceforth, than to want to give up all work because hitherto you have not taken pains enough. Besides it is better to raise our eyes to the mountains whence comes help to us, and to hope in the Lord, gladly rejoicing in our infirmities that the strength of Christ may dwell in us, than like the sons of Ephrem to turn back in the day of battle.* For they who trust in the Lord shall take wings as eagles, they shall fly and fail not, but those who give way shall vanish like smoke; and he who timidly returns to the baggage has rest indeed, but no greater security than he who fights.

4th Proposition. I seem to hear Christ saying †: *Simon, son of John*, or Peter John, *lovest thou me?*—and Peter John answering: *Thou knowest that I love thee:* then at length the Lord strictly commanding: *Feed my sheep.* There is no greater proof of love than the doing of this work. . . .

* Ps. lxxvii. 9.

† John xxi.

LETTER IV.

TO AN ABBESS.

On the excellence of mental prayer, and on the virtues of religious life.

ANNECY, 18*th August* 1614.

MY DEAR SISTER—This first time of writing to you I want to say one or two words of preface, which may serve for all the letters which I shall send you in future as occasion requires. 1. That neither you nor I will make after this any preface; for the love of God which you have will be a preface to you, and my desire to have it will be your preface to me. 2. In virtue of this same love, possessed or desired, assure yourself, my dear sister, that you and all your daughters will always find my soul open and dedicated to the service of yours. 3. But all this without ceremony, without formalities; since, although our vocations are different in rank, this holy love to which we aspire equals us and joins us in itself.

Truly, both you and your daughters are very fortunate to have at last met with the vein of that *living water which springeth up into everlasting life*,* and to desire to drink it at the hand of Our Lord, to whom, with St. Catharine of Genoa and the blessed Mother (St.) Teresa, you seem to me to be making this prayer: *Lord, give me of this water.*

May this divine goodness be for ever praised, who himself has made himself a spring of living water in the midst of your community; for our Lord is a fountain

* John iv. 14.

from which we draw by prayer the water of cleansing, of refreshment, of fertility, and of sweetness.

God knows, my dear sister, what the monasteries are in which this most holy exercise is not practised; God knows what obedience, what poverty, and what chastity are observed there before the eyes of his divine Providence, and whether the communities of daughters are not rather companies of prisoners than true lovers of Jesus Christ.

But we have not so much need to consider that evil, as to weigh at its just weight the great good which souls receive from most holy prayer. You then are not deceived in having embraced it, but deluded are the souls which being able to apply themselves to it do not. And yet in a certain fashion (it seems to me) the sweet Saviour of your soul has deceived you with a deception full of love, in order to draw you to his more particular communications, having tied you by means which himself alone could find, and conducted you by ways which himself alone has known. Lift very high then your heart, to follow his attractions earnestly and holily; and so long as true sweetness and humility of heart reign amongst you fear not to be deceived.

Brother N. is ignorant truly, but ignorant with more knowledge than many wise men: he has the true foundations of the spiritual life, and his society cannot but be helpful to you; I am sure that his superior will not refuse him to you, provided that you make use of him with discretion and without causing him too much distraction.

I have not yet been able to read the little book you sent me; I will do so at my first leisure.

You have done well to make yourself familiar with

the Blessed Mother Teresa, for in truth her books are a treasure of spiritual instruction.

Above all things, let there reign amongst you mutual, sincere, and spiritual love, that perfection of common life so much to be loved and so little loved in this age, even in those monasteries which the world admires; holy simplicity, sweetness of heart, and love of one's own abjection: but this care, my dearest sister, must be diligent and firm, and not eager or by fits and starts.

I shall be very glad to hear news of you often, and do not doubt but that I shall answer. M. N. will let me have your letters safely.

In particular it has been a consolation to me to know the goodness and virtue of your father confessor, who with the spirit of a true father towards you co-operates in your good desires, and is also very glad that others contribute also. Would to God that all the others of your Order were equally charitable and devoted to God's glory; the monasteries which are in their charge would be more perfect and more pure.

I salute again my dear Sisters Anne and Mary Salome, and rejoice that they have entered into this Order at a time when true and perfect piety is beginning to flourish again therein; and for their consolation I tell them that their relative, Madame Descrilles, who is now a novice at the Visitation, also tries hard on her part to make progress in Our Lord.

My dear sister, I write to you without leisure, but not without an extreme affection towards you and all your daughters, all of whom I supplicate to recommend my soul to God's mercy, as on my part I will not cease to wish you blessing upon blessing; and may the source of all blessing live and reign for ever in your hearts. Amen. I am with a most cordial love, your very humble, &c.

LETTER V.

TO THE BISHOP OF BELLEY.

On the evil of lawsuits and on the infringement of ecclesiastical rights.

ANNECY, *22nd August* 1614.

MY LORD—I rejoice, most truly, for your victories; for, whatever one may say, it is to the greater glory of God that our episcopal order should be acknowledged for what it is, and that this moss of exemption should be stripped from the tree of the Church, where one sees it to have done so much harm, as the holy Council of Trent has very well remarked.

But still I regret that your spirit suffers so much in this war, in which, no doubt, scarcely any but angels could preserve their innocence; and he who keeps moderation amid lawsuits, the process of his canonization is already drawn, it seems to me. "To be sage and to be in love is scarcely granted to the gods;" * but I would rather say: "To go to law and not to be out of one's mind is scarcely granted to the Saints." † Nevertheless, when necessity requires and the intention is good, one must embark, under the hope that the same Providence which obliges you to make the voyage will oblige itself to conduct you.

My greatest regret is to see that at last this bitter-

* Sapere et amarę vix diis conceditur.

† Litigare et non insanire vix sanctis conceditur.

ness of heart which you describe to me will take you away from us, and from me will take away one of the most precious consolations that I had, and from that flock an inestimable good; for of devoted prelates there are so few: *Apparent rari nantes in gurgite vasto.** *Save me, O Lord, because there is now no saint.*†

I see clearly, my Lord, by your letter and by that of M. de N., who is in truth very much my friend and singularly good father, that we cannot preserve in foreign countries the ecclesiastical liberties which the Dukes had left us. Oh may God bless France with his great blessing, and make to spring there again the piety which reigned in the time of St. Louis!

But meantime, my Lord, since this poor little clergy of your diocese and mine has the good fortune to have you to speak to the States in its name, we shall be free from all scruple if after our remonstrances we are reduced to servitude; for what more could one do except cry out in the name of the Church: *See, O Lord, and consider, for I am become vile.*‡ What abjection, that, having the spiritual sword in our hand, we must, as simple executors of the will of the temporal magistrate, strike when he orders and stop when he tells us; and that we should be deprived of the chief one of the keys which Our Lord has given us, which is that of judgment, of discernment, and of knowledge in the use of our sword! *The enemy hath put out his hand to all her desirable things: for she hath seen the Gentiles enter into her sanctuary, of whom thou gavest commandment that they should not enter into thy church.*§

* *Æneid*, i. 117. They are seen here and there swimming on the wide waves.

† Ps. xi. 1. ‡ Lam. i. 11. § *Ib.* 10.

It is not in a spirit of impatience or murmuring that I say this. I always remember that *these evils are come upon us because we have sinned, we have acted unjustly.** However, my Lord, you will see our articles, and will do I am sure, all that can be done for the preservation of the rights of God and of his Church; and while our Josue is there, we will keep our hands lifted up, and will pray that he may have a special assistance of the Holy Spirit. We will invoke our angel-protectors, and the holy bishops who have gone before, that they may be round about you, that they may give force to your remonstrances.

There was never question of sending any one to represent my diocese. Is not my diocese yours, since I am so perfectly yours? *My people is your people.*† You will see Father Dom John of St. Malachy at Saint Bernard; if you frequent his company you will find in him a fertile source of piety, of wisdom, of friendship for me, who reciprocally honour him greatly. Tell me some day at leisure the history of Madame Falin, because it is just to announce the glory of the king.‡ May God be for ever the heart of our souls. I am, my Lord, yours, &c.

* Gen. xlii. † Ruth i. 16. ‡ Tobias xii. 7. [?]

LETTER VI.

To Mother Claudine de Blonay, Abbess of the Order of St. Clare.

On having all in common: on the necessity of having extraordinary Confessors: on the advantage of freedom in spiritual communications.

THONON, 12*th September* 1615.

NEVER think, my dear sister, that I can forget your person or the temporal necessities of your monastery; these latter, indeed, I have found even greater than I had been told. Only, I see we must wait till these suspicions of contagion cease before we can profitably make our collection; and meantime I will have the letters got ready. For the rest, my heart, which loves the sanctity of your community, though I have only seen it in passing, and rather had a glimpse than a sight of it, does not permit me to leave without exhorting you in Our Lord to pursue with constancy the execution of the sacred inspiration which God has given you, viz., to make more and more perfect this virtuous company, by a pure and simple abandonment of all private possessing, by the exercise of holy mental prayer, and by a fervent frequenting of the Divine Sacraments.

And do not doubt, my dear sister, that Father Garinus will be favourable to you, if you represent to him, simply and humbly, your praiseworthy intentions; for he is a doctor of great judgment and long experience, and very zealous for the constitutions of the Church, and for working out the decisions of the Council of Trent, as are all good men. You can then tell him with confidence that you have hinted to me a word or two about the state of things with you; for I know well that he will not take this amiss, being, as he is, one of my best friends, and one who well knows that it is not my way to spoil anything, and that I am not an underminer of authority, but a man who causes no disturbance. And you can further tell him all that I have told you, of which, to refresh your memory, I will now make a repetition.

1. The renouncement of all private possessing and the exact community of all things is a point of great perfection, which should be desired in all monasteries and observed wherever superiors so will. For although those religious women, who have not this use in their houses, do not cease to be holy, custom dispensing them, they are all the same in extreme danger of ceasing to be holy, when they oppose the introduction of so holy an observance, so deserving of love and so much recommended by Father Saint Francis and Mother Saint Clare; which makes Orders rich in their poverty and perfectly poor in their riches, since *mine* and *thine* are the two words which, as the Saints say, have ruined charity. Nor is it any use to say *our* veil, *our* dress, *our* tunic or *our* linen, if in fact the use of them is not indifferent and common to all the sisters; words are little if acts do not correspond. And how can a thing be called common which no one uses but myself? Now I have seen in a monastery in which I had a very near relative that all the difficulty of this point lay in the over-niceness of some sisters as regards linen. I wondered that washing was not enough for the daughters of him who tenderly kissed the lepers, and of her who kissed the feet of the sisters when they returned from outside.

Truly when a person is particular about wearing washed linen or cloth because it was worn previously to washing by his Christian brother, I do not see how he dares to say that he loves his brother as himself; and it must be a strong self-love that he has, to make him think himself so clean in comparison with others.

Now the method of putting everything in common is very easy when all is kept together in a box or wardrobe, and a person distributes indifferently to all, according to their necessities, what is wanted; having regard to nothing except necessity and the superior's will. In some congregations they even change the beads and all the little objects of devotion, by lot, at the beginning of each year.

2. As to prayer and frequenting the Sacraments, there is no difficulty, I think, except that for the latter one must get the father Confessor not to be tired of doing the sisters the charity of hearing them in confession when required by the superior.

But there is a point of importance, of which I said a word to you, which you should for the benefit of your family ask from your superiors, and which they cannot in good conscience refuse you; it is that twice or thrice each year they must offer other and extraordinary Confessors (according to the command of the sacred Council of Trent) who must hear the confessions of all the sisters. And the Congregation of Cardinals has declared that if the superiors are negligent in this point the Bishops are to act themselves, and that this must be done several other times in the year if required. And it *is* required when the superior sees that some sisters are very much troubled, and find it very hard or repugnant to confess to the ordinary Confessor—provided that this is not constantly the case, but at times only and without abuse. But as to this last point it would seem unbecoming to ask it, because the directions of the Council suffice for the satisfaction of your congregation.

And you must receive no statements to the contrary, for nothing in this world is done which is not contradicted by petty and captious souls; and from everything, however good it may be, one can draw awkward consequences if one choose to cavil at them. We must stay on what God ordains, and his Church, and on what the Saints teach. Nor may it be said that your Order is exempt from the constitutions of the sacred Council; for besides that the Council is above all the Orders, if there is one Order which should obey the Councils and the Church of Rome it is yours, since Father St. Francis has so often inculcated this.

But, it may be said, it might be that a sister knowing she could have an extraordinary Confessor would keep back her sins till he comes, when if she had no hope of another Confessor she would not keep them back.

It is true that this might happen; but it is also true that a sister who would be so unhappy as to make bad confessions and communions while waiting for the Extraordinary will make no great scruple of making many bad ones while waiting for a change of Confessors or the coming of the superior. And in any case this drawback is not to be compared with the thousands of losses of souls which the fact of never being able to confess save to one only may cause, as experience clearly shows; and at last it is intolerable presumption in any one, whoever he may be, to think that he better understands the spiritual needs of the faithful, and is wiser, than the Council. So you must hold firmly to this point, and not let yourself be led away by considerations belonging to the human spirit.

3. There remains the question of spiritual communications, which also I tell you are very useful if properly made. And to begin with, no one, as I think, can forbid them to you; for as far as I can see in the Rule of St. Francis and St. Clare there is nothing to prevent them; what is said simply prevents any kind of abuse. And I will tell you how they are conducted amongst the daughters of Mother (St.) Teresa, who are in my opinion the most retired of all. Thus then are they made:

The sister who desires a conference says so to her superior; the superior considers whether the person with whom she desires to communicate is the proper kind of person to give her benefit and consolation; and the person, if such, is to be asked to come, and when he arrives the sister who wants to hold communication is taken to the *grille*, the blind remaining on the grille; and then free opportunity is given to communicate, every one retiring to a distance at which they cannot hear the one who is speaking but simply are able to see her. If they find a sister who wants to confer too often with the same person, beyond three times, it is not permitted, unless there is a strong appearance of great fruit, and the persons are beyond suspicion of vanity, are of mature age and practised in virtue.

You have seen, I am sure, what the Blessed Mother Teresa says on the point, and that will suffice to answer all the objections which might be alleged. And never was it the intention of the Saints to deprive souls of such conferences, which are extremely advantageous for many virtues, and are free from danger when properly arranged. This is an important matter, and a subtle temptation; we want to keep the liberty of private possession which is contrary to perfection, and will not accept the liberty of communications which well understood helps us to perfection. We find drawbacks where the Saints find none, and find none where the Saints find so many.

Further, these communications are not to be made in order to learn the different ways of living in a monastery, but to learn to practise better and more perfectly that to which one is bound; and far from injuring the public conferences they serve the better to direct and apply each conference to the particular case.

I had forgotten to say that when the Confessor Extraordinary comes, all the sisters must confess to him, in order that those who require it may not be discovered, and the evil one may not sow a crop of unkind remarks throughout the house. But those who do not want to give their confidence to the Extraordinary can before going to him make their confession to the ordinary one, and afterwards only mention to the Extraordinary some sins already confessed, to serve as matter of absolution.

I have been very long, my dear sister, but I wanted in this to declare my sentiments fully, that you may know them more distinctly. Hold firm with good courage in order to introduce into your house a holy and truly religious liberty of spirit, and to banish therefrom false and superstitious earthly liberty. Bring back these blessed souls to the observance of the holy Councils, and you will be blessed. Our Master Garinus, and all your higher superiors, discreet and reasonable persons, will help you, I do not doubt; as also will your good Confessor, who is a very virtuous and wise religious as I can tell, and one who will readily listen to reason when it is clearly pointed out to him.

I salute you a thousand thousand times in the bowels of the mercy of Our Lord, to whom I beseech you with all your dear and virtuous company, to recommend me continually. Your most humble in Our Lord, &c.

LETTER VII.

TO A BENEDICTINE MONK OF THE ORDER OF FEUILLANTS.

Suggestions as to the method of composing a Summa of Theology.

ANNECY, 15*th November* 1617.

MY REVEREND FATHER—It is the truth that I love your congregation, though with a love unfruitful up to now. May God make it as effective as it is affectionate, and not only at N., but in two or three worthy monasteries of this diocese, we shall see flourish again the sacred piety which the glorious friend of God and Our Lady, St. Bernard, had planted there.

I see indeed in your letter that you are ailing, since you say to me: *He whom thou lovest is sick;* * but still my compassion for you has an extreme sweetness,

* John xi. 3.

inasmuch as this sickness is not to death, but that the works of God may be manifested. For behold, he who loves is sick because he *languishes with love.** And therefore I am very glad to fill the office of *a daughter of Jerusalem,* and will go tell thy Beloved—behold he who loves and whom thou lovest is sick. And do you, my dear Father, in return, implore for me and over me the assistance of which, in these waters, I have so much need. Many waters, many peoples: *Save me, O Lord, for man hath trodden me under foot; and deliver me from many waters.*†

I have seen with an extreme pleasure the design of your *Summa* of Theology, which is, to my taste, well and judiciously done. If you favour me by sending me a section of it I will read it lovingly and tell you my opinion frankly and simply, cost what it may. And to give you some assurance of this at once, I say that my idea is that you should omit, as far as possible, all *methodic* words, which, though they must be used in teaching, are superfluous, if I mistake not, and unseasonable, in writing. What need is there, for example, of: "In this difficulty three questions occur to us: the first question is, *what is predestination?* the second, *to whom does predestination belong?* the third, &c.?" For, since you are extremely methodical, it will be clearly seen that you do these things one after another, without your giving notice beforehand. Similarly: "On this question there are two opinions: the first opinion is, &c." For is it not enough to give the statement of the opinions at once, beginning with a number, in this way:—

1. Scotus, Mayronis, and their followers, &c. 2.

* Cant. v. 8. † Ps. lv., cxliii.

Ocham, Aureolus, and the Nominalists. 3. St. Thomas, however, and St. Bonaventure—and so on.

Then instead of saying: "The three conclusions must now be replied to, of which the first is, &c.," is it not enough to say: "I now then say first, &c.;" 2. "I say;" 3. "I say, &c.?" So again with making prefaces in continuing subjects: "Having treated of God as one, it is proper that we now treat of God as threefold, or of the Trinity, &c.:" this is good for persons who go without method, or who need to make their method known because it is extraordinary or involved. Now this will largely hinder your *Summa* from swelling: it will be all juice and marrow, and according to my idea it will be all the more tasty and agreeable.

I add that there is a large number of questions quite useless except to furnish matter of argument. Certainly there is no great need of knowing "Whether angels are in a place by essence or by operation, whether they move from term to term without traversing intermediate space," and the like: and although I should wish to have nothing forgotten, yet it seems to me that in such questions it should suffice to express clearly your opinion, and to base it on a good foundation, and then at the end or beginning to say simply: "so and so have thought otherwise;" thus leaving more room for enlarging a little more on questions of consequence, in which you must take care to instruct your reader thoroughly.

Further, I know that when you please you have an *affective* style; for I have a lively recollection of your Benjamin at the Sorbonne. I should approve that in the places where it can suitably be done you should expose the arguments for your opinions in that style; as in the question, "Whether the Word would have taken flesh if Adam had not sinned." In either view you can draw out the opinions in the affective style. In that question, "Whether predestination is after the foreseeing of merit," whether one hold the opinion of the holy Fathers who have preceded St. Ambrose, or that of St. Augustine and St. Thomas, or that of others, the arguments can be formed in affective style without amplifying, indeed, rather the contrary; and instead of saying, "The second argument is," simply put the number 2. Again, it is a great ornament to give some good authorities, when they are full and brief; otherwise, a little with a reference.

Well now, my dear Father, what do you think of my heart? Does it not act simply with yours? But still, believe me, I am not so simple that with another I should act like this. I call to mind your meekness, natural, moral, and supernatural; I have my imagination full of your charity which *endureth all things,** and *how you willingly suffer the foolish while you yourself are wise,*† wherefore I speak in my foolishness. May God make you prosper in his holy love. I am in him, unto extremity, my Reverend Father, your, &c.

* 1 Cor. xiii. 7. † 2 Cor. xi. 19.

LETTER VIII.

TO DOM PLACID BAILLY, A BENEDICTINE MONK.

His esteem for Dom Placid's sister: the true spirit of Religious: on bearing the cross.

ANNECY, *12th June* 1618.

MY VERY DEAR FATHER—I can assure you that our dear Sister Frances Gabrielle Bailly, your sister, is as dear to me as if she were mine own, her piety having won me to this, and I praise God that she receives and gives much consolation in the congregation of our dear sisters. Our Mother here loves her entirely, and we see that she is a vessel well purified, empty, open to receive great celestial graces: for hers is an upright soul, a spirit empty and stripped of all the things of this world, which has neither thought nor aim save for its God. Oh how happy she is in this state! For little does passing time import a soul which aspires to eternity, and which only takes notice of perishing moments in order to pass by them into immortal life. Ah! my dear Father, my brother, let us live thus in this little pilgrimage, cheerfully conforming ourselves to those with whom we live, in all that is not sin. I know that your soul is of those whose eyes fail them through strong fixing on the sacred object of their love and saying: *When wilt thou console me?* *

You ask me for some instruction as to beginning a good religious life. Good heavens! my dear Father, I, who was never so much as a good clerk, is it for me to instruct holy Religious? Carry with sweetness and

* Ps. cxviii. 82.

love this your cross, which as I understand is great enough to load you with blessings if you love it.

Some little occupation hinders me from answering as I should like the sweet letter which you have written me. I only say to you that to-day is the day when I was consecrated to God for the service of souls: I solemnise this day every year with the greatest affection I can, consecrating myself anew to my God. Kindle my sacrifice with the ardour of your charity, and believe that I am at once your very humble servant, father and brother, &c.

LETTER IX.

TO A LADY.

Promises two portraits of himself: simple loving affections the best kind of prayer: to follow attractions the secret of prayer.

20th June 1618.

BY this safe opportunity I will tell you, my dear daughter, that our Mother tells the truth; I *am* extremely oppressed not so much with affairs as with hindrances which I cannot get free from. Nevertheless, I would certainly not wish, my dear daughter, that on this account you should abstain from writing to me when you please, for the receipt of your letters unwearies me and much recreates me. Only you must be somewhat good to me in excusing me if I am a little slow in answering; though I can assure you that it will never be but by necessity that I shall delay, for my spirit is pleased indeed to visit yours.

I cannot refuse you anything, my dear daughter; and therefore the two portraits which you desire shall be made. Why have I not desired to preserve the image of our heavenly Father in my soul, and the integrity of its likeness to him! My dearest daughter, you will kindly help me to ask the grace of having it repaired in me.

Your method of prayer is very good; yes, much better than if you made considerations and reasonings in it, since considerations and reasonings are only to excite the affections; so that if it please God to give us affections without reasonings and considerations it is for us a great grace. The secret of secrets in prayer is to follow attractions in simplicity of heart. Take the trouble to read, or to get read to you, if your eyes cannot serve you so far, the seventh Book of the *Treatise on the Love of God*, and you will there find all that it is necessary for you to know of prayer.

I remember very well that one day in confession you told me how you were acting, and I said to you that it was quite right, and that although you were to have a point ready, yet if God drew you to some affections as soon as you were in his presence, you were not to cling to the point but to follow the affection; and the more simple and tranquil it was the better it would be, for so it attaches the spirit so much the more strongly to its object.

But, my dear daughter, having once resolved on this do not occupy yourself, in time of prayer, with wanting to know what you are doing or how you pray; for the best prayer or state of prayer is that which keeps us so well employed in God that we think not of ourselves or of what we are doing. In a word, we must go to it simply, in good faith and artlessly, to be with God, to love him, to unite ourself with him. True love scarcely goes by method.

Remain in peace, my dear daughter, walk faithfully in the way wherein God has placed you; take good care holily to give satisfaction to him to whom he has made your companion; and like a little honey-bee, while you faithfully make the honey of sacred devotion make duly also the wax of your domestic affairs; for if one is sweet to the taste of Our Lord, who being in this world eat butter and honey,* the other also is to his honour, since it serves to make the lighted candles of edification of our neighbour.

May God who has taken you by the hand direct you, my dear daughter, whom I love tenderly; and more than paternally do I love your soul and your heart, which may God deign to make more and more his own. Amen. *Vive Jésus!*

LETTER X.

TO A RELIGIOUS SUPERIOR.

A request in favour of one of his subjects who had been expelled and wished to return.

ANNECY, 13*th July* 1618.

MY REVEREND FATHER—Brother N. came to me in the depth of his affliction, and I am able to say that he was more dead than alive, so extreme was his desolation. And I was reminded of him who did *not extinguish*

* Isa. vii. 15.

the smoking flax, and did *not break the broken reed.** He presented to me his letters of dismissal, ejection, expulsion from the Order, and by his tears easily obtained from me leave to stay some weeks in this diocese, during which I was at Lyons visiting my Lord the Archbishop, at whose house the Reverend Father V. spoke to me. To say what I think, he spoke to me according to my heart, for he recommended to me this poor man, this priest, bound by the vows of religion, that he might be somewhat comforted. After that, I did still more gladly what I wanted to do in charity for this soul.

But, my Reverend Father, it has always been with this reservation, that he should on every occasion respect and honour your Order, and should conduct himself humbly towards all those who belong to it; and on your information I will keep my hand still more firmly upon him as to this as long as he stays in my diocese, for I desire nothing but to give satisfaction to Religious, and particularly to such as yourselves.

But, my Reverend Father, you propose to me the return of this sheep into your fold; I think he would desire nothing better, and particularly if you would please to assure him that you would further his good intention with some gentle advice, and with some moderation of the penance which perhaps your constitutions impose on those who return. And if you take the trouble to acquaint me with your will in this respect, I will co-operate in this good work with all my heart; with which, saluting you very humbly, and wishing you every holy benediction, I remain, my Reverend Father, yours, &c.

* Matt. xii. 20.

LETTER XI.

TO AN ABBESS (APPARENTLY THE ABBESS OF PORT-ROYAL).

Promises of friendship and of help in spiritual matters: it is not necessary to go against our inclinations when they are not sinful.

PARIS, 25*th May* 1619.

MADAME—No, I beg you, never be afraid that you will weary me with your letters; for I tell you in real truth that they will always give me a very great pleasure, as long as God grants me the grace of having my heart in his love, or at least desirous of possessing it. So let this be said once for all. It is doubtless true, my very dear mother, that if I had not come into this city you would hardly have been able to communicate with me as to your spiritual affairs; but since it has pleased heavenly Providence that I should be here, there is no difficulty about employing this opportunity, if you think well.

And by no means think that there comes to my mind the thought that you are seeking in me any personal excellence; for although this kind of thought would be very natural to my wretchedness, still as a fact it does not come to me on these occasions; but on the contrary there is nothing perhaps which is more capable of advancing me towards humility, than to see (with wonder) that so many men and women, servants of God, have so great a confidence in so imperfect a spirit as mine is; and I take great courage on this to become such as I am thought to be, and I hope that God giving me the holy friendship of his children will give me his own most holy friendship, according to his mercy, after he has made me do penance suitable to my evilness. But I am almost wrong in saying all this to you; it is, then, that wicked spirit, who, deprived for ever of sacred love, would hinder us from enjoying the fruits of that which the Holy Spirit wants to subsist between us for this purpose, that in holy mutual communications we may have a means of advancing in his heavenly will.

It is difficult, my very dear sister, to find universal minds, which can equally well discern in all matters, nor is it requisite to have such in order to be well guided: and there seems to me no harm in gathering from several flowers the honey which cannot be found in one alone.

Yes; but, you will tell me, meantime I keep cleverly favouring my inclinations and humours. My dear sister, I do not see that there is great danger in that, since you do not follow your inclinations unless they are approved of; and though you seek favourable judges, still at the same time you cannot do wrong in following their opinions, although desired by you, provided that for the rest you sincerely expose your case and the difficulties which you have. It is enough, my very dear sister, to let oneself be guided by counsels, and it is not so necessary or expedient to desire them to be contrary to our inclinations; we have only to wish them to conform to heavenly law and doctrine. For my part, I think that we ought not to summon bitternesses into our heart as Our Lord did, for we cannot govern them as he did; it is enough that we suffer them patiently. For which reason it is not required that we always go against our inclinations, when they are not bad, but have been examined and found good.

It is no great harm to listen to persons of the world, or to hear about worldly affairs, when it is to make them good; and you must not be punctilious in the examination which you make as to this; for it is a thing morally impossible to keep long at the exact point of moderation. But, my very dear sister, I would not have you fail in prayer, at least for half an hour, unless for pressing occasions, or when bodily infirmity prevents you.

For the rest, I beg you to believe that nothing will hinder me from having the satisfaction of seeing you again except impossibility; and I will take all the leisure you may desire: so true is it that I extremely desire your satisfaction, and that God has given me a singular affection for your heart, which may his divine Majesty crown with his blessings. Then therefore will we talk at will of your conduct, and of all that you will please to propose to me, and I will not excuse myself in anything, except when I shall not have the light required to answer you. Remain then always God's, and in him I will be for ever, my very dear sister, without reserve and with my whole soul, your very humble, &c.

LETTER XII.

TO MÈRE ANGÉLIQUE ARNAULD, ABBESS OF THE BENEDICTINE ABBEY OF PORT-ROYAL.

On peaceful humility, union with Christ, and Holy Communion.

[This celebrated woman, abbess at fourteen, had already at the age of seventeen, despite the strongest opposition, introduced a reform into her own abbey, and was now engaged in the still more difficult work of reforming the abbey of Maubuisson. Unhappily she did not persevere in reforming herself. She was irresistibly attracted and subjugated by the virtues and gentle strength of St. Francis, put herself entirely and sincerely under his direction, and begged leave to quit the Benedictine Order and become a sister of the Visitation. He never encouraged her in this idea, though he permitted her to apply to Rome. Her request was not granted. After the Saint's death she fell under the influence of St. Cyran, and her strong impetuous nature, blinded by personal and family pride, hurried her into the abysses of Jansenism.

The Saint at her request went to preach at Port-Royal, where her sister Agnes was superior in her absence. During his sermon he burst into tears, and being afterwards asked the cause, he said: "It was because God let me know that your house will lose the faith. The only way to preserve it is obedience to the Holy See."

These letters also seem prophetic in their insight into the dangers which beset the path of the poor young abbess, and the means necessary to avoid them.

It is to be noted that the Saint frequently speaks of her soul as if it were one of her religious daughters—"that daughter whom I have recommended to you."]

25th June 1619.

I DO not write to you, my dear daughter, because I have not the leisure this morning; a soul who has to return to the country and came to make her general confession to me unexpectedly, took away the free time that I had. I affectionately salute your dear soul which my wretched one cares for more than I can say, never ceasing to desire it the protection of divine love; and I will certainly see it before my departure, if possible, in order that, knowing it still more particúlarly, I may, God so disposing, serve it on occasion more according to its desire.

Meantime tell that well-beloved daughter whom I have so much recommended to you, and who is so dear to my heart, that I continue to say to her that God wills to draw her to an excellent kind of life, and that therefore she must bless this infinite goodness which has regarded her with his loving eyes ; but at the same time I tell her that the way by which she is to follow this vocation is not extraordinary ; for, my dear daughter, it is a sweet, tranquil and strong humility, and a most humble, strong and tranquil sweetness. Tell her, my dear daughter, that she must in no way think whether she is to be amongst low souls or high ; but let her follow the way I have marked out for her, and repose in God, walking before him in simplicity and humility.

Let her not look whither she is going, but with whom she goes, and I tell her she goes with her King, her Spouse, and her crucified God. Whithersoever she may go she will be blessed. To go with her crucified Spouse is to abase and humble self, to put down self even unto the death of all our passions, and I say unto the death of the cross. But, my dear daughter, note that I turn back to say that this putting down of self must be practised gently, tranquilly, constantly, and not only sweetly but gaily and joyously.

Tell her to communicate without fear, in peace, with humility, to correspond with that Spouse who, to unite himself to us, has annihilated and sweetly lowered himself to become our meat and nourishment—ours, who are the food and meat of worms. O my daughter ! he who communicates according to the spirit of the Spouse annihilates self, and says to our Lord : masticate me, digest me, annihilate me, and convert me into thee.

I find nothing in the world of which we have more possession, or over which we have more dominion, than the food which we annihilate for our conservation; and Our Lord has come to this excess of love, that he has made himself food for us: and we, what should we not do that he may possess us, eat us, chew us, swallow us and swallow us again (*avale et ravale*)—do with us as he will? If any one murmur, take it humbly and lovingly: the murmurs will change into benedictions. For the rest I will speak to you in person.

Take no pains to construct carefully the letters you send me; for I do not seek fine buildings nor the language of angels, but the nest of doves and the language of love. Live all for God, my dear daughter, and often recommend to his goodness the soul of him who, with an invariable affection, is entirely dedicated to yours.

I only thought of writing to salute you, but insensibly I have gone on to write a letter. My brother salutes you very humbly, and I salute our three dear sisters. I salute the little sister, daughter of M. Thonzé, and wish her a happy perseverance.

LETTER XIII.

TO THE SAME.

On courageous humility and on equableness of mind: praise of Dom Sans' Spiritual Exercises: *it is possible to pass a day without venial sin: she is not to practise too many austerities.*

About August 1619.*

THERE shall then no more be *My Lord* with me for you, nor *Madame* for you with me; the old cordial and

* The French says, "Before 12th September 1619." [Tr.]

charitable names of father and daughter are more Christian, more sweet, and of greater force to testify the sacred love which Our Lord has willed to be between us. I say thus boldly *which God has willed between us*, because I feel it strongly, and I believe that this feeling comes from nowhere else. And besides I know that it is profitable to me, and that it encourages me to do better; that is why I will preserve it carefully. Tell you to do the same I will not; for if it please God he will inspire you with it, and I cannot doubt that he will.

So, my dear daughter, then, the truth is that I am at present in such great uncertainty as to the time of my departure, that I dare no longer promise myself the consolation of seeing you again with my mortal eyes: but if I have the leisure I will do so, with great affection; and if I see that this might be an important benefit for your soul I will do all I can to ensure it.

In any case, my dear daughter, remember what I have told you: God has cast his eyes on you to make use of you in matters of consequence, and to draw you to an excellent sort of life. Respect then his election, and follow faithfully his intention. Continually animate your courage with humility, and your humility and desire of being humble animate with confidence in God, so that your courage may be humble and your humility courageous.

Season every part of your conduct, both interior and exterior, with sincerity, sweetness, and cheerfulness, according to the direction of the Apostle *: *Rejoice in the Lord always, again I say rejoice; let your modesty be known to all men.* And if possible be equal in

* Phil. iv. 4, 5.

temper, and let all your actions display the resolution you have made to love constantly the love of God.

This good bearer, whom I love cordially because he is all yours, carries to you the book of Father Dom Sans, General of the Feuillants, in which there is great and profound spiritual doctrine, full of very important maxims. If it were to seem to you that he was leading you out of that holy joyousness which I have so strongly recommended you, believe that this is not his aim, but only to make this joy serious and grave, as also it should be: and when I say grave, I do not say taciturn, nor affected, nor gloomy, nor disdainful, nor haughty, but I mean to say holy and charitable.

The good Father holds an opinion, founded on his virtue and humility, that one cannot pass a day without a venial sin deserving of accusation in confession.* But in this point experience has made me see the contrary; for I have found several souls who when well examined had nothing which I could observe to be a sin, and amongst others the blessed servant of God, Mlle. Acarie. I do not say that perhaps some venial faults did not escape her, but I do say that she could not note them in her examination, nor I in her confession, and that therefore I had reason to make her repeat the accusation of some former fault.

You will not say this to any one, if you please, my dear daughter; for I so highly revere this good Father and all he says that I would not have it known that even in this I do not agree with him. Besides, I do not know how he has treated this point, not having read it in his book which I have not yet seen, but only having heard him say it; and further I am speaking to your heart in confidence.

* Page 131 of fourth edition: "Sur la Confession." [Tr.]

Do not burden yourself with too many vigils and austerities, my dear daughter; for I know well what I am saying in this. But go to the *royal port* of the religious life by the royal road of the love of God and your neighbour, of humility and gentleness.

If ever you write me news of your heart, you have no need to sign your name, nor to mention the place from which you write, nor to speak of yourself, but only of *that daughter whom I have recommended to you.*

I do not know why I write to you thus at large; it is my heart which does not weary of speaking to yours. But I must finish in order to go and take my bath, since I am in the hands of the doctor. May God be for ever in the midst of your heart, my dear daughter, and I am with all mine unchangeably your father and servant.

LETTER XIV.

TO A RELIGIOUS SISTER.

A monastery is a spiritual hospital, where we must suffer what is necessary for the healing of the soul: remedy against the fear of spirits.

9th September 1619.

MY DEAR DAUGHTER—Since I have seen your heart I have loved it, and recommend it to God with all my heart, and beseech you to have care of it. Try, my dear daughter, to keep it in peace by equality of its emotions. I do not say: keep it in peace, but: try to do so; let this be your principal solicitude. And carefully beware of making an occasion of troubling yourself out of this, that you cannot all at once subdue the variety of the movements of your feelings.

Do you know what a monastery is? It is an academy of exact correction, where each soul should learn to let itself be treated, worked and polished, in order that being well smoothed and planed, it may become able to be joined, fixed and glued more exactly to the will of God. To be willing to be corrected is the evident sign of its perfection; for it is the principal fruit of humility, which makes us know that we have need of it.

The monastery is a hospital of spiritual sick who want to be cured, and who to be cured offer themselves to suffer cupping, the lancet, the razor, the syringe, the steel, the fire, and all the bitterness of medicines. And in the beginning of the Church, Religious were called by a name which means healers.* O my daughter! let us be truly that, and take no account of all that self-love will tell you to the contrary; but sweetly, graciously, and lovingly, take this resolution: either to die or to be healed, and as I do not will to die spiritually I will to be healed; and to be healed I will to suffer cure and correction, and to beseech the doctors not to keep back what I ought to suffer in order to be healed.

As to other matters, my dear daughter, I am told that you are afraid of spirits. The sovereign Spirit of our God is everywhere, without whose will and leave no spirit stirs. He who has the fear of this divine Spirit, should fear no other spirit. You are under his wings like a little chicken; what fear you? I, when young, was affected with this imagination, and to free

* Therapeuts.

myself from it I forced myself little by little to go alone, my heart armed with confidence in God, to the places in which my imagination threatened me with fear: and at last I strengthened myself so much that the darkness and solitude of night are delightful to me, on account of this all-presence of God, which we enjoy better in this solitude.

The good Angels are around you like a company of soldiers on guard. *The truth of God shall compass thee with a shield; thou shalt not be afraid of the terror of the night.** This assurance will be gained little by little, in proportion as the grace of God will grow in you; for grace brings forth confidence, and confidence is not confounded.

May God be for ever in the midst of your heart, my dear daughter, to reign therein eternally. I am in him your most humble brother and servant.

LETTER XV.

TO THE ABBESS OF PORT ROYAL.

Encouragement to trust in God: she must moderate her vivacity and quickness of temper: trials are to be expected in the service of God, and to be borne patiently.

PARIS, *12th September* 1619.

I START at last, to-morrow morning, my dear daughter, since such is the will of him whose we are, to whom we live and shall die. Oh may he be praised, this great eternal God, for the mercies which he exercises towards

* Ps. xc. 5.

us! Your consolation consoles my heart, which is so closely united with yours that nothing will ever be received in the one but the other will therein have its part, yea the whole, since in truth they are, as seems to me, in perfect community, and I seem able to use the language of the primitive Church, *one heart and one soul.**

This was written when I received your second letter, but I continue answering the first.

I hope that God will strengthen you more and more: and to the thought or rather the temptation of sadness from the fear that your present fervour and attention will not last, answer once for all that those who trust in God are never confounded, and that as much for the spirit as for the body and for temporals you have *cast your care upon the Lord, and he will nourish you.*† Let us then serve God well to-day; as to the morrow God will provide for it. Each day should bear its own burden. Have no solicitude for to-morrow, for God who reigns to-day will reign to-morrow. If his goodness had thought, or rather known, that you would have had need of a more present assistance than that which I can render you from such a distance, he would have given it you, and he will always give it you, when required to supply the deficiency of mine. Remain in peace, my dear daughter; God works from afar and from close by, and calls distant things to the service of those who serve him, without bringing them near—*absent in body present in spirit*, says the Apostle.‡

I hope that I shall understand clearly what you will tell me of your prayer, in which, however, I do not

* Acts iv. 32. † Ps. liv. 23. ‡ 1 Cor. v. 3.

want you to curiously regard your process and method of making it; for it is enough that you quite simply acquaint me with any important change in it according as you remember after having made it. I approve your writing down things as they occur to send me afterwards as you may think well, not fearing that you will weary me; for you will never weary me.

Beware, my dear daughter, of that word *fool,* and remember the saying of our Lord *: *He who shall say to his brother Raca* (which is a word that means nothing, but only manifests some indignation) shall *be guilty of the council;* that is, there will be deliberation as to how he must be punished. Gradually tame down the vivacity of your spirit to patience, sweetness, and affability, amid the littleness, childishness, and feminine imperfections of the sisters who are tender with themselves, and inclined to be always teasing a mother's ears. Do not glory in the affection of fathers who are on earth and earthly, but in that of the heavenly Father, who has loved you and given his life for you.

Sleep well: little by little you shall return to the six hours, since you desire it. To eat little, work hard, have much worry of mind, and refuse sleep to the body, is to try to get much work out of a horse which is in poor condition without feeding him up.

As to the second letter—ought you not to have been tried in this beginning of higher aims? Well then, there is nothing in this but effects of the Providence of God, who has abandoned this poor creature in order to effect that her sins may be more severely punished, and that by this means she may return to herself and to God from whom it is so long since she

* Matt. v. 22.

departed. I should have wished you not to treat those persons with ridicule or sarcasm, but by a modest simplicity to have edified them by the compassion of which they are worthy, according as our Lord has taught us in his Passion: still, God be praised that the affair has passed with so much edification of other neighbours, according as the good M. du V. writes me.

My dear daughter, I say adieu to you, and conjure your heart to believe that never will mine separate from it: 'tis impossible; what God unites cannot be separated. Keep your heart high uplifted in that eternal Providence, which has named you by your name, and bears you graven in his paternally maternal bosom; and in this greatness of confidence and of courage faithfully practise humility and mildness: Amen. I am yours beyond compare, my dear daughter. Rest in God: Amen. I am starting in some little haste, because the R.* desires that I give her an answer before my return. That which is not God ought to be little in our estimation. May God be your protection: Amen.

LETTER XVI.

To the Same.

On longanimity in the pursuit of perfection: necessity of calming the heart: for himself he desires God's will only: solicitude for some of her Religious and friends.

16th December 1619.

I BEGIN where you finish, my dear and most truly well-beloved daughter; for your last letter of those

* *Reine* (Queen)?

which I have received finishes thus: I think that you know me well. Yes, it is true, without doubt, I know you well, and that you have ever within your heart an invariable resolution of living wholly to God, but also I know that your great natural activity makes you feel many vicissitudes in your impulses.

No, my daughter, I pray you do not believe that the work which we have undertaken to do in you can be so soon done. Cherry-trees soon bear their fruits, because their fruits are only cherries, lasting but a short time; but the palm, the prince of trees, does not bear fruit for a hundred years after it has been planted, it is said. A life of lower level may be gained in a year, but the perfection to which we aspire—oh! my dear daughter, it cannot come till after many years, speaking of the ordinary course.

And say this further to that daughter whom I have so much recommended to you, that in truth I cannot forget her either day or night, my soul incessantly imploring the grace of God for her: and tell her confidently that no, never will I be cast down about her weaknesses and imperfections. Should I not be cruelly unfaithful if I did not look upon her with sweetness amid the efforts which she makes to strengthen herself in gentleness, in humility, in simplicity? Let her continue her efforts faithfully, and I will ceaselessly continue to long and strive for her good and progress. The good father thanks me so kindly for the affection which I bear towards this dear daughter, without considering that it is an affection so precious to me, and so naturalised in my soul, that no one should be more pleased with me for that than he would be for my wishing good to myself.

But tell her, that dear daughter, that in her morning exercise she must put her heart in an attitude of humility, of sweetness, and of tranquillity, and that she must put herself back into it after dinner during grace, and at Vespers, and in the evening, and that during the day she must remember I have told her to do it.

Tell her that I stay here in my diocese, so long as God pleases, and that as nothing can draw me from it save some particular occasion which I shall think to be to the glory of Our Lord, so when this presents itself, I shall have no more difficulty in at once detaching myself from the favours which I receive than before they were given me. I am and will be and wish to be for ever at the mercy of God's Providence, without willing that my will should hold there other place than that of follower. You always know everything, but keep your knowledge to yourself.

I am again invited to go to Paris, and on advantageous conditions. I have said: I will neither go there nor stay here save according to the good pleasure of heaven. This country is my fatherland according to my natural birth; according to my spiritual birth the Church is. Wherever I think I can better serve the latter there I will gladly be, without attaching myself to the former.

No, my daughter, do not leave out your prayer unless for causes which it is almost impossible to control. There is no harm but on the contrary good in treating with our good Angel.

But let us say a word of our dear daughters. Alas! will poor N. also lose the fruit of her vocation? O my God! permit it not. Her poor sister is in great danger, according to what is written to me; and I assure you that my soul is very much afflicted about it; and I should like, if I could, to do much to retain these two sisters for God, who wants them provided they do not resist.

I do not write at present to our dear Sister Catherine of Genoa. I think that the assembly of L. can have done nothing against her, since you say nothing to me about it. Oh no; for God will protect that dear soul, and will not let so fierce a storm come to beat her down. Let her take good heart again and live joyfully.

As to the C. you must not be vexed at the refusal of it; the good which is to come from it is too great to allow no difficulty or contradiction over it. M. will return to himself, no doubt; I could not restrain myself from writing to him at much length, although I do not know him; I thought I ought to do this for the advantage of Our Lord's business.

Remain in peace, my dear daughter, and often pray for my amendment that I may be saved, and that one day we may rejoice in the eternal joy, remembering the attractions with which God has favoured us, and the mutual contentments which he has willed us to have in speaking of him in this world. O my daughter, may he be for ever the sole object of our heart's desires! Amen.

LETTER XVII.

TO THE SAME (THE ABBESS OF PORT ROYAL).

She is not to be discouraged by the inconstancy or rebellions of nature, or even by frequent venial failings if the will remain good: on avoiding affectation, and indiscreet austerities.

About the end of 1619.

I SEE clearly this ant's nest of inclinations which self-love nourishes and pours forth over your heart, my dear daughter, and I am well aware that the nature of your mind, subtle, delicate, and fertile, contributes towards this; but still, my dear daughter, they are only inclinations, and since you feel their importunateness, and your heart complains of them, there is no appearance that they are accepted with any deliberate consent. No, my daughter; your dear soul having conceived the great desire with which God has inspired it of being his alone, do not easily yield to the thought that it gives consent to these contrary movements. Your heart may be shaken with the movement of these passions, but I think that it rarely sins by consenting.

Miserable man that I am, said the great Apostle,* *who shall deliver me from the body of this death?* He felt within him an army composed of his natural humours, aversions, customs, and inclinations, which had conspired his spiritual death; and because he fears them he bears witness that he hates them, and because he hates them he cannot endure them without sorrow, and his sorrow makes him thus exclaim; to which

* Rom. vii. 24.

he himself answers that *the grace of God by Jesus Christ* will defend him, not from the fear, not from the terror, not from the alarm, not from the fight, but from defeat, and will prevent him from being conquered.

My daughter, to be in the world and not feel these movements of the passions are incompatible things. Our glorious St. Bernard says that it is heresy to say we can persevere in one same state here below, inasmuch as the Holy Spirit has said by Job,* speaking of man, that *he never continueth in the same state.* This is in reply to what you say of the levity and inconstancy of your soul; for I believe firmly that that soul is continually agitated by the winds of its passions, and that consequently it is always shaking; but I firmly believe also that the grace of God and the resolution which it has given you remain continually at the pinnacle of your spirit, where the standard of the cross is ever upraised, and where faith, hope, and charity ever loudly proclaim—*Vive Jésus!*

You see, my daughter, these inclinations to pride, vanity, self-love, mingle themselves with everything, and sensibly or insensibly breathe their spirit into almost all our actions; but at the same time they are not the motives of our actions. St. Bernard feeling them tease him one day while he was preaching said: "Depart from me, Satan; I did not begin for thee and I will not end for thee."

One thing only have I to say to you, my dear daughter, on your writing to me that you nourish your pride by little arts in conversations and in letters. In conversation, indeed, affectation sometimes enters so insensibly that one scarcely perceives it at all; but

* † xiv. 2.

still if one does perceive it the style should immediately be altered; but in letters this is certainly a little less, yea much less, to be tolerated; for we see better what we are doing, and if we perceive a notable affectation we must punish the hand that wrote it, making it write another letter in other fashion.

For the rest, my dear daughter, I do not doubt but that amid so great a multitude of turnings and windings of the heart there glide in here and there some venial faults; but still, as they merely pass through, they do not deprive us of the fruit of our resolutions, but only of the sweetness which there would be in not making these failures, did the state of this life permit.

Well now, be just: do not excuse, no, nor accuse your poor soul save after mature consideration, for fear lest if you excuse it without foundation you make it presumptuous, and if you lightly accuse it you dull its spirit and make it low-hearted. Walk simply and you will walk confidently.*

I must yet add on the remaining space of my paper this important word. Do not burden your weak body with any other austerity than that which the rule imposes on you; preserve your bodily strength to serve God with in spiritual exercises, which we are often obliged to give up, when we have indiscreetly overdone that with which the soul has to go through them.

Write to me when you please, without ceremony or fear; do not let respect oppose the love which God wills there should be between us, according to which I am for ever unchangeably your very humble brother and servant, &c.

* Prov. x. 9.

LETTER XVIII.

To the Same.

Sympathy on the death of her father. Importance of exterior observance: the best way to treat thoughts of vanity: on doing everything in a composed manner: the Saint praises her for manifesting her defects: on distractions in prayer.

Annecy, 4*th February* 1620.

O my dear daughter, what can I say to you on this decease? Our good mother of the Visitation has given me the news of it; but at the same time she writes to me that she had seen Madame your mother, and my dear daughter your sister Catherine of Genoa, brave, resolute, and full of courage, and that M. de Belley had received letters from you by which you testified to him your steadiness on this occasion. I did not doubt, my dear daughter, that God had a care of your heart in these occurrences, or that if he wounded it with one hand he applied his balm with the other; he strikes and he heals; *he killeth and maketh alive;** and so long as we can lift up our eyes and look at celestial Providence grief cannot oppress us. It is enough then, my dearest daughter; God and your good Angel having consoled you I no longer try to do so: *your bitterest bitterness is in peace.*† In what measure God draws to himself, one by one, the treasures which our heart had here below, that is, what we love, he draws with them our heart itself, and "since I have no longer a father on earth," said St. Francis, "I will say more

* 1 Kings ii. 6. † Isa. xxxviii. 17.

freely: *Our Father* who art in heaven." Courage, my daughter, all is ours and we are God's.

I have said Mass for this soul, and every day celebrate with a particular memory of it before God. But, my daughter—and our sisters, Catherine of Genoa, Anne and Marie, what are they doing, poor things? They are constant, are they not, for they are our sisters? Of M. d'Andilly and of M. Arnauld, my son, there can be no doubt. Certainly when I remember how M. d'Andilly spoke to me of his little Francis, I am further comforted. The peace of God be ever in our hearts. Amen.

I now answer your two last letters of the 19th November and the 14th December. It is true, I am extraordinarily burdened with affairs, but your letters, my daughter, are not business, they are refreshment and solace to my soul; let this be said once for all.

It is a great thing that exteriorly you are more observant of the rule. God formed first the exterior of man, then *he breathed into him the breath of life*, and this exterior was made into a living soul.* Humiliations, says Our Lord, very often precede and introduce humility; continue in this exterior which is easier, and little by little the interior will accommodate itself thereto.

Ah! yes, my daughter, I see your entanglements in these thoughts of vanity; the fertility, and at the same time subtlety, of your mind lend a hand to these suggestions; but what do you put yourself in trouble about? The birds came down upon the sacrifice of Abraham †: what did he do? With a branch which he kept waving over the holocaust he drove them away.

* Gen. ii. 7. † *Ib.* xv.

My daughter, a simple little pronouncing of some word of the cross will drive away all these thoughts, at anyrate will take away from them all hurtfulness:—O Lord! pardon this daughter of the old Adam, for she knows not what she does. O woman! behold thy father on the cross. You must sing very quietly: *He hath put down the mighty from their seat, and he hath exalted the humble.** I say that these renouncements must be made quite gently, simply, and as if one made them for love, and not from the necessity of the struggle.

Accustom yourself to speak softly and slowly, and to go, I mean walk, quite composedly, to do all that you do gently and quietly, and you will see that in three or four years you will have quite regulated this hasty impetuousness. But carefully remember to act thus gently and speak softly on occasions when the impetuosity is not urging you, and when there is no appearance of danger of it; as for example when going to bed, getting up, sitting down, eating, when you speak with our Sister Marie or Anne, or with our Sister Isabel: in short, everywhere and in everything dispense not yourself from it. Now I know that you will make a thousand slips a day over all this, and that your great natural activity will be always breaking out; but I do not trouble myself about this provided that it is not your will, your deliberation, and that when you perceive these movements you always try to calm them.

Be very careful about what may offend our neighbour, and not to make known what is secret to his disadvantage, and if you do so try to repair the injury as far as you can immediately. These slight move-

* Luke i. 52.

ments of envy are of no importance, yea are useful, since they make you clearly see your self-love, and since you make contrary acts.

But, my daughter, is it not good in this daughter whom I have so often recommended to you, and who in truth is dear to me as my soul, to confess that little trait of self-love? For what is there more delicate than that little aversion, which she describes, to the being called daughter by that poor mother?* (Ask her, I beg you, if she has not also a repugnance to my calling her my daughter, and if she does not want me to call her my mother?) Oh! what effort it has cost her to tell me this little weakness! I do not know indeed, my daughter, how much it costs her, but I would not for anything in the world have it unsaid, since she has hereby practised such profound resignation, and such confidence towards me. She is, however, still more agreeable when she forbids me to say this to the poor mother. O my daughter, tell her that these little communications of her soul to mine enter into a place whence they never go out save by leave of her who puts them there. Besides, my dear daughter, I do not know what this daughter has done to me, but I find such satisfaction that she describes her miseries so naturally to me that more could not be. Tell her now always to write simply to me, and that although when I was there with her she never showed me any of the letters which she wrote to her sisters, now if I were there she would make no difficulty in doing so; for she knows me much better than she did, and well knows that I am not of a mocking turn.

* Madame Arnauld entered Port Royal on the death of her husband. [Tr.]

As to prayer, my dear daughter, I approve your reading a little in your Theotimus, in order to restrain your mind, and your saying to Our Lord from time to time, quite quietly, words contradicting the distractions in which you may perceive yourself to be. But look, do not disturb yourself over these distractions—if I were a Saint, if I were speaking to the Pope, and the like; for they are distractions all the more completely for being very silly; and no other remedy is wanted than quietly to bring back the heart to its object.

I have answered everything, my dear daughter. Ah! salute with some greater tenderness from me the poor dear eldest sister; my heart regards her with pity. I know that it is so much in Our Lord that not even this rude blow has been able to drive away interior peace; but her distress and her fears will have been great. This sister is dear to me in quite an extraordinary degree. May God for ever be our all. Amen. I am in him all yours in a way that Providence alone can make you conceive. The grace, peace, and consolation of the Holy Spirit be with you. Amen.

My brother is still with Madame. May I venture to salute the little brother Simon, and the dear little sister? But my daughter Marie Angélique, without doubt I salute her with all my heart, and the good M. Manceau, and, when you see her, your great friend and my dear sister de la Croix. God be in the midst of your heart. Amen.

LETTER XIX.

TO THE SAME.

Further exhortations to composedness, tranquillity, and patience with herself.

14th May 1620.

IN spite of all that you write to me in three of your letters, my dear daughter, I do not cease to have a great confidence that the daughter whom I have so greatly recommended to you, and whom in truth I love as my own soul, will turn out a great servant of God; for she commits no fault on purpose or on account of any will that she has to follow her perverse, unprofitable, and somewhat rebellious inclinations. This then being so, there is nothing to fear; her natural impetuosity is the cause of all her trouble; for it excites her vivacity, and her vivacity excites her impetuosity. Meantime you will tell her from me that her chief care must be to keep her spirit in modesty, sweetness, and tranquillity, and that just on this account she must tone down her outward actions, her bearing, her gait, her behaviour, the movements of her hands, and, if she please, also to some extent her tongue and her speech, and that she must not be surprised if this is not done in a moment: to train a young horse to his paces, and to make him steady under his saddle and bridle, takes whole years.

But look you, my dear daughter, you are a little too severe with her, this poor daughter: you must not give her so many reproaches, since she is a daughter of good desires. Tell her that all unstable as she may be she must never be disheartened nor be vexed with herself; let her rather regard Our Lord, who from the heights of heaven regards her, as a father does his child when the child as yet quite feeble can hardly take its steps, saying: gently now, my child: and if it tumble he encourages it, saying: he is up again, he is very good, do not cry—then he goes up to it and gives it his hand. If this daughter be a child in humility, and knows well that she is a child, she will not be astonished at a fall; besides she will not fall from a great height.

Ah! my dear daughter, if you knew how much my heart loves this daughter, and with what eyes I regard her from here at every moment, you would take a great care of her, for love of me also, besides what you are to her; for you love me with a love which is strong enough to make you love all that I love.

When the great Apostle recommends to Philemon the poor young man Onesimus, and says to him a thousand such sweet words that they enrapture one with love: "If you love me," he says, "if you have given me a place in your heart, *receive also my bowels*," * —thus styling Onesimus, who had done some injury to Philemon, for which Philemon was angry. O my dear *Philemona*, my daughter I mean, if you love me, if you have received me within your heart, receive therein also my dear daughter *Onesima*, and bear with her, that is, *receive my bowels*, for this daughter is truly that in Our Lord. And if sometimes she gives you pain, bear with her patiently for my sake, but above all for the sake of him who has loved her so much, that to go and rescue her in her nothingness wherein she was, he abased himself unto death and the death of the cross.

* Phil.

And as for you, my dear daughter, how shall you not love God who loves you so greatly? What a mark of his love, my daughter, in this happy decease of that good father, for whom you have so much desired such an end! Certainly, I am in raptures over it. A thousand blessings on your heart, my dear daughter, and on all our dear sisters, and on all that is yours, in you and for you: and then I shall have my good share therein, since I am infinitely yours in Jesus Christ and for Jesus Christ.

LETTER XX.

TO A YOUNG LADY AT PARIS (PROBABLY MLLE. DE FROUVILLE).

[SEE FOLLOWING LETTER.]

The Saint shows her that under her circumstances she cannot safely stay in the world, and exhorts her to enter Religion.

31*st May* 1620.

WELL now, in God's name, my dear daughter, it is true, God wills that you should make use of my soul with an entire confidence, in all that regards the good of yours, which on this account he has made wholly dear and precious to me in his heavenly love.

Behold then, you are out of this troublesome business, my dear daughter, with an entire liberty which the eternal Providence has given you; and since you know it to be so, bless from the very depths of your soul this divine sweetness; and I will bless it with you, destining for this purpose the most holy sacrifices which I will offer upon his holy altars. For, better thank-offering I cannot make to the divine Majesty than to present to him the One for whom and by whom everything is agreeable to him in heaven and on earth.

But now, my daughter, what shall we do with this liberty which we have? We will, without doubt, wholly immolate it to him of whom we hold it; for this resolution is invariable that without any reserve or exception even for a single moment, we will live for him alone, who, to make us live with true life, even willed to die on the cross.

But how?—in what state?—in what condition of life? To stay in the state which you are in would indeed be the easiest in appearance, but in reality the hardest. That world of Paris, or indeed of the whole of France, would not let you live peacefully in this middle state. They would not cease to drive you violently outside the limits of the resolution which you would have taken about it; and to promise yourself a resolution so constant that it could not be shaken, yea overcome, would be to promise yourself a real miracle in this age, with your attractive appearance, among so many subtle advocates and intercessors which the world and its prudence would have with you, who without any pity or cessation would attack, now on one side now on another, your repose; and by dint of importunities, or of deceits or surprises, would at last procure for their aims the victory over your powers. And I well know that I need say no more on this point, since you yourself own that it is true, and know the impossibility. There remains then, as matter for consideration, marriage, or religion.

But, my dear daughter, I have needed no extraordinary penetration to discern which of the two I should counsel you to choose; for, as you clearly describe to me, and as you have already let me know, during the time when I had the benefit of hearing you speak with confidence of your soul to mine, the feeling which you have against marriage comes from two causes, of which even the one would be enough to determine a person not to embrace it—a great aversion, a most entire disgust, a very strong repugnance. O my daughter! that is quite enough, we need say no more about it. Why! those souls which have a particular inclination for marriage, let it be as happy a one as it may, find in it so many occasions of patience and mortification that only with great difficulty do they bear the burden of it. And how would you manage, entering into it wholly against your feelings? Of other difficulties I have a hundred times seen alleviations; of this one never.

The Apostles, as you know, having once heard Our Lord speak of the indissolubility of the marriage tie, said to him: * *Lord, if it be so, it is not good to marry.* And Our Lord, approving their opinion, answered them: *All receive not this word; . . . he that can receive it let him receive it.* My dear daughter, I also, having heard you speak and seen your letter on this subject, speak to you boldly and say to you: without doubt, my daughter, since the case is so it is good for you not to marry; and although all do not understand, that is, do not accept, do not adopt, this saying, do not understand its excellence, do not put it into effect, still you, my dearest daughter, you can easily effect it, you

* Matt. xix.

can easily attain this good, and understand and relish this counsel. Do so then.

Now I say this with still more assurance because I see marriage to be more dangerous in you than in another on account of that ambitious spirit which you describe to me, which would make you continually pant after aggrandisement and incessantly plunge into vanity.

But after taking this resolution without there being any subject for scruple, it is far more difficult to say to yourself next, Enter then into religion. And yet it must perforce be said to you; since neither the customs of France, nor the inclinations of your relatives, nor your age, nor your appearance, would allow you to remain as you are. I say this to you then perforce: My daughter, enter into religion; but in saying it to you I feel a secret sweetness in this force, which makes it not forced but sweet and agreeable. The Angels *pressed* * that good man Lot, and his wife and daughters, *and took his hand* and forcibly *brought him forth and set him without the city,* but Lot finds no violence in this force, indeed he says he well knows *he has found grace with* them. And Our Lord in his parable † commands his servant: *Compel them to come in,* yet not one of them that were compelled said: Let me alone, you hurt me. I am forced and compelled to say to my daughter: Enter into religion, but this compulsion does not distress my heart.

O my daughter! let us speak together in some degree heart to heart. Think you that God always gives the vocation to religion or to perfect devotion

* Gen. xix. † Luke xiv.

according to natural qualities and the inclinations of the souls whom he calls? Certainly not, my daughter, do not be afraid of that. The religious life is not a natural life, it is above nature, and it needs that grace give it and form the soul of this life. It is true that the sovereign Providence many times uses nature for the service of grace, but this is far from being always the case or almost always. He who cried so piteously: * *The good which I will I do not, but the evil which I will not, that is present in me; . . .* that is to say, *there dwelleth not in my flesh that which is good; for to will good is present with me, but to accomplish that which is good I find not . . . unhappy man that I am: who shall deliver me from the body of this death? The grace of God by Jesus Christ;* or *I give thanks to God by Jesus Christ: therefore I myself, with the mind* and in the mind *serve the law of God, but with the flesh,* and in the flesh, *the law of sin*—he, I say, showed clearly that his nature but little served grace, and that his inclinations were but slightly submissive to inspirations: and yet he was one of the most perfect servers of God whom God ever had in this world, and was so blessed at last that he could say with truth: † *I live, now not I, but Christ liveth in me,* after grace had subdued nature, and inspirations had subjected inclinations.

My daughter, these fears of finding superiors indiscreet, and these other apprehensions which you explain to me so faithfully, all this will vanish before the face of Our Lord crucified, whom you will affectionately embrace; your spirit, noble with the world's nobility, will change by force, and will make itself noble with the loftiness of the Angels and Saints. You will see

* Rom. vii. † Gal. ii. 20.

the foolishness of the human understanding and its reasonings, and will laugh it to scorn. You will love *the word of the Cross,** which the pagans have looked upon as *foolishness* and the Jews as a *scandal, but which to us, that is, to those who are saved, is the* supreme *wisdom,* the virtue and power of God.

But, my daughter, there is this very great softening of a counsel which is so absolute and seems so rigorous. You are rich; a twentieth or perhaps a hundredth part of your means would suffice to make you foundress of a monastery, and in that capacity you would have a graceful means of living in a religious manner outside the pressure of the world, whilst waiting for custom, consideration, and inspiration to give the last courage to your heart and the last perfection to your resolution, so as to be altogether a religious. Thus would you finely cheat your nature and artfully entrap your heart. Oh! as Our Saviour lives, to whom I am consecrated, this advice regards your soul only, and has no aim, either to right or to left, but your peace and repose. And meantime pray to God, my dear daughter; humble yourself, direct your life to eternity, elevate your intentions, purify your aims, often think how that a single little increase in the love of God is worthy of great consideration, since it will increase our glory for all eternity. In short, your spirit, and what God has done to have you his, and a thousand considerations, call you to no common Christian generosity. I recommend you to have confidence in the good Mother of the Visitation as in myself, for she will serve you faithfully. And I am, without end and without reserve, your very humble and unchanging servant, &c.

* 1 Cor. i.

LETTER XXI.

TO MLLE. DE FROUVILLE, AT THE VISITATION, PARIS.

[SEE PRECEDING LETTER.]

Congratulations upon her entering Religion : the incomparable advantages of that state : the Saint encourages her to make that sacrifice perfect.

ANNECY, *9th August* 1620.

IT causes an incomparable sweetness to me, my dear daughter, to see the heavenly operation which the Holy Spirit has effected within your heart, in this your strong and generous resolution to withdraw from the world. Oh how wisely you acted according to supernatural wisdom, my dear daughter!—for so was it, in the Gospel of the feast which was being kept, that Our Lady *went with haste into the mountainous country* of Juda.* This promptitude in doing the will of God is a grand means of drawing down great and powerful graces for the following out and accomplishment of every good work; and you see, my dear daughter, that after the violent shock which your heart felt when by main force it stripped itself of its feelings, humours, and inclinations, to follow that superior attraction, you are now here all happy and at rest in the blessed bush which you have chosen, to sing therein for ever the glory of your Saviour and Creator of your soul.

Raise, my dear daughter, often raise your thoughts to that eternal consolation which you will have in Heaven, for having done what you have done; though it is nothing (and I see well that you think it so), it is indeed nothing in comparison with your duty, or with those immortal rewards which God has prepared you.

* Luke i. 39.

For what are all these things which we despise and quit for God? After all, they are but brief little moments of a liberty which is a thousand times worse slavery than slavery itself—perpetual disquiets, aspirations vain, inconstant, incapable of being ever satisfied, which would have agitated our spirits with a thousand useless solicitudes and anxieties, and all this for miserable days, so uncertain, and short, and evil. Nevertheless it has so pleased God, that he who quits these nothings and vain occupations of the moment, gains in exchange a glory of eternal felicity, in which this sole consideration of having willed to love God with all our heart, and having gained a single little degree more of eternal love, will inundate us with joy.

In truth, my dear daughter, I would have carefully forborne from saying to you, trample under foot your feelings, your hesitations, your fears, your aversions, if I had not had confidence in the goodness of the celestial Spouse, that he would give you the strength and courage to take the side of inspiration and reason against that of nature and disliking.

But, my daughter, I must needs say to you—here you are sweetly all dead to the world and the world all dead in you: it is a part of the holocaust. But two parts still remain; the one is to flay the victim, stripping your heart of itself, running the knife under and cutting away all those little imperfections which nature and the world cause you; the other is to burn and reduce to ashes your self love, and wholly convert your dear soul into flames of heavenly love.

But, my daughter truly all dear, this is not done in one day; and he who has done you the grace of making the first stroke, will himself make with you the other two; and because his hand is entirely paternal, either he will do it insensibly, or if he let you feel it, he will give you the constancy, yea gladness, which he gave on the gridiron to the Saint whose feast we keep. Wherefore you must have no fear: He who has given you the will he will give you the accomplishing: * only be faithful over a few things and he will set you over many things.†

You promise me, my dear daughter, that if you are allowed you will write me all the circumstances of your happy retreat; and I promise you that you will be allowed, and that I shall receive this account with an extreme love. May God be for ever blessed, praised and glorified, my dear daughter, and I am in him and for him, most singularly, your very humble, &c.

P.S.—The good Carthusian uncle will be greatly pleased when he knows what you are.

LETTER XXII.

TO FATHER STEPHEN BINET, S.J., AT PARIS.

The Saint explains his course of action with regard to the desire of the Abbess of Port Royal to enter the Visitation.

ANNECY, 11*th November* 1621.

MY REVEREND FATHER—With a thousand thanks for the trouble you have taken to write to me, I say in answer that when at Paris I would never acquiesce in the desire that Madame de Port-Royal manifested to me of withdrawing from the Order in which she had so profitably lived up to that time; and veritably I

* Phil. ii. 13. † Matt. xxv. 21.

brought into this country not so much as a thought of it, but time after time I received by letters very earnest pleadings, with which she excited me to enter into her ideas and approve her wishes.

I temporised as much as I could, and showed myself not only cold, but altogether opposed to her dispositions, until after eighteen months a person of great consideration wrote to me in such a sense that I considered it well not to make myself the sovereign judge on this occasion, but to leave the final decision to the event. I refrained then from giving her advice, and wrote to her that since her heart found no repose in all that I had said to her she might have her petition presented for what she desired; that if His Holiness granted it there would be a very probable appearance that her desire is the will of God, inasmuch as the thing being in itself difficult could not succeed without a special concurrence of the divine favour; that if on the contrary His Holiness refused it, there would no longer be anything left save to humble herself and abase her heart. This, my reverend Father, is as far as I have gone. I clearly saw that this design was extraordinary, but I also saw an extraordinary heart. I saw indeed the inclination of this heart towards commanding; but I saw that it was to conquer this inclination that she wanted to bind herself to obedience. I saw indeed that she was a woman, but I saw she had been more than a woman in commanding and governing, and that she might well be so in obeying properly.

As for the interest of the Visitation, certainly, my reverend Father, I protest before God and your Reverence that I never thought of it, or if I thought it was so little that I have no recollection of doing so. I confess indeed that I have a particular loving affection for the institute of the Visitation; but Madame de Chantal, your dear daughter and mine, will tell you that for it I would not have withdrawn the most excellent and most esteemed creature in the world from her just vocation, even though she might become a canonised Saint in the Visitation. I rejoice when God draws good subjects to it, but I will never employ either word or art, however holy it might be, to attract any one, unless it might be some feeble prayer before God. The inconstancy of woman is to be feared, but one cannot guess, and constancy is in this case equally, and better than equally, to be hoped for.

Oh! my Father, how extraordinarily our ancient friendship makes my soul familiar and effusive with yours! I am running on too much. I let myself go by the advice of others; I will also willingly accommodate myself to the advice of those who will take the pains to examine this affair, but above all your own, which therefore I will very affectionately wait for and very lovingly receive, being ever, my reverend Father, your most humble, &c.

LETTER XXIII.

TO THE ABBESS OF SAINTE CATHERINE.

[This was a Cistercian Abbey near Annecy.]

On certain measures of reform taken somewhat precipitately by some of her daughters.

29th August 1622.

I ANSWER your letter frankly, my very dear cousin, my daughter. It is true that I have long perceived the desires which several of your daughters had for a reform, and as far as my conscience permitted I have told you of it from time to time. But it is also true that I should have wished them to have a little more patience, since we are on the eve of seeing a general order for the reform of all the monasteries of this province this side the Alps, in particular of the monasteries of women, amongst whom little failings are more blamed than great ones among men. But, my dear cousin, the thing has now come out. That there have been some acts of impatience, immortification, disdain, disobedience, self-love, certainly cannot be denied: still for all that the substance of the affair does not cease to be good and according to God's will. All the defects which occur in a good work do not spoil its essential goodness; wherever good comes from we must love it. My inclination was to wait before doing this till the order came from Rome, in order that there might be less resistance. The fervour of the charity of some, or if you like the ardour of the self-will of others, has chosen another means which seemed to them shorter. It must not on this account be rejected, but we must contribute to it all that holy, sincere, and true charity will suggest to us; and we must take care not to let our own interest or self-love use our own prudence contrarily to the will of the heavenly Spouse. But of all this we must talk more at length, God helping.

Madame my dear cousin, my daughter, that this matter was so designed I knew before my departure from this town; that it had come to execution I knew in Argentine; but you were the first to give me information as to particulars, although I have since learnt even more. It matters little whether good be done in one way or in another, provided that it be done in such sort that a greater glory may come to Our Lord from it. I am, madame my dear cousin, your, &c.

LETTER XXIV.

To a Young Lady.

Exhortation to enter the religious life. The marriage at Cana.

I HAVE learnt then, by the mouth of our dear cousin, in how many ways our Lord had tested your heart and tried your steadiness, my dear daughter. Well now, we must holily animate and invigorate ourselves amidst all these storms. Blessed be the wind, whencesoever it come, since it makes us speed to a good port.

These, my dear daughter, are the conditions with which we should give ourselves to God; namely, that he may at once do his will with us, with our affairs and with our plans, and may break and contravene ours, as it shall please him. Oh how happy are they whom God turns as he likes, and leads according to his good pleasure, whether by tribulation or by consolation! But still the true servants of God have always more esteemed the way of adversity, as being more conformed to that of our Head, who would only succeed in our salvation and the glorifying of his own name by the cross and ignominies.

But, my dear daughter, do you realise well in your heart what you write to me, that God by thorny ways conducts you to a state which had been offered to you by easier means? For if you had this knowledge you would extremely cherish this state which God has chosen for you, and would love it so much the more because he has not only chosen it but leads you to it himself, and by a way by which he has conducted all his dearest and greatest servants. Beseech him that this sentiment which he gives you may not die out, but that it may increase to perfect maturity. As for me, I bless your dear soul, which Our Lord wants for himself, and I have for you all the holy love which can be expressed. Our dear cousin is tender in this affection, and has a heart perfectly yours.

This bridegroom of Cana in Galilee makes his marriage feast, and intends to be bridegroom; but he is quite too fortunate, for Our Lord gives him an exchange, and converting the water into very good wine makes himself the Bridegroom and the soul of this poor first bridegroom his spouse. For whether it was St. John the Evangelist or some other, and not on the eve but on the day of marriage, Our Lord carries him off to follow him, draws to himself his chaste soul, and makes him his disciple; and the bride, seeing that this Saviour could have many spouses, would be of the number: and for one sole nuptial banquet, where the wine ran short, behold two excellent ones; for the souls of both one and the other are espoused to Jesus Christ.

It is so that we read that Gospel; and it has come to my heart to say this word to you: blessed are they who thus change their water into wine; but it must be by the agency of the most holy Mother. I beseech her ever to give you her sweet and maternal protection. I am in her your most affectionate servant, &c.

LETTER XXV.

To a Carmelite Superioress.

That the Providence of God is certain to give the means of fulfilling the duties it puts upon her.

My dear Daughter—What a consolation for you that it is God himself who has made you superioress, since you are such by the ordinary ways! Wherefore his Providence is under obligation to you, on account of its being the disposer of things, to hold you with its hand, that you may do well what it calls you to. Be sure of this, my dear daughter; you must walk with good confidence under the guidance of this good God, and not except yourself from that general rule that *God who has begun in you a good work will perfect it,** according to his wisdom, provided that we are faithful and humble.

But, *here now, it is required amongst the dispensers that one be found faithful;*† and I tell you that you will be faithful if you are humble. But shall I be humble? Yes, if you will it. But I will it. You are it then. But I feel distinctly that I am not. So much the better, for this serves to make it more certain. It behoves not to subtilise so much, but to walk simply; and as he has charged you with these souls, charge him with yours, that he may carry it all himself, both you and your charge on you. His heart is large, and he wants yours to have a place there. Rest yourself then on him; and when you commit faults or defects do not distress yourself, but

* Phil. i. 6. † 1 Cor. iv. 2.

after having humbled yourself before God, call to mind that *God's power is made perfect in infirmity.**

In a word, my dear daughter, it is necessary that your humility be courageous and brave in the confidence which you must have in the goodness of him who has put you in office; and to cut right off those many doublings which human prudence under the name of humility is accustomed to make on such occasions, remember that Our Lord does not will us to ask our annual bread, or monthly, or weekly, but daily. Try to do well to-day, without thinking of next day; then next day try to do the same, and not think of all you will do during the whole time of your office; but go from day to day fulfilling your charge, without increasing your solicitude; since your heavenly Father, who has care to-day, will have care to-morrow and after to-morrow, of your guidance, in proportion as, knowing your infirmity, you hope only in his Providence.

It seems to me, my dear daughter, that I act with great confidence indeed in thus speaking to you, as if I did not know that you know all this better than I do: but it matters not, for it makes more impression when a friendly heart says it to us. I am your, &c.

LETTER XXVI.

To a Religious Sister.

He thanks her for a nosegay she had sent him: advice on patience, fidelity, confidence in God and mortification.

May our dear crucified Jesus be for ever a bouquet *between your breasts*,† my dear daughter. Yes, for

* 2 Cor. xii. 9. † 1 Cant. i. 12.

those nails of his are more desirable than carnations, and his thorns than roses. God knows, my daughter, how greatly I desire you to be holy and all sweet-scented with the perfumes of this dear Saviour. This is to thank you for your nosegay, and to assure you that little things are great to me when they come from your heart, to which mine is all devoted, I assure you, my dear daughter.

The Our Father which you say for your headache is not forbidden; but oh! my daughter, no indeed, I should not have the courage to ask Our Saviour by the pains which he had in his head that I should have none in mine. Ah! did he endure that we should not endure? St. Catherine of Sienna, seeing that her Saviour offered her two crowns, the one of gold the other of thorns:—"Oh! I desire the painful one," said she, "for this world, the other shall be for heaven." I would rather use the crowning of Our Lord to obtain a crown of patience around my aching head. Neither is it any harm to eat on the Fridays of Lent nothing which has had life; it savours, however, a little of levity of mind, if done merely on that ground; but if done out of mortification it is good. Live wholly amongst the thorns of the Saviour's crown; and, my daughter, like a nightingale in its bush, sing *Vive Jésus!*

I have obeyed your desire, but you will see that this paper of the book has drunk all that I have written; and I quite think your heart will do the same, for this is the delicious wine of the soul, which holily inebriates and enraptures it.

May this divine and celestial love ever confidently advance; and while observing a loving fidelity and loyalty towards this dear Saviour do not distress yourself about not doing well enough: no, my daughter; but acknowledging your lowness and abjection, cast your spiritual care upon the divine goodness, which accepts our little and poor efforts, if they are made with humility, confidence, and loving fidelity. Now I call that a loving fidelity by which we will, as far as depends on us, to forget nothing of what we should think to be most agreeable to the Beloved, and this because we love his pleasure more than we fear his chastisements.

This our flesh is marvellously disinclined for anything that pricks it, but still the repugnance which you feel does not show any lack of love; for, as I think, if we thought he would love us better flayed we would flay ourselves, not without repugnance but despite repugnance. I should approve that by manner of experiment one should make two or three efforts to overcome oneself, with some little violence, at least now and then; for he who never overrules these repugnances becomes every day more tender of self.

The poor mother of our Visitation is cruelly afflicted with a breaking-out which she has on the mouth; but she rejoices over it, and says that provided she applies her heart to God she finds sweetness in this burning pain. She is a good daughter, and very resigned, and loves you dearly: as so indeed do I, who am all yours in God. My dear daughter, live all in him. Your, &c.

LETTER XXVII.

TO THE ABBESS OF MONTMARTRE, OF THE ORDER OF ST. BENEDICT.

Encouragement and advice on the reformation of her Abbey.

MADAME—I received a double consolation from the letter which you wrote me some months ago; for it testifies to me your good-will, which I greatly desire, and gives me information of the graces which God does to your monastery, which form the dearest news that I can receive, inasmuch as I extremely honour and esteem that house, through a certain inclination which God has given me for it.

I hope that in our days, your sacred mountain will be found spread with flowers worthy of the blood with which it has been watered, and that their perfume will render so many testimonies to the goodness of God that it will be a true Mount of Martyrs.

The favour which the king did you in the octave of your great Apostle, in giving up the nomination, is a good presage of it, and so is the being supported by the favour of those virtuous souls who concur with you in the desire of a complete reformation. I often recommend at the altar this holy design to him who has originated it, and who has given you the affection of embracing it that he may give you the grace of making it perfect. I seem to see the gate open to it: I only beg you, madame (and pardon the simplicity and confidence which I use), that because the gate is narrow and hard to pass, you would take the trouble and the patience to lead all your sisters through it one after the other; for to want them to pass in a flock and a crowd, I do not think it can well be done; some go not so quick as others. You must pay regard to the old ones; they cannot so easily accommodate themselves, they are not flexible; for the nerves of their spirits, like those of their bodies, are already contracted.

The care which you ought to bring to this holy work ought to be a sweet, gracious, compassionate, simple and gentle care. Your age, methinks, and your own disposition require it; for rigour is not becoming in the young. And believe me, madame, the most perfect care is that which approaches nearest to the care which God has of us, which is a care full of tranquillity and quietness, and which in its highest activity has still no emotion, and being only one yet condescends and makes itself all to all things.

Above all, I beseech you, make use of the help of some spiritual persons, of whom you will easily find a choice at Paris, the city being very large. For I will say to you, with the liberty of spirit which I ought to use everywhere: your sex needs to be led, and never did it succeed in any undertaking save by submission; not that it has not very often as much light as the other, but because God has so appointed. I am saying too much about it, madame, since I do not doubt your charity or humility; but I do not say enough about it for the extreme desire which I have of your happiness, to which alone you will please attribute this manner of writing; for I have not been able to restrain my spirit from artlessly presenting to you what this affection suggests to it.

For the rest, madame, doubt not that I am communicating and applying to you many sacrifices which

Our Lord permits me to present to him. I beseech you to exchange them with your prayers and most fervent devotions: you will never give them to one who is with better heart nor more than I, madame, your very humble and very affectionate servant in Jesus Christ, &c.

LETTER XXVIII.

TO A RELIGIOUS SISTER.

Tenderness in devotion is not in our own power: the spiritual nosegay: it is better to use the opportunities which we have than to desire new trials of our fidelity: self-renunciation.

No, my dear daughter, I do not find it at all surprising that you desire my letters; for, besides that God wants it (which is the great point of our mutual intercourse), I feel so much consolation from your communication with me that I easily feel that you gain a little from mine; and we need not wait for any other subject, either you or I, beyond that of a holy spiritual conversation between our souls, and the debt which we owe one another of contributing mutual consolations.

I say nothing, my good daughter, about your heart, and your having no tears; no, my daughter, for the poor heart cannot help it, since this does not arise from a want of resolutions or lively desires to love God, but from a want of sensible feelings, which does not depend on our heart, but on certain conditions which we cannot command. For just as, in this world, my dear daughter, we cannot make it rain when we like, nor prevent it from raining when we do not wish it to rain, so is it not in our power to weep when we will through devotion, nor again not to weep when the impetuous tears well up. The lack of tears does not for the most part arise from our own fault, but from the Providence of God, who wants us to make our way by land and by desert, and not by waters, and who wills that we accustom ourselves to labour and hardship.

Hold your nosegay in your hand; and if haply some sweet and salutary perfume arise from it, do not refrain from gratefully smelling it; for it is only gathered in order not to leave you all day without comfort and spiritual pleasure. Keep yourself quite firm in this disposition of making your heart entirely God's,—for there is no better.

On no account desire persecutions for the trial of your fidelity, for it is better to wait for those which God will send than to desire any; and this your fidelity has a thousand other kinds of exercises, in humility, sweetness, charity, the service of your poor sick one—but a hearty, loving, and earnest service. God gives you a little leisure to make ready your provision of patience and vigour, then the time will come to use them.

Oh my daughter, take off all the garments of your captivity by continual renunciation of your earthly affections; and say not that the King does not give you royal ones to draw you to his holy love. *Vive Jésus!* my dear daughter. This is the interior word under which we must live and die, and with which I protest that I am ever wholly yours.

LETTER XXIX.

To a Religious Sister.

On patience with self and sweetness with our neighbour.

My dear Daughter—I will answer you in a few words, since I know what you would have said to me by your letter almost as if I had heard you speak with the mouth; for still it is that you are ever that same person which you used to describe to me in past years.

To which I answer, first, that you should meekly bear with yourself, humbling yourself much before God, without any vexation or discouragement.

Secondly, you should renew all the purposes which you have previously made of amending yourself; and although you have seen that in spite of all your resolutions you have remained involved in your imperfections, you must not on this account give up undertaking a good amendment, or resting upon the assistance of God: you will be all your life imperfect, and will always have much to correct in it; wherefore you must learn not to get tired in this exercise.

Thirdly, labour to acquire sweetness of heart for your neighbour, considering him as a work of God, and one who will enjoy, if it please the celestial goodness, the Paradise which is prepared for you: and those whom Our Lord bears with we ought tenderly to bear with, cherishing a great compassion for their spiritual infirmities.

Accept willingly this little visit which the divine goodness has made to you. We must be faithful in little occasions to obtain fidelity in great ones.

Remain in great peace, and feed your soul with the sweetness of heavenly love, without which our hearts are without life, and our life without happiness. On no account give way to sadness, the enemy of devotion. For what cause should a servant of him who will be our joy for ever make herself sad? Nothing but sin should sadden and distress us; and to this sorrow for sin it is necessary that holy joy and consolation should be attached. I salute you a thousand times, and am without end, my dear daughter, your, &c.

LETTER XXX.

To a Religious Sister.

Patience and silence during trouble, with the thought of Christ crucified and of eternity.

God then is good to you, my dear daughter, is he not? But to whom is he not good, that sovereign love of hearts? Those who taste him cannot be satisfied with him, and those who draw near to his heart cannot restrain theirs from blessing and praising him for ever.

Keep this holy silence which you tell me of, for truly it is good to be sparing of our words, for God and for his glory. God has held you with his kind hand during your affliction. Well then, my dear daughter, you must always act so. "Alas!" said St. Gregory to an afflicted bishop, "how can our hearts which are henceforth in heaven be disturbed by the accidents of earth?" It is rightly said: the mere sight of our dear Jesus crucified can in a moment soften all our pains, which are but flowers compared with his thorns. And then our grand goal is in that eternity, and compared with this what power can that have with us which ends with time?

Continue, my daughter, to unite yourself more and more with this Saviour; plunge your heart into the depths of the charity of his, and let us always say with all our heart: Let me die and Jesus live! Our death will be happy if it is made in his life. *I live*, says the Apostle;* but he corrects himself: no, *now not I*, but my Jesus *lives in me*.

Blessed may you be, my dear daughter, with the blessing which the divine goodness has prepared for the hearts which abandon themselves as a prey to his holy and sacred love. And courage, dear daughter; God is good to us; if everything be evil to us what should it matter? Live joyously by his side; it is in him that my soul is wholly dedicated to yours. The years pass away, and eternity comes towards us. May we so employ these years in divine love, that we may have eternity in his glory. Amen.

LETTER XXXI.

To a Religious Sister.

On struggling with perseverance against the prevailing faults of impatience and hastiness.

Another time you must keep your heart quite open and have no kind of apprehension; for it will be much more useful to confer mouth to mouth than by writing.

These inclinations which you have are precious

* Gal. ii. 20.

occasions which God gives you of nobly showing your fidelity towards him, by the care which you will have to repress them. Make efficacious prayers and affections contrary to them; and immediately you feel you have gone astray, repair the fault by some contrary action of sweetness, humility, and charity towards the persons whom you have a repugnance to obey, submit to, wish well to, love cordially: for, in a word, since you know on what side your enemies press you the most, you must steady yourself and well fortify and guard yourself there. You must continually lower the head and charge against your customs or inclinations, must recommend this to Our Lord, and in everything and everywhere calm yourself down, scarcely thinking of anything else than the effort after this victory. For my part, I will by Our Lord to give you it and the triumph of his holy Paradise. He will do it, my dear daughter, if you persevere in the pursuit of his holy love, and take care to live humbly before him, amiably towards your neighbour, and sweetly towards yourself. And I will ever be cordially, your, &c.

LETTER XXXII.

To a Religious Sister.

The Saint tells her what nosegay she can give to her guardian angel, her heavenly Valentine or Cavalier: he exhorts her to patience in the difficulty of teaching a self-willed little girl.

You ask me, my dear daughter, what bouquet you can give to your Valentine. It should be made of some little acts of virtue which you should practise expressly for the sake of this heavenly Valentine; and at the end of the morning's meditation you shall offer it to him that he may consecrate it to your dear Beloved. You can also sometimes gather some from the garden of Olives, or from the mount of Calvary —I mean those bouquets of myrrh of your St. Bernard—and beg your heavenly Valentine to receive them from your heart, and to praise God for them, which is as if he spread abroad their perfume; for you can neither smell his divine flowers worthily enough, nor highly enough extol their sweetness.

Again you can ask him, this dear Valentine, that he also would take this bouquet and let you smell it from his hand, and also that he would give you some other in exchange; that he would give you scented gloves, covering your hands with works of charity and humility, and bracelets of coral and chains of pearls. In such way should you have loving tendernesses with these blessed knights of the King of Glory.

I think it was St. Thomas Aquinas that you drew for the month, the greatest Doctor that ever was; he was a virgin, and the sweetest humblest soul that could be conceived.

But let us speak a little of this heart of my dear daughter. If it were in front of an army of enemies would it not do wonders, since the sight and presence of a troublesome and ill-behaved little girl troubles her so greatly? But do not distress yourself, my dear daughter. There is no annoyance so great as the annoyance which is composed of many trifling, but pressing and continual, worries. Our Lord permits us to fail in these little occasions, that we may humble ourselves, and may know that if we have overcome certain great temptations it has not been by our strength, but by the assistance of his divine goodness.

I see well that through these little troubles there are very many chances of exercising the love or acceptance of our own objections. For what will be said of a daughter who has not made this little girl get on, not trained her well nor given her good manners? And then what will our sisters say to see that for the smallest disagreeableness that a creature causes us we get ruffled, we bemoan ourselves, we grumble.

There is no help for it, my dear daughter; St. Athanasius's good woman would have bought this state of things for gold; but my daughter is not so ambitious; she would rather have the occasion removed from her, than try to make good out of it. Well, let us betake ourselves to humility, and for the little time that this exercise will last try to bear it in the presence of God, and to love this poor little thing for the love of him who has so loved her that he has died for her. Do not correct her, if you can help it, in anger; take cheerfully the pain she gives you, and believe me to be, yours entirely, &c.

LETTER XXXIII.

To a Religious Sister.

On patience under a humiliating infirmity.

I ASSURE you, my dear Mother, my daughter, that I would greatly wish to bear in my body and in my heart all the pains which you suffer from your remedies; but as I am unable thus to relieve you, holily embrace these little mortifications, receive these abjections in a spirit of resignation, and, if possible, of indifference. Accommodate your imagination to reason, and your natural feelings to your understanding, and love the will of God in these subjects which are of themselves disagreeable, as if it were in the most agreeable of things. You do not receive your remedies by your choice nor through sensible feeling; you do so then through obedience and by reason:—is there anything so agreeable to our Saviour?

But there is some abjection:—And St. Andrew and so many Saints have suffered the nakedness of the cross. O little cross! thou art dear to me, because neither sense nor nature loves thee, but higher reason alone.

My dear mother, my heart salutes yours filially and more beyond comparison than filially. Be a little sheep, a little dove, all simple, mild and affectionate, without art or second thought. God bless you, my dear mother; may your heart be ever in him and to him. Do not employ your mind in matters of business, and receive humbly and lovingly the little attentions which your infirmity requires. *Vive Jésus et Marie!* I am he whom this same Jesus has made your, &c.

LETTER XXXIV.

To a Religious Sister.

Congratulations on the anniversary of her profession: it is a high point of humility to be humble with those who look down upon us; unceasing efforts to be made against our faults.

YES indeed, my good and dear daughter, let us bless God together for this happy day on which, by a quite new fire, you renewed the holocaust of your heart, offered and vowed henceforth to the divine Majesty; and may this day be therefore counted amongst the memorable days of our life. May it hold the second rank after that of our baptism. Day of the renewal of our interior temple; day in which by a favourable exchange we consecrated our life to God to live no more but in his death; foundation-day, God helping, of our salvation; day the harbinger of the holy and desirable eternity of glory; day whose memory will not only rejoice us at temporal death but also in immortal life. Ah! my dear daughter, truly, methinks, did God then make you to be born again in my interior arms, which certainly embraced you with tenderness, and my heart was quite dedicated to yours.

I well know that you very often have occasion for exercising the love of contempt, of rebuffs, and of your own abjection. Do this indeed; for it is the great point of humility to see, serve, honour and converse with, as opportunity occurs and at proper time (for one must not make oneself troublesome in our attempts) those whom we have an aversion for, and to be humble, submissive, sweet and tranquil amongst them. This is a very admirable point; for you see, my daughter, the humilities which are least seen are the finest. But still for the exterior also I should greatly desire, on account of religious propriety, that you amend yourself of this haughty and unrestrained way of speaking.

It is nothing to feel these movements of anger and impatience, if they are mortified as soon as you see them arise, that is, if you try to put yourself back into restraint and calmness of heart; for thus, although the combat should last all day, it would be practice but not loss for you. Have good courage, my daughter. I clearly see that Our Lord wills to love us and to make us his. I hope in Our Lady that no fire will ever inflame our hearts save that of the holy love of his Son, for whose sake I am in all truth, yours entirely, &c.

LETTER XXXV.

To a Lady on the Point of Entering into Religion.

Consolation in the difficulty which she finds in separating herself from the world: she is to give up worldly delicacies and vanities: his own practice in this respect. On a superstitious practice of curing by words.

What joy, my very dear daughter, did my heart receive to see the frankness and simplicity of your heart at this beginning time. Do not be troubled about these tears; for although they are not good, still they come from a good place. If our resolutions were trifling and liable to be revoked, we should not have these strong feelings in these abnegations or in these high determinations which we have made. David wept those abundant tears over the dead Saul, though he was his greatest enemy; we may weep a little over this world, which is dying, yea, which is dead for us, and to which we mean for ever to die.

O my daughter, my good daughter, how glad I am to see you suffering a little these pains of spiritual child-birth! No, never did any soul bring forth Jesus Christ without pain, save the Blessed Virgin, to whom he gave in exchange great pains as he died. But, my daughter, you will see that after these pangs you will have a thousand sorts of consolations. And as for me, do you not think that my heart grows tender with yours? Indeed yes, I assure you, but with a gentle and sweet tenderness, to see that your pains are a presage of future favours which God will do you if constantly and faithfully you persevere in this enterprise, the worthiest, the most generous, the most useful that you could ever undertake.

Continue then, my dear daughter; keep your heart quite open to me; doubt not of my fidelity; trust in me, without fear, without reserve, without exception: for God who has willed it will keep me with his holy hand, that I may serve you properly.

This same God knows that on your departure he put it into my mind to tell you that you must cut off your musk and your perfumes; but I waited, after his method which is sweet, to leave place for the movements which little by little spiritual exercises are wont to make in souls which consecrate themselves entirely to the divine goodness. For truly my soul extremely loves simplicity; but the knife by which to cut off these useless shoots I generally leave in the hands of God, and here now he is going to use it on you as to these powders, this gilded paper. May his mercy be ever blessed!—for merciful it is, I clearly see.

Yes, give these powders and this gilded paper to some lady of the world, who should however be of such confidence that you can tell her the subject of this little renunciation; and do not be afraid that this may scandalise her. On the contrary, it will edify her soul, since I am presupposing that it is a lady who has a good one. You are right, my dear daughter, in renouncing all this; believe me, these little renunciations are very agreeable to God. And truly, I must tell you this, since I have begun to communicate my soul with simplicity. I have never so much as worn knitted socks,* nor coloured or scented gloves, since I gave myself to God, nor used gilded paper, or powders: these are daintinesses too trifling and vain. Oh! what a heart do you give me towards you, walking so bravely.

Yes indeed, my dear daughter, it is certainly true; these eternal and irrevocable renunciations, these immortal adieux which we have said to the world and to its friendships, cause some grief to our heart; and who would not shrink under the action of this keen-edged knife cutting between, and separating, the soul and the spirit and the flesh's heart from God's heart, and ourselves from ourselves? But thanks be to God the knife has been applied, and it is over: no, never shall there be a rejoining of one with the other, by his grace whom to join ourselves with inseparably we have separated ourselves for ever from all else.

Give up entirely these cures by words: such things are nonsense, which I might permit to a heart less resigned than yours; but to yours, my daughter, I say at once: put away these childish trifles, which if not sins are useless amusements, tending to superstition.

My daughter, as to all these worldly visitors who come to you, receive them with a sweet and cheerful countenance. But in order that you may mutually give news, entertain them as if you came from the other world; for if you talk to them in the language of the parts where they live, it will be no great news to them.

For a month after my consecration to the episcopal office, coming from my general confession and from

* At this time still a luxury in Savoy. [Tr.]

amid the Angels and the Saints, amongst whom I had made my new resolutions, I only talked as a man strange to the world, and it seems to me that this was graceful in me: and although affairs have a little quieted these ebullitions of the heart, yet the resolutions, by God's grace, have remained with me.

Be brief when you cannot do good. May this great God ever strengthen more and more in us the reign of his love! I am in him, but with a quite special affection, yours. If I had the advantage of leisure I would write more, for I do not weary of this sweet conversation on God, on his love of our souls. Earnestly demand of the little new-born Jesus his holy simplicity for your heart, that nakedly and purely it may be his. Your very affectionate father and servant, &c.

BOOK V.

General Instructions to Sisters of the Visitation.

[The following instructions were written down, not by the Saint, but (with the exceptions that will be noted) by the persons to whom they were addressed. Some have been already given in the previous letters, but will profitably be repeated as showing what St. Jane Frances and the first Mothers of the Visitation considered most noteworthy in their saintly Founder's teaching.]

I.

TO MOTHER DE CHANTAL.

What was to be the spirit of her religious life.

I DESIRE you to be extremely little and low in your own eyes, sweet and yielding as a dove; to love your abjection and practise it faithfully. Employ willingly all the opportunities of this which occur. Be not quick in speaking, but answer with slowness, humbly, sweetly, and say much by keeping silent with modesty and equableness.

Support and greatly excuse your neighbour, with great sweetness of heart.

Do not reflect upon the contradictions which happen

to you; do not look at them, but at God in all things, with no exception. Acquiesce in all his orders most simply.

Do all things for God, making or continuing your union by simple turning of your eyes or outflowings of your heart towards him.

Do not agitate yourself over anything; do all things tranquilly in a spirit of repose; for nothing whatsoever lose your interior peace, even if everything should be turned upside down: for what are all the things of this life compared with peace of the heart?

Recommend everything to God, and keep yourself still and reposeful within the bosom of fatherly Providence.

In all sorts of occurrences be faithfully unchanging in this resolution of remaining in a most simple unity and unique simplicity of adherence to God by a love of the eternal care which divine Providence has over you. When you find your spirit outside of this bring it back gently and very simply.

Remain unvaryingly in most simple unity of spirit without ever clothing yourself with any cares, desires affections or designs at all, under whatsoever pretexts.

Our Lord loves you, he would have you all his. Have no longer any arms to carry you but his, nor other bosom to rest in but the bosom of his divine Providence. Direct not your eyes elsewhere, nor let your spirit stay save in him alone.

Keep your will so intimately united to his that there may be nothing between; forget all the rest, troubling yourself about it no more: for God has desired your beauty and simplicity.

Have good courage, and keep yourself very humble,

abased before the divine Majesty; desire nothing but the pure love of Our Lord.

Refuse nothing, painful though it may be; clothe yourself with Our Lord crucified; love him in his sufferings, and make ejaculatory prayers over them.

Do this indeed, my dearest mother, my true daughter: my soul, my spirit blesses you with all its affection; and may Jesus Christ himself do in us, with us, and through us, and for his own sake, his most holy will. Amen.

I have, thanks to God, my eyes fixed on this eternal Providence, whose decrees shall be for ever the laws of my heart.

II.

To the Same.

Questions and answers on the same subject.

[This is the famous "*livret*" so highly esteemed in the Visitation. The translation is made from the actual autographs of the two Saints.]

In the name of Jesus and of Mary.

1. First, you should ask of your very dear lord, if he will approve your renewing in his hands every year, at the renovation time, your vows, your general abandonment, and committing yourself into the arms of God, and if he will specify particularly what he considérs to affect you most closely, so as at last to make this abandonment perfect and without exception, and to enable you truly to say: *I live, now not I, but Christ lives in me.** And

* Gal. ii. 20.

to reach this let your good lord not spare you, nor permit you to make any reserve, either in little or in much, let him appoint the daily exercises and practices required for this, in order that in truth and reality the abandonment may be perfect.

Answer. I answer, in the name of Our Lord and of Our Lady, that it will be good, my very dear daughter, that you should make every year the renewal proposed and freshen again the perfect abandonment of yourself into the hands of God. For this end I will not spare you; and you yourself must cut off superfluous words which refer to the love, even just, of all creatures, and in particular of relatives, house, country, and above all of father, and as far as possible all lengthened thought of all these things, save on the occasions when duty obliges you to order or procure things needed; so that you may perfectly put in practice that word *: *Hearken, O daughter, and see, and incline thy ear: and forget thy people and thy father's house.* Before dinner, before supper, and at night when going to bed, examine whether according to your actions of the present moment, you can sincerely say: *I live, now not I, but Christ lives in me.*

2. Whether the soul, being thus committed, ought not, as far as possible, to forget all things for the continual memory of God, and to repose in him alone by a true and entire confidence?

Answer. Yes, you should forget all that is not of God and for God, and remain entirely at peace under the guidance of God.

3. Whether the soul should not, particularly in prayer, try to stop all kinds of reasoning, effort, reflec-

* Ps. xliv. 11.

tion on self, curiosity and the like, and instead of regarding what she has done, what she will do, or what she does, look at God and so simplify her spirit and empty it of everything, and of all care about herself, remaining in this simple view of God and of her nothingness, quite abandoned to his holy will, in the effects of which she should remain content and tranquil, not disturbing herself at all to make acts either of the understanding or of the will. I say that even in the practice of virtues and in faults and falls there must be no moving from this, it seems to me; for Our Lord puts in the soul the sentiments required and perfectly enlightens it; I mean in everything, and better a thousand times than it could be by all its reasonings and imaginations. You will say to me: why then do you stir from it? O God! it is my misery, and in spite of myself, for experience has taught me that this is very hurtful; but I am not mistress of my spirit, and without my leave it wants to see and manage everything. This is why I ask from my dear lord the help of holy obedience to stop this miserable truant, for it seems to me that it will fear an absolute command.

Answer. Since Our Lord, this long time, has drawn you to this sort of prayer, having made you taste those desirable fruits which spring from it, and made you know the harm of the contrary method, remain firm, and with the greatest quietness you can, bring back your spirit to this unity and simplicity of presence and of abandonment with God. And inasmuch as your spirit desires that I should employ obedience, I say thus to it: My dear spirit, why will you practise the part of Martha in prayer, since God makes you understand that he wants you to exercise that of Mary? I command you then that you simply remain either in God or with God, without trying to do anything there, or seeking from him anything whatever, except in proportion as he inspires you. Do not return at all upon yourself, but be there near him.

4. I come back then to ask of my dear father, whether the soul being thus committed to God ought not to remain quite at repose in its God, leaving to him the care of what regards it, whether interiorly or exteriorly, and remaining as you say in his Providence and will, without care, without attention, without choosing, without any desire save that Our Lord would do in her, with her, and by her, his most holy will, without any hindrance or resistance on her part. O God! who will give me this grace which is the sole one I ask for save you, good Jesus, by the prayers of your servant?

Answer. God be gracious to you, my dear daughter. The infant which is within its mother's arms needs only to let her act and to fasten itself to her neck.

5. Whether Our Lord has not a quite special care to ordain all that is requisite and necessary to the soul thus committed to him?

Answer. Persons in this state are dear to him as the apple of his eye.

6. Whether she should not receive all things from his hand, I say all, down to the very smallest, and also to ask his counsel about all, about all?

Answer. In this God wants us to be as a little child. We have only to take care not to use a superfluous attention when we seek out the will of God in all the particular details of small, ordinary, and trifling actions.

7. Whether it will not be a good exercise to be-

come attentive without laborious attention, to remain tranquilly in the will of God, in the many little occasions which contradict us and tend to put us out of humour (for as to great ones these are seen from afar) —as, to be disappointed of some consolation, which seems to us useful or necessary, to be hindered in doing a good action, a mortification, this or that, whatever it may be, which seems to be good, and instead to be turned aside by things useless and dangerous, and sometimes bad.

Answer. Not consenting to evil things, indifference for the rest should be practised on every occasion, under the leading of God's Providence.

8. To make oneself faithful and prompt in the observance of rules, when the sign is given? Here are so many occasions of little mortifications! We are surprised in the middle of something we are telling, in the midst of some action which it is hard to interrupt; only three strokes more are wanted to finish the work, one letter to make, just to warm oneself—what not?

Answer. Yes, it is good not to attach yourself to anything so much as to the rules, in such sort that, unless for some important occasion, you go where the rules draw you, and make it stronger than all these trifling attractions.

9. To let oneself be absolutely governed as to what regards the body, receiving simply all that is given us or done for us, good, bad, disagreeable; to take what is, according to our judgment, too much, without saying anything or showing any kind of disapprobation; to take the indulgences of sleep, rest, warming oneself, exemption from some painful action or mortification; saying sincerely what one can do, but if they insist giving in

without a word? This point is great and difficult for me.

Answer. You must say sincerely what you feel, but in such a way as not to take away the courage of replying from those who have care of us. For the rest, to make yourself so perfectly tractable is what I very strongly desire of our heart.

10. To yield with great sweetness to the will of the sisters, and of all others, as soon as one knows it, although one can easily avoid it and question it; this is somewhat difficult and tends to leave nothing for oneself. For how often would one desire a little solitude, rest, time to oneself?—but one sees a sister coming shyly along (*qui côtoie*), who would like this quarter of an hour for her, a word, a caress, a visit, anything.

Answer. One must take reasonable time for oneself; and this done take up again the opportunity of gratifying the desires of the sisters.

11. Such is what has come to my mind as to points in which it seems to me that I could exercise and mortify myself. My dearest lord will approve it if he think fit, and will ordain what pleases him, and, my God helping me, I will obey him.

Answer. Do it and you shall live. Amen.

12. I ask for the honour of God help to humble myself. I have the thought to make myself very particular in never saying anything whence there can come to me any sort of glory or esteem.

Answer. Without doubt, he who talks little of himself does extremely well; for whether we speak of self in excusing ourselves or in accusing ourselves, whether in praising or in dispraising ourselves, we shall see that our words serve ever as a bait to vanity. If then some great charity does not draw us to speak of ourselves and of what belongs to us, we ought to keep silent on the subject.

The book of *The Love of God*, my dearest daughter, is made specially for you; for which reason you may, indeed you should, lovingly practise the teachings which you have found there. The grace of God be with your spirit for ever. Amen, Amen.

13. I do not want to forget this, as I have often been in trouble about it. All preachers and good books teach that we should consider and meditate the benefits of Our Lord, his greatness, our redemption, particularly when the Holy Church brings them before us. The soul, however, which is in the above state, desirous to try to do it, is in no manner able, whereby she distresses herself greatly. But still it seems to me that she does it, and in a very excellent manner, namely, by a simple remembrance or very delicate representation of the mystery, with very sweet and delicious affections: my lord will understand better than I can say it. But further, sometimes also one finds oneself dry as to the remembrance of his benefits, or on some occasion, when reasoning is required, as when one would confess or renew one's vows, and contrition is necessary: meantime the soul remains without light, dry and without sentiment; and this causes great pain.

Answer. Let the soul stay on the mysteries in the manner of prayer which Our Lord has given it; for preachers and spiritual books understand it not otherwise. And as for contrition, it is very good when dry and arid; for it is an act of the superior, yea the supreme, part of the soul.

III.

To the Mothers-superior of the first Monastery of the Visitation, Rue St. Antoine, Paris.

On the excellence and duties of their charge.

Since it is the height of Christian perfection to lead souls to God, a work which has drawn Jesus Christ down from heaven to earth in order to labour at this and to consummate his work in death and by the cross, it is easy to judge that those whom he employs in this function ought to esteem themselves to be highly honoured, and to acquit themselves thereof with a care worthy of the spouses of him who was crucified and died as a king of love, crowned with thorns, amid the army of his elect, encouraging them to the spiritual warfare which must be sustained here below, to arrive at the heavenly country promised to his children.

Thus, my dear daughters, those whom God calls to the guiding of souls ought to keep within their mystic hives, where the heavenly bees are gathered together to produce the honey of holy virtues; and the superior, who is amongst them as their queen, should be solicitous to be present there in order to teach them the way to make and store it. But it is necessary to do this work and this holy business with an entire submission to holy Providence, and a spirit of perfect courage, in the continual practice of humility, sweetness and meekness of heart, the two dear virtues which Our Lord recommended to the Apostles who were destined to the superiorship of the universe—drawing from the bosom of the celestial Father the means suitable to this office.

For it is not with your own milk nor from your own breasts that you feed God's children; it is with the milk of the breasts of the divine Beloved, you doing nothing more than showing them and saying: take, suck, draw, live: and he will do your part with you if you do his with him; now his is the sanctification and perfection of souls, for whose sake he has willed not to fly the labour required for glorifying the name of his Father.

Work at this then humbly, simply, and confidently; never will there arise from it any hurtful distraction; for this divine Master who employs you at this work has bound himself to give you his most holy hand in all the duties of your office, provided that you correspond on your side, by a most humble and courageous confidence in his goodness. He calls to his service things that are not as those that are, and makes use of nothingness as of much for the glory of his name. Wherefore you must make your own abjection the chair and the chain of your superiorship, making yourself in your nothingness valiantly humble and humbly valiant in him who made the grand manifestation of his all-mightiness in the humility of his cross.

He has destined you a help, assistance, and grace most sufficient and abundant for your upholding and support. Do you think that so good a Father as God is would want to make you nurse of these daughters without giving you abundance of milk, butter, and honey? The Lord has put these souls into your arms and on your bosom, to make them worthy of being his true spouses, by teaching them to look solely upon his divine eyes, to renounce little by little the thoughts which nature suggests of itself, and so to make them think solely of him. A daughter destined to the government of a monastery is charged with a great and important affair, above all when it is to found and establish. But God extends his almighty arm in the measure of the work which he imposes, and prepares for her great benediction, in order to cultivate and govern the sacred seed-plot.

You are the mothers, the nurses, and the waiting-women of these daughters of the king. What a dignity has this dignity! What a reward, if you do this with the love and the breasts of mothers! It is a crown which you are making, and which you will enjoy in beatitude; but God wants you to carry it entirely within your heart in this life, and then he will put it on your head in the other.

Spouses of old wore on their marriage day only such crowns and garlands of flowers as they had themselves gathered and woven. Mourn not, my dear daughters, the loss of your spiritual advantages or of the particular satisfactions which you would receive in your own devotions, so long as you can cultivate properly these dear plants; be never weary of being mothers, although the toils and cares of maternity are great: for God will reward you in the day of the heavenly nuptials, crowning you with himself, since he is the crown of his Saints.

IV.

To the Same.

Same subject: means to be used.

Since you hold, my dear daughters, the place of God in the guidance of souls, you must be jealously careful to adapt yourselves to it. Observe his ways, and not your own, and carefully second his drawing in each one, by helping them to follow it with humility and submission, not in their own way but in God's; and this you will know better than they so long as self-love is not annihilated in them, for it often causes us to go astray, and to turn the divine drawing to our ways and the pursuit of our inclinations.

For this object always have upon your lips and your tongues the fire which your Beloved, burning with love, came on earth to cast into hearts, to the end that it may consume the whole exterior man and remake it into an interior one, wholly pure, ardent, simple, and strong to bear the trials and exercises which his love will send them for their good, to purify, perfect, and sanctify them. And in order to encourage them to this, show them that it is not with spiritual as with material rose-trees—in the latter the thorns remain and the roses fade, in the former the thorns will pass away and the roses will remain; that they have no hearts save in order to be children of God, loving, blessing, and serving him faithfully in this mortal life; and that he has united them together that they may be extraordinarily brave, hardy, courageous, constant, and eager to undertake and carry through great and difficult works.

For regarding henceforth your houses as the seed-plots of many others, you must root there the great and perfect virtues of a masculine, strong and generous devotion, abnegation of self love, mortification of the senses, and sincere charity; taking from them that petty delicacy and softness which disturb our peace and make us flatter our humours and inclinations. To this will serve the continual changes which are practised in your Order, as of rank, cells, and annual offices; which tend to deliver them from being attached to this or that other employment, and from the imperfection of a vain and jealous imitation, and to strengthen them to desire not to do all that the others do, but only whatever superiors may command them, and to make them walk in that single and simple intention of serving the divine Majesty with one same will, same undertaking, same design, in order that Our Lord and his most holy Mother may thereby be glorified.

But if some were to set themselves against this guidance, you can take occasion to bring them to it by pointing out to them their ignorance, their unreasonableness and lack of judgment in thus giving heed to the fancies and false imaginations which depraved nature suggests; you may tell them how opposed the human spirit is to God, whose secrets are revealed only to the humble; that there is not question in religion of philosophers and clever men but of graces and virtues, and of these not to talk learnedly about them, but humbly to put them in practice; and you must command to them, and make them do things hard to do and understand, and humiliating things, so as to detach them insensibly from themselves, and engage them to a humble and perfect submission to the orders of superiors, who for their part ought to have a great discretion, duly observing time, circumstances, and persons.

For whereas it is a very hard thing to feel oneself crushed and mortified at every turn, yet the skill of a sweet and charitable mother gets the bitter pills swallowed with the milk of a holy friendship, continually offering to her daughters a bosom rich in spiritual fulness, kind looks, and joyful gracious welcomes, that they may run to it with joy, and so may let themselves be moulded like balls of wax, which will without doubt grow soft in the fire of this ardent charity. I do not say that they are to flatter, but that they are to be sweet, amiable, and affable, loving their sisters with a cordial, maternal, fostering, and pastoral love, making themselves all to all, mothers to all, the succour of all, the joy of all; which are the only sufficing conditions, and without which nothing suffices.

Hold the balance justly among your daughters, and let not the gifts of nature make you distribute unfairly your affections and good offices. How many persons are there of disagreeable exterior who are very agreeable in the sight of God! Beauty, gracefulness, the gift of speech, often form a great attraction to persons who still live according to their inclinations; but charity regards true virtue and interior beauty, and spreads itself cordially over all without distinction.

Do not be disturbed to find obstacles arise in your government. You must quietly bear everything, and then lay it before God and take counsel with your assistants; afterwards doing what is thought best, and with a holy confidence that divine Providence will order all things to his glory. But do this so sweetly that your inferiors may not take occasion to lose the respect which is due to your office, nor think that you need them for your governing; in order, also, to follow the rule of modesty and humility, and what is laid down by the Constitutions. Because, you see, we must as far as possible take care that the respect of our inferiors for us does not diminish love nor love diminish respect, and if some sister should not fear you or treat you with sufficient respect, point out to her by herself how that she ought to honour your office and to co-operate with the rest to preserve in dignity the charge which binds all the congregation together in one body and in one spirit.

Hold fast to the strict observance of rules, to the orderliness of your persons and of your houses. Have a great respect paid to sacred places and things. Do not dispute over the more or the less of temporals, since this best befits the sweetness which Our Lord teaches to his children. The Spirit of God is generous; what one would gain by contention would be lost in reputation: and peace is holy merchandise, worthy to be bought at a high price.

Preserve sweetness with equal-mindedness amidst the troubles and multiplicity of affairs. Every one expects from you good example joined to gentleness of charity; because from this virtue, as from the oil of the lamp, the flame of good example rises, and there is nothing which gives so much edification as gentle charity.

Willingly take advice which is not contrary to the design which has been resolved upon, following in all things the spirit of a sweet gentleness, and thinking more of the interior of souls than of the exterior. For, at last, *the beauty of the king's* daughters *is within*,* and this superiors must cultivate, if the daughters do not themselves take this pains, lest they sleep on their way and let their lamps go out through negligence: for it would undoubtedly be said to them as to the foolish virgins who presented themselves to enter the nuptial feast: *I know you not*.† Tell me not that you are weak; charity, which is the nuptial garment, will cover all. Persons who are in this state excite those who know them to lighten their burden, and even cause a particular tenderness of love towards them, provided that they are seen to carry their cross devoutly and in sweetness.

I recommend you to God that you may obtain his sacred grace in your government, in order that entirely according to his will and by your hands he may work upon souls, whether by hammer, chisel, or pencil, to form them all according to his good pleasure; giving you for this end the hearts of fathers, solid, firm, and constant, not without that tenderness of mothers, which makes them desire sweetnesses for their children according to the divine order, which governs everything with a strength all sweet and an all strong sweetness.

* Ps. xliv. 14. † Matt. xxv. 12.

V.

To Mother Joly de la Roche, Superioress at Orleans.

"*Collection of the particular instructions which Monseigneur has given me for my amendment.*"

My judgment is, that it would be extremely useful for you to try to keep your soul in peace and in tranquillity; and for this you must on rising in the morning begin that exercise; doing your actions quite quietly, forecasting in your morning exercise what you have to do, taking pains throughout the day not to let your spirit dissipate itself: continually observe whether you are in this state of tranquillity, and as soon as you see yourself out of it, take great care to put yourself back into it, and this without reasoning or effort.

At the same time I do not mean that your spirit is to be always on the strain after this peace; for all must be done with a simplicity of heart entirely founded on love, keeping yourself with Our Lord as a little child with its father: and when it happens that you commit faults, whatever they may be, ask Our Lord's pardon for them very quietly, saying to him that you are well assured he loves you dearly and will pardon you: and this always simply and sweetly.

This ought to be your continual exercise; for this simplicity of heart will hinder you from thinking distinctly (I say distinctly, because we are not so far masters of our thoughts to be able to have only those we like) of anything but what you have to do or what is marked out for you, and will not let your spirit run off to the willing or desiring other things, and will make all those desires of pleasing and fears of displeasing our mother disappear, till there remain solely the desire of pleasing God, who is and shall be the one object of our soul.

When it happens that you do something which might annoy or disedify the sisters, if it be a matter of grave importance excuse yourself, saying, if true, that you had no bad intention; but if it be a little thing, of no consequence, do not excuse yourself; ever acting with sweetness and tranquillity of spirit in this, as also when you are spoken to about your conduct. And although the inferior part may be excited and disturbed, do not put yourself in trouble about this, but try to keep peace amid war; for perhaps it will never be in your power to escape feeling correction: but you are well aware that such feelings, like any other temptation, do not make us less agreeable to God, provided that we do not consent to them.

You mistake in thinking that you ought to make forcible acts, in order to free yourself from the feelings and troubles of the inferior part: on the contrary, you must take no heed of these, but simply go on your way, not so much as looking at them. If they beset you too closely you must show them some contempt, as it were despising them, and this by a simple look of the superior part; after which you must think no more about them whatever they may say.

And it is the same with thoughts of envy and jealousy, and also with the anxiety you have about your bodily comforts, and the like trifles, which are ordinarily passing through our minds: you must cut off from your soul every care except that of keeping in peace and tranquillity, even the care of your own perfection; for I remark that this too great solicitude about becoming perfect hurts you a good deal; for as soon as you happen to commit some fault you get troubled over it, because it always seems to be against your purpose of making yourself better. In the same way if some fault is pointed out to you you fall into discouragement.

Now all this you must do no more, but must steady yourself on this—not to let yourself be troubled for any cause whatever. Still if you happen to let yourself become so, despite your resolution, even then do not give way to disturbance of mind; but put yourself back into tranquillity as soon as you see where you are, and ever in the same way that I have described, quite simply, without effort or agitation of mind.

And do not think that this is an exercise of some days; oh! no, for it requires much time and much pains to attain this peace. But still it is true that if you can keep faithfully to it, Our Lord will bless your labour. His goodness draws you to this exercise; that is a thing quite certain: and therefore you are seriously obliged to be faithful in it, in order to correspond with his will. It will be hard for you, inasmuch as you have a lively spirit, and one that stops and busies itself over every object which it meets; but the difficulty must not make you fall into discouragement as if unable to reach the object of your strivings. Do quite simply and quietly what you can, not troubling yourself about anything else.

In like manner, when some order which you give is not as well received as you would like, pass on, thinking on what you have to do. Look at Our Lord, and try to go to the God of all things, doing your best to multiply ejaculatory prayers, interior looks, turnings of the heart to God, fervent movements of the spirit towards him; and I assure you that this will be very useful to you.

God wants you wholly and without any reserve, and to the very utmost stripped and denuded of self. Therefore must you take the greatest care to put off your own will; for that only it is which hurts you, as it is very strong in you, and you are strongly attached to the willing of what you do will.

Adopt then this exercise very faithfully, since I tell you this with the charity of God and the knowledge which I have of your need. Which need is that you regard the Providence of God in the contradictions which will be offered to you, God permitting them in order to detach you from all things, to fasten you better to his goodness, and to unite you to himself: for I know that he wants you to be his own, yes, and in a very special manner.

Make yourself therefore quite indifferent as to whether you get what you ask or not, and cease not still to ask with confidence. Remain in indifference as to having or not having spiritual goods: and when you feel that you lack confidence to approach Our Lord, on account of the multitude of your imperfections, then bring into play the superior part of your soul, saying words of confidence and love to him, with the greatest fervour and frequency you can.

Take great care not to distress yourself when you have committed some fault, and not to give way to self-pity, for all this simply comes from pride; but humble yourself promptly before God; and let it be with a sweet and loving humility which may bring you at once to have recourse with confidence to his goodness, making you sure that it will aid you to amend.

I do not want you to be so tender, but like a strong woman to serve God with a good courage, looking at him alone; and therefore when those thoughts, as to whether people like you or not, come into your mind, do not even look at them, assuring yourself that they will always like you as much as God wills. And let this suffice you, that God's will be accomplished in you, who are obliged with a particular obligation to perfect yourself, for God wants to make use of you. Effect it then, and for this purpose try to greatly love your own abjection, which will hinder you from disturbing yourself about your defects.

Take pains to keep your soul in peace and occupied with high things, faithfully diverting it from the attention which you give to yourself, principally when you are put out and when you are discouraged. Occupy yourself in telling Our Lord that you desire to have courage, and that you will never consent to what a troubled spirit may suggest to you: you will do better still to divert your mind from the subject, making it think that you have no trouble, taking no more notice of it than if you did not feel the pressure of this feeling.

The more you think yourself poor and destitute of all sorts of virtues, the stronger purposes you must have to do right. Do not be disturbed about the evil sentiments you may have, strong as they may be; but take care, at such times, to multiply ejaculatory prayers and returns of the soul to God; and as you have a great need of sweetness and humility, take care to put your heart very often during the day in the posture of a humble sweetness.

And when you are reproved or corrected for something, try gently to love the correction, and be not vexed if the inferior part is disturbed; but make the superior part rule, in order that you may do what is wanted from you on the occasion.

Be not so much in love with your peace as, when it is broken by some command or correction or contradiction, to become troubled; for that peace which is not willing to be shaken is an object of self love.

And now I tell you you must have a most particular care to make yourself equable in your humours, never letting any change appear in your exterior. What a pity is it thus to show your imperfections, since this prevents God from being served by you as he desires! This equableness of your exterior behaviour is required for the perfect employment of the talents which God has given you. Often consider then what a sorrow it will be and should be to you, to see that you fail in corresponding with God's will, since he has left it to your efforts to acquire what is to perfect and complete your talent.

Work faithfully for this, join all the forces of your spirit to attain it, and take care that mortification shine out in your exterior, so that seculars may find more reason to observe that than your appearance or good style.

You ought to have a very great care to bend yourself towards the side of humility, since you have so great an inclination to pride and self-esteem. Doubt not that having got this virtue, you will have in the same proportion all those which you need. Abase yourself very often in the abyss of your nothingness before Our Lord and Our Lady. But remember what I said in the conference on humility; as often as it brings not forth that fruit it is indubitably false—abase yourself in the knowledge of your littleness, and at once afterwards raise up your spirit to consider what God wants from you.

VI.

To the Same.

Advice for the Charge of Superioress.

God wants you to serve him in the guidance of souls, since he has disposed things as they are, and has given you the capacity of governing others.

Have a great esteem for the ministry to which you are called; and to fulfil it properly never fail to say daily when you awake, that word which St. Bernard so often said: "Whereto art thou come?" What does God want from thee? Then at once abandon yourself to divine Providence, that it may do with you and in you all it pleases without any reserve.

Have a particular devotion to Our Lady and your good Angel. Then, my daughter, remember that you require more humility to command than to obey. But take care also not to attend so minutely to what you do. Have a right intention to do all for God, and for his honour and glory, and turn yourself away from all that the inferior part of your soul would like to do: let this tease as much as it likes round about your spirit; do not even look at what it is doing or what it wants to say, but keep yourself firm in the superior part of your soul, and in the resolution of willing to do nothing save what is for God, and is agreeable to him.

Further, you must give great attention to that word which I have put in the Constitutions, viz., that the superioress is not so much for the strong as for the weak; though she must have care of all, so that the more advanced may not fall back. Have at heart the support of the imperfect daughters who are in your charge: never show yourself discomposed, whatever sort of temptation or imperfection they may discover to you; but try to give them confidence to tell you entirely all that is troubling them.

Be very tender with regard to those who are more imperfect, to help them to profit by their imperfection. Bear in mind that a very impure soul can attain a perfect purity if well assisted. God having given you both the duty and the power of doing this, by his grace, apply yourself earnestly to do it for his honour and glory. Note that those who have the greatest number of bad inclinations are those who can reach a greater perfection. Avoid having particular affections.

Do not be at all discouraged to find in yourself many very bad inclinations, since by the goodness of God you have a superior will which can overrule all this.

Take great care to maintain your exterior in a holy equableness. And if you have any trouble in your mind, let it not appear outside. Preserve a grave demeanour, being sweet and humble, but never showing levity, particularly with young people.

Such, I think, is what you must pay attention to, in order to give God the service which he has desired from you. But I greatly want you to consider very often the importance of the charge which you hold, not only of being superior, but also of being in the place where you are. The glory of God is concerned here, and also the reputation of your Institute; on which account you must lift high your heart, making it understand the importance of what you are called to.

Annihilate yourself in the very depths of your being, to see that God wills to use your littleness to do him a service of such great importance. Acknowledge yourself to be much honoured by this honour, and go on earnestly to beseech Our Lady to deign to offer you to her Son, as a creature absolutely given up to his divine goodness, resolving that in future you will by means of his grace live a life entirely new, making from henceforth a perfect renewal of your whole soul, detesting for ever your past life, with all its old habits. Proceed then, my dear daughter, full of confidence that after having made this perfect act of holy abandonment of self into the arms of the most holy Virgin, thus consecrating and sacrificing yourself again to the service of her Son's love, she will keep you all the time of your life under her protection, and will present you again to his goodness at the hour of your death.

Then I say to you: speak as little as possible of yourself; and I say this in good earnest, bear it well in mind and pay attention to it. If you are imperfect, humble yourself to the bottom of your heart, and do not talk of it, for that is only pride which inspires you to say much about it, so that people may not find in you as much as you say. Speak little of yourself, I keep saying, little.

Have a great care to preserve your exterior amongst

your daughters in such a medium between gravity and humble sweetness, that they may see that while you love them tenderly you are still the superior; for affability must not hinder the exercise of authority. I entirely approve that superiors should be superiors, making themselves obeyed, provided that modesty and patience be observed.

Keep a holy gravity with seculars; for as you are young you must carefully observe this. Let your laugh be moderate, even with women, with whom you can have a little more affability and cordiality. By this gravity you must not understand that you are to be severe or frowning; for a gracious serenity is always to be observed before young people, even though of ecclesiastical profession. For the most part keep your eyes cast down, and be brief in words with such persons, always taking care to profit their souls by showing forth the perfection of your Institute. I do not say your own but that of your Institute, not in words, save very simply; only praising it in the way that one speaks of oneself, or of one's relatives, that is, briefly and simply.

Praise highly other Orders and forms of Religion, and put your own below others, though you must not conceal that you live in peace, and must say, simply, when occasion presents itself, the good which is going on. Always make much of the Carmelite Sisters, and enter into friendship with them wherever you may be, always testifying that you have a great esteem for them and love them dearly.

Incline much to the Jesuit Fathers, and communicate gladly with them; as also with the Fathers of the Oratory, and the Minims; take counsel with any of these when you have need, and particularly with the Jesuit Fathers.

Do not be at all so reserved as to raising the veil as the Carmelite Sisters are, but still use discretion in this, letting it be seen when you raise it, that you do so to gratify those who speak to you, observing not to go nearer the *grille*, still less to pass your hands through, unless for certain persons of quality who desire it.

As regards prayer, you must take care that the subjects of it be the death, life, and Passion of Our Lord; for it is a very rare thing that we cannot make profit out of the consideration of what Our Lord has done. After all, he is the sovereign Master, whom the Eternal Father has sent into the world to teach us what we ought to do; and therefore, besides the obligation which we have to form ourselves on this divine model, we ought for this reason to be strongly induced to consider his works in order to imitate them, for it is one of the most excellent intentions we can have in all we have to do and do, to do it because Our Lord has done it, that is, to practise the virtues because Our Lord has practised them and as he has practised them. To comprehend this rightly we must faithfully ponder, observe and consider how this thought—because our Father did it in such a way I wish to do it—includes love towards our divine Saviour and most beloved Father; for the child who really loves his good father has a great inclination to conform himself closely to his ways and to imitate him in all he does.

There may, however, be some exceptional souls who cannot dwell upon nor engage their minds with any mystery; they are drawn to a certain gentle simplicity before God, and held in this simplicity, without other consideration save to know that they are before God, and that he is their whole good; and so they remain profitably. That is good: but I think it is clearly enough expressed in the book *On the love of God*, which you can go to if necessary, or to the other books which treat of prayer.

But speaking generally you must make all the sisters, as far as possible, keep in that state and method of prayer which is the most safe; viz., that which tends to the reformation of life and change of manners, which is the prayer that I named at first as being made over the mysteries of the life and death of Our Lord. And credence must not always be given to young sisters just entering religion, when they say they are in this or that lofty state; for very often it is only a delusion and amusement of the fancy. Wherefore they should be put in the same way and the same exercises as the others; for if their prayer is good they will be very glad to be humiliated and to submit themselves to the guidance of those who are in authority over them. There is everything to fear in these kinds of exalted prayer, but one can walk securely in the more common, which is to occupy ourselves with simplicity about our Master, to learn what he wants us to do.

The superioress can on some great and special occasion impose a two or three days' fast on the Community, or, say, only on the stronger members; or the discipline in preference to fasting—for this is a mortification which does not hurt the health, and therefore all can take it, after the fashion which is used here. But you must take care not to introduce austerities into your houses; for this would be to change your Institute, which is principally for the weak.

The superioress should certainly visit the cells of the sisters from time to time to prevent their having anything in private possession, but still this must be done so discreetly that the sisters may have no just reason to think that the superior has any distrust of their fidelity, whether in this or in any other thing: for this discretion must always be observed so as neither to hold them too tight nor leave them too free; and you cannot think how necessary a thing it is to keep in this moderation.

For my part, I should greatly approve that you do nothing but simply follow the community in all things, whether in mortifications or in whatever it may be. It seems to me that it ought to be the principal practice of a superior, this going before her daughters in the simplicity of doing neither more nor less than they do. For this causes her to be greatly loved, and marvellously keeps the spirit of her daughters in peace. I greatly desire that the history of Jacob be ever before your eyes, that you may do like him, who accommodated himself not only to the steps of his children, but even to those of his little lambs.

As to Communion, I should wish you to follow the advice of confessors; when you desire sometimes to communicate beyond your usual practice, take their counsel. You may well communicate once a week oftener than the community, as well as in your turn like the others; and even as to communicating more frequently on exceptional occasions, you must do what those who have care of you think good, for you must let them direct you here. It will be good for you, my dear daughter, to habituate yourself to give a report of yourself every month, or every two or three months if you like, to the extraordinary confessors, or to the ordinary if he is competent, or to such other as you choose; for it is a great advantage to do nothing save by the counsel of others.

I do not think there is any practice to which you should pay more attention than to that of most holy charity towards your neighbour, by sweetly bearing with them and lovingly serving them; but in such sort that you take care always to preserve the authority and gravity of a superior, accompanied with holy humility. When you have decided that something ought to be done, walk securely and fear nothing, regarding God as often as you can. I do not say, be always attentive to God's presence, but multiply as much as ever you can the turning of your spirit to God. "It is this last point which, with all my heart, I have promised my God to practise faithfully, by the help of his grace, having taken Our Lady as protectress of this my resolution." *

VII.

To the Same.

The Saint's last advice to her on her departure from Annecy.

[*Written with his own hand.*]

Go, my very dear daughter; God will be propitious to you. Three virtues are dearly recommended to you: most humble sweetness, most courageous humility, per-

* These words have been put in inverted commas as being apparently the words of Mother Joly de la Roche. [Tr.]

fect confidence in God's Providence; for as to equableness of mind and of outward demeanour, it is not a particular virtue, but the interior and exterior ornament of a spouse of Our Saviour. Live thus then all in God and for God, and may his goodness be ever your repose. Amen.

Act thus, my most dear daughter. May God's be the praise of the trial by which Providence exercises you in sending you this sickness: it will sanctify you, by his holy grace. For as you will never be a spouse of Jesus Christ glorified unless you have first been one of Jesus crucified, you will never enjoy the nuptial joy of his triumphant love unless you have felt the suffering love of the bed of his holy cross.

Meantime you must pray God ever to be your strength and your courage in suffering, as your modesty, sweetness, and humility in his consolations.

VIII.

On the Vocation to a Religious Life.

A good vocation is simply a firm and constant will which the called person has to serve God in the way and in the places that Almighty God has called him to: that is the best mark that one can have to know when a vocation is good. Not that it is necessary that such a soul should do from the beginning all that it must do in its vocation with so great a firmness and constancy as to be exempt from all repugnance, difficulty or disgust, in the matter of its vocation; still less that this firmness and constancy must be such as to make it exempt from committing faults; nor has it to be so firm as never to come to waver or vary in its undertaking to practise the means which may lead it to perfection: since all men are subject to such passions, to change, to vicissitude, and are not to be judged by these different movements and accidents, so long as the will remains firm as to the point of not quitting the good which it has embraced, though it may feel some disrelish and coldness.

So that to have the sign of a good vocation there is not needed a sensible constancy, but an effective one. To know whether God wills one to be a religious man or woman, one is not to wait for him sensibly to speak to us, or to send us an angel from heaven to signify to us his will; nor is there any need to have revelations on the subject. Neither is there need of an examination by ten or twelve doctors of the Sorbonne to try whether the inspiration is good or bad, to be followed or not; but one must properly cultivate and correspond with the first movement, and then not be troubled if disrelish or coldness supervene.

For if one try to keep the will always firmly fixed upon seeking out the good which God shows us, he will not fail to make all turn to his glory. From whatever side the motive of the vocation may come, it is enough to have felt the inclination or movement in the heart to seek after the good to which one is called, and to remain firm and constant in its pursuit, although this may be with repugnance and coldly.

And in this one ought to have a greát care to love souls, and to teach them not to be alarmed at these vicissitudes or changes, and to encourage them to remain firm under them; saying to them that they must not distress themselves about these sensible feelings, nor examine them so much, that they should content themselves with this constant will, which amidst all does not lose its affection for that first design, that they must only be careful to cultivate it well, and to correspond with this first movement, not concerning themselves as to what side it comes from, because our God has many ways of calling his servants to his service, now making use of sermons, now of the reading of good books, now of the vexations, misfortunes, afflictions, and crosses which befall us, now of the world which gives us cause to be angry with it and abandon it—for from all these causes there have come great servants of God. Others again come to religion on account of some natural defect of body, as for being lame, short of an eye, ugly; others are brought to it by their fathers and mothers in order to benefit their other children by this relief: but God often displays the greatness of his clemency and mercy by making use of such intentions, which of themselves are far from good, to make of such persons great servants of his divine Majesty.

In a word, he makes the lame and the blind to enter to his banquet, to show us that two eyes and two legs are not needed for going to Paradise. Many of those who have come into religion in this way have produced great fruit and persevered faithfully in their vocation. Others who have been duly called have, however, not persevered in it, but after having remained some time have given up all. Of whom we have an example in Judas, of whose good vocation we cannot doubt, since Our Lord himself had chosen and called him like the others, and he could not be deceived in choosing him, for he had the discernment of spirits.

It is a certain thing that when God calls any one by prudence and divine Providence he obliges himself to furnish all the helps necessary to make him perfect in his vocation. When he calls any one to Christianity he obliges himself to furnish him with all that is required for being a good Christian. In the same way when he calls any one to be priest, bishop, or religious, he obliges himself at the same time to furnish him all the means required to be perfect in his vocation.

In this, however, we must not think that it is we who obliged him to do this in making ourselves priests or religious, seeing that we could not oblige Our Lord save as he obliges himself for himself, led by his infinite goodness and mercy: so that in making me a religious Our Lord is obliged to furnish me all that I need have to be a good religious, not by obligation but of his infinite mercy and Providence; though the Divine Majesty never fails in care and Providence touching all this.

And to make us believe this the better, he has obliged himself to it in such sort that we must never entertain the opinion that there is any fault of his when we do not succeed well, nor must we think that he does not sometimes give the same helps and succour even to those whom he has not called—so great is his mercy and liberality. But although he gives all the means necessary to become perfect in the vocation to which he calls us, this does not say that he gives them to us all at once, so that those who are called are perfect in the very instant of their entrance into their vocation; for then religious Orders would not be named from hospitals as anciently they were named, or the religious themselves (from the Greek word, Θεραπευται) Therapeuts, which means healers in hospitals, because they healed one another. We must not then think that in entering into Religion one becomes perfect all of a sudden, but that one enters there to tend to perfection.

It is not then the sad deportments, or the tearful faces, or the sighing bosoms which have always the best call; nor those who kiss the Crucifix most frequently, who are never willing to leave the Church, or who are always in the hospitals; nor those again who begin with great fervour. We are not to regard the tears of the tearful, nor the groans of the melancholy, nor the gestures of exterior ceremonies, to know those who are properly called; but we are to look for those who have a firm and constant will to be saved, and who for that end work faithfully to recover spiritual health. Nor must we hold as a mark of a true vocation the fervour which causes persons to be discontented with their actual state, and to flatter themselves with certain desires, which are usually vain though specious, of a greater sanctity of life; for while one is busying oneself to seek out what very often is not one's vocation, one omits what would render us perfect in that which we have embraced.

IX.

On the Reception and Probation of Sisters.

1. *For the state of postulant.*

With regard to the first reception into the monastery in the secular dress, as one cannot know much of the candidates because they all bring a good exterior and show themselves as prompt in words as St. James and St. John to drink the chalice of Our Lord, so one cannot well refuse them. And indeed one must not make too great question about receiving them. All that one can do is to observe their manner, and by conversation with them learn something of their interior.

As to what regards corporal health and bodily infirmities of any kind, little if any consideration is to be made of them, inasmuch as the weakly and infirm can be received in the Visitation as much as the strong and robust; and it is partly made for them, provided that the infirmities are not so bad as to make them altogether incapable of observing the rule and of doing what belongs to their vocation.

2. *For taking the habit, or clothing.*

As regards the receiving them into the habit or novitiate, one must do so with as much more difficulty and consideration as one has had more opportunity of remarking their character, actions, and habits. To be yet sensitive, or hasty, or subject to other passion of the kind, should not be a bar to their admission to the novitiate, provided they have a good will to amend, and to submit to use the medicines and appliances suited to their cure; and even though they have a repugnance to them, or take them with great difficulty, this does not signify, so long as they do not cease to use them; nor again that they are somewhat rough and awkward in their manners, from having been brought up badly and without due training; this, I say, ought not to hinder their reception; for though they may have more trouble and difficulty than others who have a gentler and more tractable nature, yet still if they much desire to be cured and testify a firm will to receive a cure, though at a great cost—to these refuse not your votes notwithstanding their falls; for these persons, after long labour, produce great fruits in Religion and become great servants of God, and acquire a strong and solid virtue: for the grace of God supplies the void, and ordinarily where there is less nature there is more grace.

3. *For profession.*

As regards receiving them to profession there is required a greater consideration. Three things must be observed.

The first, that they be healthy, not in body but in heart and spirit; that is, that they have the heart well disposed to live in an entire docility and submission.

The second, that they have a sensible (*bon*) mind—not of those superior minds which ordinarily are vain and full of self-satisfaction, which in the world were abodes of vanity, and which come to religion not to humble themselves, but as if they came there to give lessons in philosophy and theology, wanting to lead and govern everything. Against these you must be very specially on your guard. But a sensible mind is a medium mind, which is neither too great nor too little; these minds are to be valued, because these spirits always do a good deal, and yet without knowing it; they apply themselves to work, and give their attention to solid virtues; they are tractable, and there is not much difficulty in leading them, for they easily understand.

The third thing to be observed is whether the sister has worked hard during the year of novitiate; if she has well borne and profited by the application of the remedies suitable to cure her infirmity; if she has carried into effect the resolutions which she made on entering Religion, and afterwards in her novitiate, of changing and amending her bad habits, faults of character, and inclinations. If one sees that she perseveres faithfully in her resolution, and that her will remains firm and constant to continue, and if it is observed that she has applied herself to reform and to form herself according to the rules and constitutions, and that this will remains still in her, viz., to desire always to do better, it is the sort of conduct which deserves reception, and even if she fall into grave faults on occasion, and maybe rather often, this should not cause her to be refused.

For although in the year of her novitiate she was to work at the reformation of her manners and habits, that does not say that she must commit no faults, nor that she must be perfect at the end of a year: as the Apostles, although they were called, and had for a long time laboured at the reformation of their life, did not cease committing faults, and this not only in the first year but also in the second and in the third.

X.

TO MOTHER ROSSET.

On her duties as superior (at Bourges).

OUR Blessed Father told me that the arms we must carry with us when we go to any foundation are no others but holy humility; with which virtue he said I must be wholly endowed, because humility is entirely generous, and makes us undertake with an invincible courage all that regards the service of God and the advancement of his glory. And the less ability we feel in ourselves to do it, the more should we clasp and fasten and bind ourselves to Our Lord, trusting and leaning on him alone, on his assistance and on his grace, which his goodness will not fail to give us in order to enable us to do our duty according to his holy will, if we are filled with humility and distrust of self. For it is quite certain that we can do nothing ourselves, but it is also the truth that in God all things are possible to us. We are not *procurators* nor superiors of the talents and gifts which God has placed in us, but only *dispensers* * to distribute them to others, carrying everywhere the spirit of the Visitation, in order to pour it out for our neighbour, trying to polish, purify, and adorn the spirits of those whom Our Lord will commit to our charge, which are very diverse. With them we must practise a great sweetness, simplicity, and long-suffering patience as we watch them journeying at slow pace, and always falling into imperfections: at the same time we must inculcate upon these souls true humility, generosity, sweetness, and charity, which is the true spirit of our rules, in order that by this means they may arrive at the perfection of sacred love, and of union with the divine Majesty, which is the end for which he has called them to Religion.

* Referring to offices exercised in the Visitation. [Tr.]

XI.

TO SISTER CLAUDE-SIMPLICIAN FARDEL.

Description of the true daughter of the Visitation.

[It is the Saint's answer to the question: "My Lord, if you were a sister amongst us, what would you do to be quickly perfect?"]

IT seems to me that with the grace of God I would keep myself so attentive in fulfilling the little and minute observances which are established amongst you, that by this means I would try to gain the heart of God. I would keep the silence well, and also I would sometimes speak, even in time of silence, I mean whenever charity required, but never otherwise. I would speak very gently, and would give particular attention to this because the constitution so orders. I would open and shut doors very quietly, because so our Mother wishes, and we firmly will to do all we know she wants us to do.

I would keep my eyes well cast down, and would walk very tranquilly; for, my dear daughter, God and his angels ever regard us and love extremely those who are living well. If I were employed in anything or had an office given me, I would love it and would try to fulfil it duly; if I were not employed in anything but left alone, I would not give my attention to anything save to be very obedient and dearly to love Our Lord. Oh! methinks I would love him with all my heart, this good God, and would closely apply my spirit to observe well the rules and constitutions. O my daughter, indeed we must do this well, the best we can; for is it not true that we have become religious only for this, you and I? I am indeed very glad that there is a sister here who wants to be a religious for me; and specially glad that it is my Sister Claude-Simplician, for I love her much. So let us then do the best we can; nothing ought to keep us from doing properly what is in our constitutions, for we are able to do it by the grace of God. But we must not be troubled about our faults, for what can we do without the help of our good God? Nothing whatever.

I think also that I would be very cheerful, and that I would never excite myself. That, thank God, I do already; for I never let myself become excited. I would keep myself very little and lowly; I would humble myself and would practise humiliations according to the opportunities I had, and if I were not humiliated I would at least humble myself because I had not been humbled. I would try my best to keep myself in the presence of God, and to do all my actions for his love, for, my daughter, here we are taught to do thus. And what have we to do but that in this world? Nothing at all; we know all that is required if we know this. And now at this present we have to quit ourselves. Let us begin in good earnest, God will help us. If we have good courage we shall do much, God helping.

But do you know this further, my daughter Simplician? I hope that I would gladly allow people to do with me whatever they liked, and I would often read the chapters on humility and on modesty in our constitutions. Yes, my dear daughter, these you must read well.

XII.

TO MOTHER FAVRE.

[This was written down by the Saint himself.]

Method of receiving postulants to the habit.

I WILL second you as well as I possibly can, my dear daughter, in your good intention; though between us there is neither second nor first, but a simple unity. I have thought that perhaps it would be well to-morrow, before going to holy Mass, that you should call all your daughters to you, and then make the two who are going to be received come forward, and in presence of the others should say to them three or four words to this effect:

You have asked us to receive you amongst us, to serve God in the unity of the same spirit and the same will; and, hoping in the divine goodness that you will make yourself greatly devoted to this end, we are about to receive you this morning into the number of our novice sisters, in order afterwards, according to the advancement which you may make in virtue, to receive you to profession at the time we think good. But before going further, think well with yourselves again of the importance of what you undertake, for it would be much better not to enter amongst us than after having entered to give some cause for not being received to profession: but if you have a good will you must hope that God will aid you.

Now, entering amongst us, know that we only receive you to teach you as well as we can, by example and words, to crucify your flesh by the mortification of your senses and appetites, of your passions, humours, and inclinations, and of your own will: in such sort that all this may henceforward be subject to the law of God and to the rules of this congregation.

And to this effect we have committed the labour and particular care of exercising and instructing you to Sister de Brechard here present, to whom therefore you will be obedient, and whom you will hear with such respect and honour that one may know it is not for the creature's sake that you submit yourself to the creature, but for the love of the Creator whom you acknowledge in the creature; and if we should appoint another, whoever she may be, to be your mistress, you must obey her with all humility for the same reason, not looking into the face of her who may govern you, but into the face of God who has so ordained it.

You enter then into this school of our congregation to learn to duly bear the cross of Our Lord by abnegation, self-renunciation, mortification of your senses; and as for me I will love you cordially as your sister, mother, and servant, and all our sisters will hold you as their well-beloved sisters.

Meantime you will have Sister de Brechard as mistress, whom you will obey, following her directions with humility, sincerity, and simplicity, which our Lord requires in all those who join this congregation.

You would quite deceive yourselves if you thought you were come to have greater repose than in the world, for on the contrary we are only assembled here to work diligently in uprooting our evil inclinations, correcting our faults, acquiring virtues. But blessed is the labour which will give us eternal repose.

Now I do not say, my dear daughter, that you must say these words, nor all this, but what you will see fit, less for these candidates themselves than for the edification and stirring up of others.

I should also think it good that after you have received some promise from them that they will conduct themselves well, you should add:

Blessed are those who will give you good example and console you in your undertaking. Amen.

Such is what I have thought of, and you can make use of it as you think fit. Good-night, my dear mother, truly my daughter. *Vive Jésus, et Marie!* Amen.

XIII.

Short Sayings from Various Letters.

1. *The spirit of one Professed.*

I REJOICE that you are now professed. Oh blessed be God for having so greatly loved you!—for I have no doubt that with the grace of Profession he has given you the height of courage, the lively realisation of eternity, the love of sacred humility, and the sweetness of the love of his divine goodness, required for the perfect practice of Profession.

2. *On humility and openness.*

There is no danger in what has happened to you, since you manifest it; but note, my dear daughter, that God has begun his visitations in your soul with the feeling and practice of littleness, lowness, and humility, in order to sanction the advice which is given you, to bring yourself down to this state, and to be truly a little child. I say in every way little, in your own eyes, in exercises, in obedience, simplicity and abjection of yourself; little and a true infant, which hides neither its good nor its bad from its father, its mother, its nurse.

3. *On the same.*

My dear daughter, dwell in this, and love this holy simplicity, humility and abjection, which the divine Wisdom has so highly esteemed, that It has left for a time the exercising of Its royalty, to practise that of poverty and abasement of self, even to that desired supreme degree of the cross, where the Mother of Wisdom having imbibed this affection has spread it thereafter in the heart of all her true daughters and servants.

4. *A perfect life.*

Serve God with a great courage and as far as ever you can by the exercises of your vocation. Love all your neighbours, but particularly those whom God wishes you to love the most. Bow yourself down to the acts whose outside seems less worthy, when you know that God wills it; for in whatever way the holy will of God is done, whether by high or by low deeds, it matters not. Often sigh after the union of your will with that of Our Lord. Have patience with yourself in your imperfections. Do not make yourself anxious, and do not multiply desires for actions which are impossible to you. My dear Sister, walk on uninterruptedly and very quietly; if our good God makes you run, he will enlarge your heart: but on our part let us stay at this one lesson: *Learn of me, because I am meek and humble of heart.**

5. *On prayer.*

My dear daughter, if you relish your point in prayer, it is a sign that God wishes you to follow this method, at least at the time. If, however, God draws us, at the beginning of prayer, to the simplicity of his presence, and we find ourselves engaged therein, let us not quit it to return to our point, it being a general rule that we must always follow his drawings, and let ourselves go whither his spirit leads us. The effervescence and violent expansions of the heart cannot always be avoided, but when one perceives their approach it is good to lessen these movements and calm them, by relaxing a little our attention and yearnings; forasmuch as prayer is the more fruitful the more calm, simple, and delicate it is, that is, the more wholly it takes place in the supreme point of the spirit.

6. *On the same.*

My dear cousin, my daughter, you must not lose courage; for you ought to be so much in love with God that even though you may be unable to do anything before him or in his presence, you will not be any less glad to place yourself there, simply to see and regard him sometimes. And some little time before

* Matt. xi. 29.

going to prayer, put your heart in peace and repose, and conceive a hope of doing well; for if you go to it without hope, and already disgusted, you will have a difficulty to excite your appetite again. . . . When your heart is wandering and distracted, bring it back quietly to its point, restore it tenderly to its Master's side; and if you did nothing the whole of your hour but bring back your heart patiently and put it near Our Lord again, and every time you put it back it turned away again, your hour would be well employed, and you would perform an exercise very agreeable to your dear spouse, to whom I recommend you with the same heart with which I am all yours.

7. *On the great virtues.*

You tell me, my dear daughter, that in your house is made particular profession of evenness of mind. For God's sake, I implore you, try to thoroughly establish this spirit throughout, with that of sweetness and real humility. I regard henceforth your house as a seed-plot of many others; wherefore you must aim at rooting therein the great and perfect virtues of abnegation of self-love, love of one's own abjection, mortification of natural humours, sincere charity—that Our Lord and his most holy Mother may be glorified in us and by us.

8. *On the divine office.*

You do well to give your honoured brother all the satisfaction you can, since he shows you so much love. And since he desires it, you are right in occupying yourself all day in work, but as for putting off your

Vespers until you retire at night after supper, my dear niece, I do not advise you this. Not that it is any great sin, for it is at most only venial, but because it will be of more edification to all your community and more benefit to your soul if you retire for half-an-hour before supper to say your Vespers, letting it be seen that this is your dear labour, and well-beloved business.

9. *On bearing with our Neighbour.*

When will the bearing with our neighbour have its due power in our hearts? It is the last and most excellent lesson of the doctrine of the Saints: blessed the soul who learns it. We desire to be borne with in our miseries, and always find them worthy of toleration; those of our neighbour always seem to us greater and heavier to bear.

10. *On Poverty.*

My Saint is St. Francis, with the love of poverty; but I know not how to love it, this attractive poverty, for I have never seen it very close: still, having heard it spoken so well of by Our Lord, with whom it was born, lived, was crucified and rose again, I love and honour it beyond measure.

BOOK VI.

Letters for Various Festivals.

LETTER I.

TO MOTHER DE CHANTAL.

On Advent.

1st December 1610.

YOU desire, my very dear daughter, some good thoughts which may help our sisters to spend Advent well, and with as much devotion as they have desire of it.

What shall I say to you, my dear daughter, except that Holy Church conducts to-day her children to Saint Mary Major, to make the station and begin Advent there. Let us do the same, my daughter; let us enter in spirit into the intention of Holy Church, and in this unity, let us retire near to the holy Virgin, our good Mother and mistress. We shall see, in this month, three objects which are not only capable of occupying our souls, but which should enrapture our hearts with holy love. The first object is Mary conceived without sin; the second, St. John, child of grace, crying out in the desert that the ways must be made straight for the Spouse who is about to come; the third, the same Spouse and Saviour arriving by his holy birth to make us sing joyfully at Christmas, Emmanuel, God with us.

There is enough to meditate upon, until I see you with the dear little flock, which may God bless.

LETTER II.

TO A SUPERIORESS OF THE VISITATION.

[*Mother Favre?*]

Preparation for Christmas. On the sweetness of Christ's zeal, and how he receives all who will to come to him.

19th December 1619.

O MY daughter, God has shown you a great mercy in bringing back your heart to a gracious forbearance with your neighbour, and in having cast the holy balm of sweetheartedness towards others into the wine of your zeal. See, I answer at last, though late, the letter which you wrote me after my passing visit to you, and I answer briefly, simply, lovingly, as to my most dear daughter whom I have loved almost from her cradle, because God had so disposed. Only this was wanting to you, my dear daughter: your zeal was quite good, but it had the defect of being a little bitter, a little severe, a little exacting; now we have it purified from this; it will henceforth be sweet, mild, gracious, peaceful, forbearing.

Ah! when we look at the dear little Infant of Bethlehem—whose zeal for souls is incomparable, for he comes to die that he may save them—he is so humble, so sweet, so amiable. Live joyfully and courageously, my dear daughter; I mean in the superior part of your soul; for the Angel who heralds the birth of our little Master announces in his song, and sings as he announces, that he proclaims joy, peace, happiness for men of good will; in order that no one may be ignorant that to receive this Infant it is enough to be of good will, although one may not up to this have been of good deed. For he came to bless good wills, and little by little he will make them fruitful and of good effect, provided that they let him govern them, as I hope that we shall do ours, my dear daughter. Amen. And I am entirely yours, &c.

LETTER III.

To a Sister of the Visitation.

On the birth of Christ.

My dear Daughter—Behold most sweet little Jesus, who is going to be born in our commemoration, on this approaching feast. And since he is born to visit us on the part of his Eternal Father, and the shepherds and kings will in return come to visit him in the cradle, I think that he is the Father and the Child both together of Saint Marie of the Visitation.

Well then, caress him fondly; give him good hospitality, with all our sisters, sing beautiful canticles to him, and above all adore him, fervently and sweetly, and in him his poverty, his humility, his obedience and his sweetness, in imitation of his most holy Mother and of St. Joseph: and take of him one of those precious tears, sweet dew of heaven, and put it on your heart, in order that it may never know sorrow save what rejoices this sweet Infant; and when you recommend to him your soul, recommend equally to him mine, which is certainly all yours.

I salute affectionately all the dear company of our sisters, whom I look upon as simple shepherdesses watching over their flocks, that is, their affections, and going at the summons of the Angel to do homage to the divine Infant, and as offering him as a pledge of their eternal service the fairest of their lambs, which is their love, without reserve or exception.

LETTER IV.

TO MOTHER DE CHANTAL.

Thoughts on Christmas night.

AH! how sweet is this night, my most dear daughter! "The heavens," sings the Church, "rain down honey over all the world." And for my part I think these divine Angels who make the air thrill with their admirable song, have come to gather this heavenly honey from the lily as it lies on the breast of the most sweet Virgin and of St. Joseph. There is a fear, my dear daughter, lest these divine spirits should make some mistake between the milk of that virginal bosom and the honey from heaven which lies upon it. How sweet to see the union of honey and milk (*le miel succer le lait*).

But pray, my dear daughter, am I not ambitious enough to think that our good Angels, yours and mine, were amongst that dear band of heavenly musicians who sang that night? Ah! if they would but please to intone again in the ears of our heart that same heavenly song—what joy! what jubilee! I beg them to do so that there may be glory to God on high, and peace on earth to hearts of good will.

Returning then from the sacred mysteries, I thus say good day to my dear daughter; for I think that even the shepherds, after having adored the sacred Babe whom heaven itself had announced to them, rested a little. But oh what sweetness, as I think, was in their sleep! They seemed still to hear the sacred melody of the Angels who had saluted them so excellently in their canticle, to see the dear Infant and the Mother whom they had visited.

What shall we give to our little King which we have not received from him and from his divine liberality? Well, I will give him at holy High Mass the well-beloved daughter whom he has given me. O Saviour of our souls, make her to be all gold in charity, all myrrh in mortification, all incense in prayer, and then receive her within the arms of your holy protection, and let your heart say to hers: I am thy salvation for ever and ever. Amen. Your very affectionate father and servant, &c.

LETTER V.

TO A RELIGIOUS SISTER.

The Infant Christ the magnet of souls: how all may help to preach him.

AND believe, my dear daughter, that for me also it is a very particular consolation to receive letters from you and to send you mine. It is well with you when you are near that sacred crib, where the Saviour of our souls teaches us so many virtues by his silence; yes, what does he not say to us while he keeps silent? His little heart, panting with love for us, ought indeed to inflame ours. But see how lovingly he has written your name in the bottom of this divine heart, which is throbbing there on the straw with the ardent passion which he has for your advancement; nor does he breathe a single sigh to his Father in which you have not a share, nor is there a single act of his mind which is not for your welfare.

Loadstone draws iron, amber attracts straw and hay: whether we are iron in hardness or straw in feebleness, we ought to join ourselves to this sovereign little Babe, who is a true drawer of hearts. Yes, my daughter; let us not return into the country from which we came out; let us leave for ever Arabia and Chaldæa, and remain at this Saviour's feet. Let us say with the heavenly Spouse: * *I have found him whom my soul loveth; I hold him and I will not let him go.*

O my daughter, does your envy of me come from this, that I preach to the world the praises of God?

* Cant. iii. 4.

Ah! what a satisfaction to the heart to proclaim the goodness of what one loves! But if you want to preach with me, do so, I pray you, my daughter, by ever praying to God to give me words according to his heart and your wishes. How often does it happen that we say good things because some good soul gets us the grace to do so! Does she not preach sufficiently, and with this advantage, that knowing nothing about it she is not puffed up?

We are like organs, where he who gives the wind really does the whole work and gets no praise for it. Often then breathe a prayer for me, my daughter, and you will preach with me; and on my part, believe me, I join my soul to yours every day by the link of the most holy Sacrament, which I only receive with you and for you. So make, my daughter, make a thousand times a day these holy aspirations to God, protesting that you are wholly and entirely, for ever and eternally his. May Jesus ever live, for he is our life! May his holy love live and reign for ever in our hearts!

LETTER VI.

TO A RELIGIOUS SISTER.

On the birth of the Infant Jesus.

YOU may think, my dear daughter, how my soul which loves yours extremely, fancies always that it can write to you, for truly I have a very great pleasure when my soul can entertain itself with yours. But these great feasts impose silence upon us inasmuch as they themselves ring with divine words, which tell us of the mystery which they represent. Indeed I know not what to say in presence of this divine Infant, for he speaks no word from his heart, full of fondness for ours, he reveals not himself except by lamentations, tears, and sweet looks: his sacred Mother is almost always silent, and marvelling at what is said to him. Oh! what great things does this silence speak to me! It teaches me to make mental prayer; it teaches me the loving fervour of a heart filled with affection, which cherishes these sweet thoughts while fearing to lose their sweetness if it utter them.

Meantime keep near this Mother, and do not leave her for a single moment, while she starts from Nazareth and goes to Bethlehem; while without eagerness but not without ardent movements of the soul she awaits the outcoming of the beautiful bird of Paradise. My dear daughter, you will see her, this fair Lady, this blessed daughter of Sion, Mother of the King of glory though she is, going about to beg hospitality in Bethlehem, and with no sort of shame, but glorying in this grace and blessed necessity.

I promise you that in this midnight Mass, in which it will seem to me that I shall see a crib on the altar, and the sweet Babe with his two eyes filling with tears more precious than pearls, I will offer him to God his Father with his Mother's approval, and will ask him for you, that he may ever be the heart of your heart and the sole Beloved of your soul. O my daughter, tightly clasp this divine Infant in your arms, and give him that milk of humility and cordial sweetness which is his food. Ah! how sweet this mystery is! Your St. Bernard's first rapture was by the vision of it, and by this means his heart and his mouth became full of the milk of the holy Virgin and the tears of this sweet little Infant. Salute your little cousin from me, and likewise salute one another. As soon as you see the august little Infant born in your soul, tell him earnestly that I sacrifice to him my soul with yours eternally. Amen.

LETTER VII.

TO MOTHER DE CHANTAL.

On the mystery of Christmas.

FINDING myself in these great feast days tied by a thousand engagements, it is really all but impossible for me to go and visit you, my dear daughter. I would, however, have gladly done so in order to entertain you all with some considerations on the holy mystery which we celebrate; but, my dear daughter, nothing will fail you, since you will be in the presence of that sacred Infant whose image you will have in your memory and imagination as if you saw him born in his poor little crib at Bethlehem. O my daughter, how many holy affections does this birth make rise within our hearts, above all of the perfect renunciation of the goods, the pomps, the consolations, of this world.

I do not know whether I find any mystery which so sweetly mingles tenderness with austereness, love with rigour, sweetness with severity. Never was seen a poorer or happier bringing forth; never so glorious or so well satisfied a Mother. Certainly she who bears the Son of God has no need to beg from the world exterior consolations. Saint Paula also preferred to live as a poor hospice-sister in Bethlehem, rather than to be a rich lady at Rome, for it seemed to her that she heard day and night in her dear hospital the infantine cries of the Saviour in the crib, or, as St. Francis used to say, of the dear Babe of Bethlehem, who inspired her with contempt for worldly grandeur and affections, and called her to most holy love of abjection. This dear little Saviour knows well, my dear daughter, that since the morning my heart cries out and begs Jesus for yours. Yes, sweetest Jesus, precious balm which givest all sweetness to Angels and to men, enter, possess the soul of this dear daughter. Enjoy these affections fully, in order that the odour of his sweet-scented name may spread out into all your actions. Ah! my daughter, you are all dear to me, because you hold nothing dear but Jesus, and since as I know well it is through him that I am very dear to you, let me therefore be still more so this year. But above all may Jesus be so more and more unto most holy eternity. Amen.

LETTER VIII.

To a Widow Lady.

On the Feast of the Circumcision.

My Daughter—I am so greatly pressed that I have not the leisure to write you anything more than the great word of our salvation, Jesus. Yes, my daughter, can we not at least once pronounce that sacred name of our heart. Oh what a balm would it spread throughout all the powers of our spirit! How happy should we be, my daughter,, to have in our understanding Jesus only, in our imagination Jesus only. Jesus would be everywhere in us and we everywhere in him. Let us make trial of this, my very dear daughter, let us pronounce it as often as we can; and if for the present it is but with stammering, still at last we shall be able to pronounce it properly.

But what is the pronouncing it properly, that sacred name?—for you ask me to speak plainly to you. Alas! my daughter, I do not know. I only know that to express it duly there needs a tongue all of fire; that is, there needs nothing less than love divine, which by itself expresses Jesus in our life by impressing him in the depths of our heart. But courage, my daughter; undoubtedly we shall love God, for he loves us. Make yourself happy in this, and permit not your soul to be troubled about anything. I am, my dear daughter, I am in this same Jesus, yours most absolutely.

LETTER IX.

To a Sister of the Visitation.

On the Circumcision: wishes for the New Year.

My dear Daughter—When Holy Scripture wishes to speak of a person who is good, gentle, innocent and devoted to God, it says: he or she is a son or daughter of one year. O my daughter, if we have not hitherto corresponded with the love of this gracious Saviour, by a holy and inseparable union of our affections with his holy will, let us now so act that at the end of this year we may be able to be called children of one year.

I was saying yesterday, my dear daughter (for I wish to share our preachings with you), that when God desired to take under his protection the children of the Israelites, in order that the exterminating Angel should not slay them as he slew those of the Egyptians, he ordained that their doors should be sprinkled and marked with the blood of the Paschal lamb, and that so his divine Majesty marked for us with the blood of his Circumcision the gate and entrance of this year, in order that in it the exterminator of our children might have no power over them. Now you know who are our children; for I speak of those of the heart, our good purposes, our good desires, the fruits of our divine love.

I hope, my dear daughter, that we shall be of inviolable fidelity to this Saviour, and that these following years will be like the fertile years of Joseph, who by the way in which he employed them made himself viceroy of Egypt: for we will so employ our years, our months, our weeks, our days, our hours, our moments, that the whole will be used for God's service, and will be profitable to eternal life, to reign with the Saints. But, my daughter, will we not be no longer those old ourselves that we were formerly, but be other ourselves, who will be without exception, without reserve, without condition, sacrificed for ever to God and to his love? Like the phœnix we will be renewed in this fire of divine love, for which we have, with an unalterable divorce, for ever given up and rejected the world and every kind of vanity.

Our little fits of anger, of sadness, these little shiverings of the heart, are remains of our maladies, which the sovereign Physician leaves in us in order that we may fear a relapse, and may remain in an entire submission. We will all the same continue to restore our strength day by day, and these little movements of the passions will grow weak, with God's help. Have courage, my daughter, for this little Jesus loves you much. I am in him all yours.

LETTER X.

To a Religious Sister.

The new year : the Infant Saviour.

Annecy, *8th January* 1620.

O my dear Daughter—Let us employ this new year well, to acquire eternity. I see you, me seems, near the Infant of Bethlehem, and while kissing his feet begging him to be your King. Abide there, my dear daughter, and learn of him to be meek, humble, simple and amiable.

Let your soul, like a mystical bee, never leave this dear little King, but make its honey around him, in him and for him ; indeed let it draw its honey from him, whose lips are all overflowing with grace, and on them, far more happily than they were seen on those of St. Ambrose, holy bees, collected in a swarm, do their sweet and gracious work.

LETTER XI.

TO A BERNARDINE SISTER, HIS COUSIN.

On the Epiphany.

OUR Lord loves you, my dear cousin, and loves you tenderly. If he does not make you feel the sweetness of his holy love, this is to make you more humble and more abject in your own eyes; but do not thereupon give up having recourse to his holy graciousness in all confidence, above all at this time when we represent ourselves to him as he was a little babe at Bethlehem. For why, my dear daughter, does he take this sweet and attractive state of a little child save to provoke us to love him with confidence and to confide in him with love?

Remain close to the Crib, this holy octave of the Kings. If you love riches, you will there find the gold which the Kings have left there; if you love the smoke of honours, you will find there that of the incense; and if you love the delicacies of the senses, smell there the odorous myrrh which perfumes the whole stable. Be rich in love for this dear Saviour, honourable in the familiarity with him to which you will aspire by prayer, and be filled with delight in the joy of feeling within yourself by holy inspirations and affections that you are most solely his. As to your little attacks of anger, they will pass away; or if they do not pass, it will be for your exercise and mortification.

At last, my dear cousin, since without reserve you will to be all for God, do not let your heart remain in trouble; and amidst all the dryness which can come to you, abide steadily in the arms of the divine mercy.

And as to these apprehensions which arise within you, they are from the enemy, who, seeing you now determined to live in Our Lord without reserve and without exception, will make all kinds of efforts to disturb you and to make the path of holy devotion hard. But you, on the contrary, must enlarge your heart by a frequent repetition of your protestation that you will never give in, that you will persevere in your fidelity, that you love the rigours of God's service better than the sweetness of the world's, that you will never abandon your Spouse.

Beware, my dear daughter, of giving up holy prayer, for you would play the game of your adversary; but constantly continue in this holy exercise, and wait for Our Saviour to speak to you, for he will some day say to you words of peace and consolation, and then you will know that your labour has been well employed and your patience useful.

Good night, my very dear daughter; glory in being all for God, and always protest that you are wholly his. Say often, *Vive Jésus.*

LETTER XII.

TO THE SAME.

On the Feast of Candlemas.

YOU tell me, my very dear daughter, that your grief over the great and irrevocable adieux which we have said to the world is past: it is well said, my daughter;

let us leave that world on one side, it is worthless. Ah! may this Egypt, with its garlics, its onions, and its gross flesh, be ever disgusting to us, that we may so much the better relish the delicious manna which Our Saviour will give us in the desert which we have entered. May Jesus then live and reign!

You desire not to tell untruths; this is a great secret for drawing the Spirit of God into our interior. *Lord, who shall dwell in thy tabernacle?* said David:* *He who speaks the truth with all his heart*, he answers. I quite approve of speaking little, provided that this little which you say is said graciously and charitably, and not morosely or affectedly. Yes, speak little and sweetly, little and well, little and simply, little and sincerely, little and kindly.

My daughter, you must from time to time exercise yourself in this self-renunciation and nakedness of heart, and ask it of God in all your exercises; but when there comes some other movement—of love, of union with God and of confidence—you must follow these without disturbing them by abnegation, for which you will leave a space at the end and in its place.

What sweetness it was yesterday to consider that fair Mother, with the little Babe hanging at her breast, as she goes to offer him in the Temple, and with that pair of doves, more favoured, methinks, than the greatest princes of the world, in being sacrificed for the Saviour. Ah! who will give us the grace that our hearts also may be so one day? But is not this Simeon glorious in thus embracing that divine Infant? Yes; but I cannot be pleased with him for the bad turn he wanted to do us; for being out of himself he wanted

* Ps. xiv. 1, 3.

to carry him away with him into the other world. *Now,* he says, *dost thou dismiss thy servant in peace.** Ah! but we still, my dear daughter, were sadly in need of him. Let us embrace him, let us live and die in these sweet embraces. Put this sweet Jesus on your heart, like a Solomon on his throne of ivory; make your soul often go before him, like a queen of Saba, to hear the sacred words which he continually inspires and breathes out. But take notice, this heart ought to be of ivory in purity, in solidity, in dryness, clear of the humours of the world, firm in its resolutions, pure in its affections.

I am not going, my very dear daughter, to that place which you had been told of, for I still live in obedience, which is imposed upon me not of God, but by the world; still it is permitted by God, and so I acquiesce in it. Live all for him who to be all ours made himself a little Child. I am in him all yours.

LETTER XIII.

TO MOTHER DE CHANTAL.

On St. Joseph.

MY DEAREST DAUGHTER—Here is the Litany of the glorious father of our life and of our love. I intended to send you it written with my own hand, but, as you know, I am not myself. Still I have taken the time to revise it, to correct and to put in the accents, that our daughter de Chastel may more easily sing it without making mistakes.

* Luke ii. 29.

But you, my daughter, who will not be able to sing the praises of this Saint of our heart, you will ruminate them, like the spouse, between your teeth; that is, while your mouth is closed your heart will be open to the meditation of the greatnesses of this spouse of the Queen of all the world, named father of Jesus, and his first adorer, after his divine Spouse.

LETTER XIV.

TO THE SAME.

On the Ascension of our Lord.

I GIVE you joy, for that Our Saviour has ascended into heaven, where he lives and reigns, and where he wills that one day we should live and reign with him. What triumph in heaven, and what sweetness on earth! Let *our hearts* be where their *treasure is*,* and let us live in heaven, since our life is in heaven. O my daughter, how lovely that heaven is, now that Our Saviour shines as its sun, and his bosom is a fount of love, at which the Blessed drink as they will! Each one goes to look into it, and there he sees his name written, in a character of love that love alone can read, and love alone has graven.

O my God, shall not our names, my dear daughter, be there? They shall undoubtedly; for although our heart has not love, yet it has the desire of love and the beginning of love; and is not the sacred name of Jesus written in our hearts?—it seems to me that nothing

* Matt. vi. 21.

can efface it. And so we must hope that ours will reciprocally be written in the mind of God. What a joy, when we shall see these divine characters which signify our eternal happiness! For my part, I have been able to think of nothing this morning except this eternity of goods which awaits us, but in which all would seem to me little or nothing but for this unchanging and ever actual love of that great God who ever reigns there.

Oh! my dear mother, how I marvel at the contradiction that is in me, in having sentiments so pure and actions so impure! For truly it seems to me that Paradise would be amidst all the pains of hell if the love of God could be there, and if the fire of hell were a fire of love, it seems that its torments would be desirable. I saw this morning that all the joys of heaven are truly nothing compared with this royal love. But whence is it that I do not love properly, since from this moment I can love properly? O my daughter, let us pray, strive, humble ourselves, invoke upon ourselves this love.

Never did the earth see eternity on its orb till this holy feast, when Our Lord, glorifying his body, gave, as I think, a desire to the Angels to have a like body, with whose beauty the heavens and the sun are not to be compared. Ah! how happy are our hearts to be expecting one day a share in so much glory, provided that they serve the Spirit well during this mortal life.

LETTER XV.

To the Same.

On the Feast of Pentecost.

Arise and depart, *O north wind, and come, O south wind; blow through my garden, and let the aromatical spices thereof flow.** O my most dear daughter, how do I desire that gracious wind which comes from the south, from divine love, that Holy Spirit which gives us the grace of aspiring after him and of breathing for him! Ah! how I should like to give you some gift, my dear daughter! But, besides that I am poor, it is not fitting that on the day when the Holy Spirit makes his presents we should be engaged in making ours; we must only be ready to receive gifts in this great day of largess.

How great a need have I of the Spirit of strength! for I am indeed weak and infirm. Still *I glory in it, that the power of Christ may dwell in me.*† I would rather be infirm than strong before God, for the infirm he takes into his arms, while the strong he leads by the hand. May eternal wisdom be ever in our heart, that we may relish the treasures of the infinite sweetness of Jesus Christ crucified.

Tell our dear daughter that she must like me glory in weakness, which is the most proper condition for receiving strength: for to whom should strength be given if not to the weak?

Good night, my very dear daughter. May this sacred fire which changes all into itself deign to

* Cant. iv. 16. † 2 Cor. xii. 9.

entirely transmute our heart, so that it may in future be nothing but love, and that so we may be no longer loving but love itself; no longer two but one single self, since love unites all things in a sovereign unity. Adieu, my dear daughter; let us persevere in the desire of this unity, which God, having made us enjoy it here below as far as our infirm condition can allow, will make us enjoy more perfectly in heaven.

LETTER XVI.

To a Lady.

On the Feast of Pentecost.

My dear Daughter—Doubt not but that I love you more than ever, because I see you in the way of entering into that path of true devotion wherein one begins to detach one's heart from all the things of the world, in order to be all God's, that he may be able absolutely to dispose of you, that you may love only what God loves, that you may do his will and follow his counsels, that you may avoid with an extreme care all that can offend him, mortify your passions, regulate your life on the maxims of Jesus Christ, be humble and patient.

For the great secret of maintaining a good devotion is to have much humility. Be humble, and God will be on your side, and will sustain your good will. Give yourself to him without concealment and without reserve, asking him from the bottom of your heart that if up to now you have not served him well enough, he would have the goodness to pardon you and to fortify you in the resolution which you have taken of detaching yourself from all the affections of the world, and of attaching yourself to nothing save the love of God, and serving him faithfully with all your heart.

I should like also to communicate to you, my dear daughter, something of what I have just written to Mother Agnes * at the Carmelites, on the dispositions for receiving well the Holy Spirit at this great feast of Pentecost—that uncreated love, which without regard to his own advantage is everywhere occupied in seeking our good, often sending forth his fairest flames when we were least thinking of this holy splendour, to engage us to love him with all our power; and because this love is a gratuitous gift of his love, therefore ought we to love it with all our strength. We must not disturb ourself about our offences, for this Divine Spirit is often more liberal of his gifts to those who have been more ungenerous with their heart and affections towards him.

But, my dear daughter, we must testify to Jesus Christ all our confidence, with the holy Apostles and disciples, on whom he did not will to send his Holy Spirit till after he had ascended into heaven. If you ask me why this was, you must first know that the Holy Spirit is the wine of heaven, according to St. Bernard, who said that in heaven there was an overflowing abundance of this wine, I mean the joy of the Holy Ghost and beatific jubilee—but they had not that sacred bread of Christ's humanity. The earth, on the other hand, had this sacred bread, which it made its delight and its joy; it had not that sweet

* *La grande mère Agnès.*

and sparkling wine of the Holy Ghost, which was to inebriate our souls and crown them with joy.

And hence that admirable inference of Jesus Christ's, when he showed his Apostles that it was not right to keep the humanity of Jesus Christ, and at the same time to have this admirable wine of heaven. There must be then, said Jesus Christ, a holy bargain between you and the Angels: you shall infallibly have from heaven that mighty wine of the Holy Ghost, if you share with it your sacred bread which is still on the earth and as it were in your hands—that is, the humanity of Jesus Christ. I think, my dear daughter, that this is enough to open your heart wide for the reception of the Holy Ghost, and of those tongues of fire and adorable flames. Adieu. I am entirely yours.

LETTER XVII.

TO A BERNARDINE SISTER.

On the Feast of the Blessed Sacrament.

YOUR heart will be pure, my dear little daughter, since your intention is pure; and the idle thoughts which surprise you cannot sully it in any way. Remain at peace, and patiently support your little miseries. You are God's without reserve; he will guide you well. If he does not deliver you from your imperfections so quickly, it is in order to deliver you from them more profitably, and to exercise you the longer in humility, that you may be firmly rooted in that beautiful virtue.

He who receives the most Holy Communion receives

the living Jesus Christ, whose body, soul and divinity are in this divine Sacrament: and inasmuch as his divinity is the very same as that of the Father and the Holy Ghost who are but one sole God with him, he who receives the most Holy Eucharist receives the body of the Son of God, and consequently his blood and his soul, and consequently the most Holy Trinity.

But still this divine Sacrament is principally instituted that we may receive the body and the blood of Our Saviour with his life-giving life; as clothing covers primarily the body of man, although, because the soul is united to the body, it consequently covers the soul—the understanding, the memory, and the will.

Walk quite simply in this belief, and often salute the heart of this divine Saviour, who to testify to us his love, has willed to clothe himself with the appearances of bread, in order to remain most familiarly and most intimately in us, and near our heart.

Let us clearly see in spirit the holy Angels who surround the most Holy Sacrament to adore it, and who in this holy Octave pour forth sacred inspirations more abundantly on those who with humility, reverence, and love approach to receive it. My dear daughter, these divine spirits will teach you how to act to celebrate well these solemn days, and will teach you above all the interior love which will make you know how great is the love of our God, who to make himself more ours, has willed to give himself as food for the spiritual health of our souls, in order that nourished by him they may become more perfect.

LETTER XVIII.

TO MOTHER DE CHANTAL.

On the Feast of the Blessed Sacrament.

IT is true, my dear sister, my daughter, that I have been a little tired in body; but in spirit and heart how could I be, after having held to my breast, close clasped to my heart, so divine an *epithem* as I did this morning during the whole procession? Alas! had I had my heart all empty by humility, and lowly bowed down by abjection, I should undoubtedly have drawn this sacred pledge to myself; he would have hidden himself within me; for he is so deeply in love with these virtues, that he is forcibly drawn towards them when he sees them.

The sparrow hath found herself a house, and the turtle a nest for herself, where she may lay her young, says David.* Oh! how this affected me when they sang that Psalm! I said: O dear Queen of heaven, chaste turtle-dove, is it possible that your little one has now for its nest my bosom? That word of the spouse also touched me greatly: *My beloved to me and I to him; he abideth between my breasts;* † for there was I holding him: and those words of the Beloved: ‡ *Put me as a seal upon thy heart.* Ah! yes, my daughter; but having taken away the seal I do not see the impression of its characters in my heart. Is there a sweetness to be compared with it?

As to the business, I know not what to say except that one can in an hour determine oneself to the less

* Ps. lxxxiii. 4. † Cant. i., ii. ‡ Ib. viii. 6.

evil; and the resolution having been taken one should content oneself with this that on whatever side one turns the affairs of this world, there will always be much to be desired and to be discussed; so that after one has formed one's determination one should not occupy oneself in sighing after the imagination of better things, but in properly overcoming present difficulties, which moreover we cannot escape without encountering others greater, since every place is full of them. Good night, my very dear daughter: may the divine Saviour, the sole love of our hearts, be our eternal repose. Amen.

LETTER XIX.

TO A RELIGIOUS SISTER.

On the Feast of St. John Baptist.

WELL, my dear daughter, if you cannot easily communicate often really, you can communicate as often as you like spiritually. And so you ask me for a good thought on St. John. This one is extremely sweet to me. On many occasions he had recognised our Lord: from the womb of his mother, rejoicing with joy at his presence and at the voice of his Mother, he already bore witness to the pleasure which he would have in seeing him, hearing him, conversing with him: yet he was deprived of it all. And for all that the Scripture witnesses, he never spoke with him as much as a full twice; but knowing that this divine Saviour was preaching and was communicating himself to all the world in Judæa, he remained solitary in a desert close by, not venturing to go to see him really, though he ever saw him spiritually.

Was there ever a like mortification, to be so close to his sole and sovereign love, and, for love of him, to remain without seeing him, hearing him, listening to him? Well, my dear daughter, you will do the same close to the Sacrament in which Jesus is; for you will only enjoy him in spirit, like St. John.

Yes, one could not say whether it was a heavenly man or an earthly Angel. His coat of armour, made of camel's hair, represented his humility, which covered him all over; his girdle of tanned skin (*peau morte*) about his loins signified the mortification with which he restrained and bound up all concupiscence. He ate locusts, to show that whereas he was on earth, still he was perpetually elevating himself unto God. Wild honey served him for condiment, because the love of God sweetened all his austerities; but this love was wild or not from cultivation, because he had not learnt it from masters, but from the trees and rocks, as St. Bernard says.

Ah! my daughter, let us eat of both the wild and the hive-honey; let us amass that holy love at every opportunity, both by the example of our sisters, and by the consideration of other creatures; for all cries out to the ears of our heart: love, love. O holy love, come then, wholly and solely possess our hearts.

Truly, our good ladies of the Visitation are doing wonders, and those who see them are quite delighted with them. *Vive Jésus!* I am in him entirely yours, my dear daughter.

CHAPTER XX.

To Mother de Chantal (?).

On the Feast of St. John Baptist.

My most dear Mother—I should indeed like to have some beautiful bouquet from the desert of our glorious St. John, to present it to your dear soul; but mine, more sterile than the desert, has not been able to find one to-day, although indeed it has had this morning, and still has, a certain insensible little sense of willing no longer to live according to nature, but as far as possible according to Christian faith, hope, and charity, in imitation of that angelic man whom we see in those desert depths contemplating nought but God and himself.

Oh how blessed is the spirit of him who sees but these two objects, the one of which carries him up to the sovereign love, and the other lowers him to extreme abjection! For what could that great hermit say, in a place where there was only God and self, save: "Who art thou, Lord, and who am I?" I beseech Our Lord, who is the Lamb whom our great St. John pointed to us, to clothe you entirely with the most holy wool of his merits, my dear mother, my daughter.

Oh! what admirable purity of heart, what indifference to all things in this admirable human angel or angelic man, who seems almost not to love his Master in order to love him better and more purely! I do not know how he had the strength of heart to remain in his desert after he had seen Our Saviour, and had seen him go away from the place. Yet he continues his preaching, and with a holy hardness he does not permit himself to be overcome by the tenderness and sweetness of the love of the presence of his sovereign good, but for his love serves him in his absence with a love austere, constant, and strong. May God and the great St. John deign to visit you in the sweetness of their consolations, with all our daughters.

As to your grating, I think that for the present you had better make it of wood, while you are in a hired house, and have a door on it so that it need not all be opened. For at a profession, the revised Pontifical printed by order of the Pope directs the sister to go outside in order to come and take the vows. And as to getting the altar ready, one must see if one can continue to go outside for this; I see no difficulty, but we must go by the ideas of others.

Certainly, if my dear sister Anastase is to be professed on the day of the Visitation, I shall be very glad to officiate. One of these Prelates (*Seigneurs*) can be asked for another day, using the Sunday within the Octave.

LETTER XXI.

To the Same (?).

On the Feast of St. John Baptist.

My very dear Daughter—Why have I not some worthy sentiment of joy for this angelic man, or human Angel, whose birth we are celebrating! What sweetness should I have in occupying myself with it! But I assure you that the greatness of my idea of him hinders me from giving myself this satisfaction.

I find him more than virgin, because he is a virgin

even with the eyes, which he has fixed on the insensible objects of the desert, nor does he even know by the senses that there are two sexes; more than confessor, because he confessed the Saviour before the Saviour confessed himself; more than preacher because he preaches not only with the tongue but with the hand and the finger, which is the highest excellence of preaching; more than doctor, because he preached without having heard the source of doctrine; more than martyr, because the other martyrs die for him who died for them, but he dies for him who is still living, and pays back, according to his little measure, the death of his Saviour before it was given him; more than evangelist, for he preaches the Gospel before it was given; more than apostle, for he goes before him whom the Apostles follow; more than prophet, for he points out him whom the prophets predict; more than patriarch, for he sees him whom they believed in; and more than angel, and more than man, for the angels are pure spirits without bodies, and men have too much body and too little spirit: this man has a body and is but spirit.

I have an extreme pleasure while contemplating him in that gloomy but blessed desert which he wholly perfumes with his devotion, and in which, night and day, he pours forth ecstatic soliloquies and discourses before the great object of his heart—that heart which, seeing itself alone with its sole love, rejoices in the presence thereof, finds in solitude the multitude of eternal sweetnesses, and there sucks the heavenly honey, which it will soon after go to distribute to the souls of the Israelites, by the river Jordan.

Behold, my daughter, what an admirable Saint he

is! He is born of one barren, he lives in the desert, he preaches to the hard and stony heart, he dies among the martyrs, and amidst all this asperity, he has a heart wholly filled with graces and benedictions! But this further is admirable, that Our Lord having said * that *amongst those that are born of women there is not a greater prophet than John the Baptist*, adds: *But he who is lesser in the kingdom of God is greater than he.* O my dear daughter, it is true; for the lowest Christian when communicating is greater than St. John: and how is it that we are so little in sanctity?

Good night to you, my dear daughter, and to all the dear flock of our daughters. May the good St. John deign to bless them, with their dear mother.

LETTER XXII.

TO THE SAME (*Mother de Chantal*) (?).

On the Feast of St. John Baptist.

Is it not right, my dear sister, that not being able to see you I should at least go and wish you a happy feast in spirit? Behold what a great Saint here presents himself before the eyes of our mind! When I consider him in that desert, I do not know whether it is an Angel who appears to be a man, or a man who aspires to be an Angel. What acts of contemplation, what upliftings of spirit does he make there!

His food is admirable: for the honey represents the sweetness of the contemplative life, all drawn from the flowers of the sacred mysteries. The locusts re-

* Luke vii. 28.

present the active life; for the locust never walks on the earth and never flies in the air, but by a mysterious blending of movements is seen sometimes leaping and sometimes touching the earth in order to take breath: and those who follow the active life alternately leap and touch earth: it lives on dew and does nothing except chirrup. My dear daughter, although according to our mortal condition, it is necessary to touch the earth so as to take order for the necessities of this life, yet our heart ought to relish nothing save the good pleasure of God in all this, and ought to refer all to the praise of God.

And that this earthly angel should be clothed with camel's hair—what is the signification of all this? The camel with its hump, naturally fitted to bear burdens, represents the sinner. Alas! however good Christians may be, they must still remember that they are surrounded with sin; and if the sin does not touch them, at least there is always present some skin —of thoughts, temptations, and dangers. Ah! how proper a dress for preserving holiness is the robe of humility!

Behold, I pray, this holy young man buried in solitude. He is there by obedience, waiting to be called to go to the people. He keeps himself separated from the Saviour—whom he knew and kissed by affection from the womb of his mother—in order not to be separated from obedience; knowing well that to find the Saviour outside obedience is to lose him altogether. Further, he is born of a barren and aged woman, to show us that dryness and sterility can produce within us grace; for John means *grace.*

But particularly notice, my dear daughter, that immediately his father Zachary had written the name of this glorious infant on the tablets, he begins to prophesy, and to sing the beautiful canticle: *Blessed be the Lord God of Israel.** Without doubt, this name, well graven on our hearts, I mean, the honour and imitation of this Saint, will make us prophesy and bless God with full benedictions.

I love this beautiful woodland nightingale, who being all voice and all song, and coming forth upon the ways of Judæa, first announces the coming of the sun. I beseech him to give you of his honey, of his locusts, and to share with you his mantle.

LETTER XXIII.

To the Same (?).

On the Feast of St. John Baptist.

Look at a rose, my most dear daughter. It represents the glorious St. John, in whom the scarlet dye of charity is more brilliant than the rose, which he resembles also in this that he lived amid the thorns of many mortifications.

But think how this great man had graven in the midst of his heart the holy Virgin and her Child, from the day of the Visitation, in which he first of mortals felt how amiable were the Mother of this Child and the Child of this Mother. Outside this Mother and this Child, nothing ought to engage the heart of my daughter or of her father. May the glorious and

* Luke i. 68.

divine Jesus live and reign for ever in our spirits, within the arms of his holy Mother, as on his established throne.

Behold then, my dear daughter, how you have here a spiritual nosegay, where you see two lilies in a rose, one born within the other, both making blessed, with the odour of their sweetness and the perfection of their beauty, the rose of those hearts which by a perfect pricking mortification live stripped, despoiled, and free of all things, for their sakes. Ah! who will give us the grace of duly relishing the honey which this mother-bee makes in the midst of this sweet flower! Good night, my most dear mother; good night to all our sisters.

LETTER XXIV.

TO THE SAME (?).

On the Feast of St. Peter.

OUR great St. Peter, awakened from his sleep by the Angel,* gives you good day, my very dear mother. What sweetness is shown in the history of this deliverance! for his soul is so enraptured that he knows not whether or no he is dreaming. May our Angel touch our side to-day, awaken us to loving attention to God, deliver us from all the chains of self-love, and consecrate us for ever to this heavenly love, that we may be able to say: *Now I know indeed that the Lord hath sent his Angel, and hath delivered me.*

Peter, lovest thou me? †—not that he doubted it, but

* Acts xii. † John xxi.

for the great pleasure which he takes in often hearing us repeat and protest that we love him?

My dear mother, do we not love the sweet Saviour? Ah! he knows well that if we do not love him we at least desire to love him. Oh if we love him, let us feed his sheep and his lambs; this is the mark of faithful love. But with what must we feed these dear little lambs? With love itself; for they either live not, or they live with love; between their death and love there is no alternative; they must die or love; for *he that loveth not*, says St. John,* *abideth in death.*

But do you notice an agreeable thought? Our Lord goes on to say to his dear St. Peter: † *When thou wast younger thou didst gird thyself, and didst walk where thou wouldst; but when thou shalt be old thou shalt stretch forth thy hands, and another shall gird thee and lead thee whither thou wouldst not.* Young apprentices in the love of God gird themselves, and take mortifications as seems good to themselves; they choose their penance, their subject of resignation and devotion, and do their own will at the same time as that of God; but old masters of the craft let themselves be tied and girded by others, submitting themselves to the yoke which others impose on them, go by ways which according to their own inclination they do not choose. It is true that they stretch forth their hands, for in spite of the resistance of their inclinations they voluntarily let themselves be governed against their wills, and say that *obedience is better than sacrifices:* ‡ and behold how they glorify God, crucifying not only their flesh but their spirit.

Truly, yesterday while they were singing the Invi-

* 1 John iii. 14. † John xxi. 18. ‡ 1 Kings xv. 22.

tatory, and saying, "The King of the Apostles—come and adore him," I had such sweet and agreeable sentiments that more could not be, and immediately I desired that it should flow out over our whole heart. O may God Our Saviour be ever all things unto us! Keep your heart uplifted into the bosom of this divine goodness and Providence, for it is the place of its repose. It is he who has made me all yours, and you all mine, that we might be more purely, perfectly, and solely his. Amen.

LETTER XXV.

To a Superioress of the Visitation.

On the mystery of the Visitation.

Feast of St. Paul.

How very glad am I, my dear daughter, that these two daughters of our heart cannot fast to-morrow, and that in exchange they should have their little involuntary mortifications!—for I singularly love the trouble which the sole election of the heavenly Father sends us, as compared with that which we choose ourselves. But you who are so robust must of course fast on bread and water; that you must understand, my dear daughter—for you do not understand it unless I say it to you—that you must understand of the year to come, if it do come, for as to this year you must really be a Jew with the Jews, a Gentile with the Gentiles, must eat with those who eat, laugh with those who laugh, says the great Apostle of to-day.*

Feed therefore your little sheep, my dear daughter;

* Rom. xii. 15.

and to-morrow you will see the poor little future Mother of the Son of God, coming sweetly to consult with her dear and holy husband and to get his consent to her making that pious visit to her aged cousin, Elizabeth. You will see how she says adieu to her dear neighbours for the three months which she expects to spend in the country and amongst the mountains—for that word is well noted. I think that they all let her go with a tender sorrow; for she was so amiable, and so greatly inspired love, that no one could be with her without love nor leave her without sorrow.

She undertakes her journey with a little eagerness, for the Gospel says, *she went with haste.** Ah! the first fruits of the movements of him whom she has within her womb cannot fail to be made with fervour. O holy eagerness, which troubles not and which hastens us without making us precipitate.

The Angels are ready to accompany her, and St. Joseph to lovingly conduct her. I should greatly love to know something of the converse of these two great souls, for you would indeed be pleased that I should tell it you. At any rate, I think that the Virgin entertains herself with nothing but that of which she is full, and breathes only after the Saviour. St. Joseph in his turn aspires only towards the Saviour, who by secret rays touches his heart with a thousand unusual sentiments; and as the wines shut up in their cellars give out the scent of the flowering vines without perceiving them, so the heart of this holy patriarch gives out without perceiving them the perfume, the vigour, and the strength of this little Child who is in flower in his lovely vineyard.

* Luke i.

Oh! what a glorious pilgrimage! The Saviour serves them as staff, as food and flask of wine—of wine I say which cheereth Angels and men,* and inebriateth God the Father with a love beyond measure. I leave you to think, my daughter, how good an odour this lovely lily spread throughout the house of Zachary, during the three months she was there, how every one was embalmed with it, and how in few but most excellent words she poured forth from her sacred lips honey and precious balm! For what could she pour out save what she was filled with?—now she was full of Jesus. Oh! my daughter, I marvel at myself that I am still so full of self after having communicated so often. Ah! dear Jesus, be the child of our inward hearts that we may nowhere breathe or smell of anything but you. Alas! you are so often in me, why am I so seldom in you? You enter within me, why am I so much outside of you? You are within my bowels, why am I not within yours to discover and collect that great love which inebriates hearts? My daughter, I am entirely engaged with this dear Visitation, in which Our Lord like a wholly new wine makes this loving affection seethe throughout the womb of his sacred Mother.

LETTER XXVI.

To a Sister of the Visitation.

On the Feast of the Assumption.

Ah! how lovely is this dawning of the eternal day, which, rising towards heaven, goes on, methinks, ever

* From Judges ix. 13.

increasing in the benedictions of its incomparable glory! May the odours of eternal sweetness, spread over the hearts of her servants, fill those of my dearest mother, as my own heart, and may our dear little congregation, entirely devoted to the praise of her Son and of the sacred breasts that gave him suck, enjoy the blessings prepared for the souls who honour her.

Yesterday evening I had a most particular sense of the advantage which one has of being a child, though unworthy, of this glorious Mother, star of the sea, *fair as the moon, bright as the sun.**

My dear mother, I had a special consolation in seeing how she gave a robe of unequalled whiteness to her servant St. Ildefonsus, bishop of Toledo; for why will she not give one to our dear heart? You see I return everywhere to my flock: let us undertake great things, under favour of this Mother; for if we are a little fervent in her love she is careful not to leave us without the object that we aspire to.

Ah! when I remember that in the Canticles† she says: *Compass me about with apples,* I would gladly give her our heart; for what other apple can this fair fruit-tree want of me?

I return from my sermon, in which I should greatly like to have spoken more holily and lovingly of our glorious and sacred Mistress: I beseech her to deign to pardon me.

May God give us the grace to see ourselves one day consumed with divine love. Meantime, good night, my dearest mother.

The 15th August, day of the glorification of our most honoured mistress. May she be for ever our love.

* Cant. vi. 9. † *Ib.* ii. 5.

LETTER XXVII.

To a Superioress of the Visitation.

On the Nativity of the Blessed Virgin.

7th September 1616.

I LIVE in hope, my most dear daughter, that if my ingratitude close not Paradise to me, I shall one day enjoy by complacency that eternal glory in the enjoyment of which you will delight, after having holily borne the cross in this life, which Our Saviour has imposed upon you in the charge of serving him faithfully in your own person, and in the person of the many dear sisters, whom he wishes to be your daughters in him.

I salute them, these most dear daughters, in the love of the most holy Virgin, on whose cradle I invite them to throw flowers every morning during this holy octave; holy anxieties to imitate her, thoughts of serving her for ever, and above all lilies and roses of purity and ardent charity, with violets of most sacred and desirable humility and simplicity.

LETTER XXVIII.

To a Bernardine Sister, his Cousin.

On the Feasts of All Saints and All Souls.

WE must bear with this inconvenience of the love of our relations, who think there is no comparison between the satisfaction of being with them, and that which is found in the course of God's service. So be in mental solitude, my dear cousin, my daughter, since you cannot be in real solitude. All is sweet to the sweet, and all is holy to the holy. You know in what manner one is to resist all these little attacks of impatience, vexation, and the rest.

Bless God, my dear daughter, for these little trials which occur to you in order to try your fidelity. Hear Mass in your heart when you cannot hear it elsewhere, and adore the Holy Sacrament.

As to the great feasts which are approaching, you have nothing further to do after your Office and services save to keep your spirit in the heavenly Jerusalem, amid those glorious streets which you will ever see resounding with God's praises. Behold that variety of Saints, and ask of them how they got there; and you will learn that the Apostles arrived thither chiefly by love, the Martyrs by constancy, the Doctors by meditation, the Confessors by mortification, the Virgins by purity of heart, and all in general by humility. On the day of the Departed you will enter into Purgatory, and will see those souls full of hope, who will exhort you to advance in piety all you can, in order that at your departure you may be the less kept back from going to heaven. Good night, my dear daughter.

BURNS AND OATES, LIMITED, LONDON.

CPSIA information can be obtained at www.ICGtesting.com
Printed in the USA
LVOW082137120712

289902LV00007B/99/P

9 781290 216975